Bridging the Gap:
College Reading

D1372619

Bridging the Gap:
College Reading

Brenda D. Smith
Georgia State University

Scott, Foresman and Company
Glenview, Illinois

Dallas, Tex.   Oakland, N.J.   Palo Alto, Cal.   Tucker, Ga.   London, England

To my helpers: my husband and my students

Library of Congress Cataloging in Publication Data

Smith, Brenda D   1944
    Bridging the gap.
    1.   Reading (Higher education)   2.   Study,
Method of.   I.   Title.
LB2395.S578   428.4′3   80-23273
ISBN 0-673-15364-9

Acknowledgments for quoted material and illustrations are included on pages 284-290 at the end of the book. These pages are an extension of the copyright page.

6-RRC-85 84 83

Preface

Frequently when I ask former reading students about their progress in regular courses, they answer, "I didn't realize how difficult it would be. There's so much to read and remember." After hearing such a response I always wonder, "What can I do that I'm not already doing to prepare students for the complexity of college textbooks?" In writing this book my objective has been to try to help students make the transition—bridge the gap—from general reading to the kind of specialized reading required in freshman college courses. *Bridging the Gap: College Reading* is meant to be "on-the-job training." It gives the instructor of reading a chance to apply reading skills to actual subject-matter areas.

All of the excerpts in this book are taken from freshman college textbooks and represent a wide variety of college courses. To appeal to student interest, I field-tested the materials on students and generally chose the selections that they gave "Four Star" ratings.

The presentation of skills in the text moves from the general to the specific. For example, initial chapters discuss concentration and previewing, while later chapters are concerned with inference, bias, and graphic material. The comprehension skills build sequentially from the word and sentence levels to an understanding of a paragraph and then an entire passage. Underscoring, outlining, and overviewing techniques are used to emphasize main idea, significant details, and structure.

Each chapter introduces a new skill, and contains short practice exercises to teach the skill. In nine of the ten chapters, the skill is applied to three longer textbook selections which are arranged on three different readability levels. The chapter on vocabulary introduces methods for unlocking word meaning; vocabulary items appear at the end of each reading selection to give the student a chance to practice those methods.

Some of the special features of this book are:

1. Actual textbook selections are used for practice exercises.
2. Each chapter contains selections on three different levels of readability for greater individualization.
3. Each selection has both explicit and inferential multiple-choice questions.
4. Each selection has an essay exam question for writing practice.
5. A word count appears at the end of each selection for those who wish to time the selections and calculate the speed of reading.
6. Vocabulary is presented in context, and exercises are included on prefixes, suffixes, and roots.
7. Even though skills build and overlap, each chapter can be taught as a separate unit to fit individual class needs.
8. Pages are perforated so that students can tear out and hand in assignments, especially underlining and outlining exercises.

The instructor's manual to accompany this book, available from the publisher, contains the answers to all of the exercises as well as suggestions for additional practice.

I would like to express my appreciation to a number of people who helped me put this book together. My initial helpers were my husband and my students. Dick, my husband, read every passage and worked every exercise, a time-consuming task to say the least. My many former students "road tested" my material and gave me suggestions and support.

I am particularly indebted to Hermann Lacher for his kindness and persistence and to my editor, Paul Jones, for his insight and enthusiasm. Paula Fitzpatrick deserves a great deal of credit for her sharp editing eye and her diligence, as does Virginia Swanton for shepherding the book through the production stages.

Others I wish to thank who have given me valuable suggestions are Bill Bean, Daytona Beach Community College; Dixie Goswami, University of Tennessee; Patricia Grant, County College of Morris; Paul R. Kazmierski, Rochester Institute of Technology; Lee Kolzow, William Rainey Harper College; Martha Maxwell, University of California, Berkeley; Alan Meyers, Truman College; and Nancy V. Wood, University of Texas at El Paso.

Brenda D. Smith
Georgia State University

Contents

Bridging the Gap:
College Reading

Chapter One

concentration

Answer the following questions honestly:

1. Do you believe the power of concentration is an innate gift that some are born with and others are not?
2. Do you believe that the ability to concentrate is hereditary, like blue eyes or brown hair?
3. If your father's side of the family is fidgety and can't concentrate, does that mean that you will be also?

The answer to all three questions is an obvious *no.* Concentration is a skill that is developed through self-discipline and practice, not a mystical power, a hereditary gift, or a defective gene. It is a *habit* that requires time and effort to develop and careful planning for consistent success.

Concentration is no more than *paying attention*—that is, focusing your full attention on the task at hand. Someone once said that the mark of a genius is the ability to concentrate completely on one thing at a time. This is easy if the task is fun and exciting, but it becomes more difficult when you are required to read something that is new and not very interesting to you. At this point your mind begins to wander, and the words on the page remain just words to pass over rather than becoming meaningful thoughts and ideas.

Improving Concentration

Analyze the following concentration pop quiz and decide if it has any value for you:

You are completely absorbed and fully engrossed in reading an assignment. Someone calls your name, but you do not hear. The caller proceeds toward you and taps you on the shoulder. You are so deeply involved in your work that you *leap* into the air with a *shout* of surprise.

- *Pop Quiz Questions:*

   1. How far into the air do you jump?
   2. How loud do you yell?

- *Score:*
   The higher you jump and the louder you yell, the higher your concentration score will be.
- *Evaluation Question:*
   Is this quiz completely silly or does it ring true?

If someone gave you this pop quiz, you would find the test to be both silly and true. Think of a time when a similar incident has happened to you. The type of intense concentration that forces us to close the rest of the world out is the state we would all like to achieve each time we sit down with a textbook. Too often the opposite is true.

Students frequently ask, "How can I keep my mind on what I'm doing?" or "I finished the assignment, but I don't know a thing I read." The solution unfortunately is not a simple trick, but rather it involves a series of both short- and long-range plans as well as a genuine desire to learn.

The Culprits: The Causes of Poor Concentration

1. External Distractions
   Who was that who just walked by? What is the name of the song playing? What time is it? Where is my chewing gum?
2. Internal Distractions
   Will I ever pass this course? Who is going to the party Saturday night? When is the next car payment? Is my blue shirt clean?
3. Lack of Curiosity
   Who cares about this stuff? Could it be any more boring? How many more pages do I have to go?

The Cures: Planning for Good Concentration

External Distractions

External distractions are the temptations of the physical world that divert your attention away from the books. They are the people in the room, the noise in the background—the general where and when that you choose for studying. To control these external distractions, create an environment that says, "Now this is the place and the time for me to get my work done."

Place • Start by establishing your own private study cubicle; it may be in the library, on the dining-room table, or in your bedroom. Wherever it may be, choose a straight chair and face the wall. Get rid of gadgets, magazines, and other temptations that trigger the mind to think of *play*. Stay away from the bed because it triggers *sleep*. Spread out your papers, books, and other symbols of studying and create an atmosphere in which the visual stimuli signal *work*.

Time • To be successful, your study hours must be as rigid and fixed in your mind as your class hours. Leave nothing to chance because too often an unplanned activity never gets done. At the beginning of each new term, establish a routine study time for each day of the week and stick scrupulously to your schedule.

Schedule • On the next page is a weekly activity chart. Analyze your responsibilities and in the squares on the chart write your fixed activities such as class hours, work time, meal time, and bedtime. Next, think about how much time you want to spend studying and how much on recreation and plug those into the chart. For studying, indicate the place that you will be at that particular time. Successful people do not let their time slip away; they manage time, rather than letting time manage them. Plan realistically and then follow your schedule.

TIME	SUNDAY	MONDAY	TUESDAY	WEDNESDAY	THURSDAY	FRIDAY	SATURDAY
8:00-9							
9:00-10							
10:00-11							
11:00-12							
12:00-1							
1:00-2							
2:00-3							
3:00-4							
4:00-5							
5:00-6							
6:00-7							
7:00-8							
8:00-9							
9:00-10							
10:00-11							
11:00-12							

Ratio • Even though it is not necessary to write this on the chart, remember that you need short breaks. Few students can study uninterrupted for two hours without becoming fatigued and losing concentration. Try the *50–10 ratio*—study hard for fifty minutes, take a ten-minute break, and then promptly go back to the books for another fifty minutes.

Habit • Forming study habits is similar to developing the habit of brushing your teeth; the important word is *consistency*. Always study in the same place at the same times and do not tolerate exceptions. After a number of repeated experiences, the places and times should become subconscious psychological signals for concentration.

Internal Distractions

Internal distractions are the concerns that come repeatedly into your mind as you try to keep your attention focused on the assignment. Rather than the noise or the conversation in a room, they are the questions of self-doubt or the nagging responsibilities on your mind that disrupt your work.

Confidence • Saying "I'll never pass this course" or "I can't get in the mood to study" is a beginning step toward *not* being successful. Concentration requires self-confidence. If you didn't think you could do it, you would not be in a college class reading this book. Don't allow self-doubt to cloud your concentration.

Have faith in yourself and in your ability to be what you want to be. How many people do you know who have passed the particular course that is worrying you? Are they smarter than you? Probably not, so you can do as well as they did. Turn the negative feelings into a positive attitude and say, "If Joan did it, so can I" or "Larry did O.K. and he's no smarter than I am." Believing that you can do it is a prerequisite for actually doing it, so open your book with a firm determination and enough self-confidence to make it impossible for a single doubt to flicker through your mind.

Responsibilities • Unfortunately, students, just like everyone else, have to run errands, pick up laundry, make telephone calls, and pay bills. The world does not stop just because George has to read four chapters for a test in "Western Civ." by Wednesday. Consequently, when George sits down to read, he worries about getting an inspection sticker for his car or about picking up tickets for Saturday's ball game rather than concentrating completely on the assignment.

Make a List • For the most part, the interferences that pop into the mind and break reading concentration are minor concerns rather than major problems. To gain control over these mental disruptions, make a list of what is bothering you. What is on your mind that is keeping you from concentrating on your studies? Jot down on a piece of paper each mental distraction and then analyze each to determine if immediate action is possible. If so, get up and take action. Make that phone call, write that letter, or finish that chore. Maybe it will take a few minutes or maybe half an hour, but the investment will have been worthwhile if the quality of your study time—your concentration power—has increased. Taking action is the first step in getting something off your mind.

For the big problems about which you can do nothing immediately, ask yourself, "Is it worth the amount of brain time I'm dedicating to it?" Take a few minutes to think and make notes on possible solutions. Jotting down necessary future action and forming a plan of attack will help relieve the worry and clear the mind for studying.

Right now, list five things that are on your mind that you need to remember to do. Alan Lakein, a specialist in time management calls this a "To-Do List." In his book, *How to Get Control of Your Time and Your Life* (New York: Signet, 1974), Lakein says that his research studies show that successful business executives start each day with such a list. Rank the activities on your list in order of priority and then do the most important things first.

To-Do List	**Sample**
1._____	1. Get hair cut
2._____	2. Book report due
3._____	3. Buy stamps
4._____	4. Call power co.
5._____	5. Pay phone bill

At the end of the day the list may not be completed, but the leftovers can be transferred to tomorrow's list. Keep your "To-Do Lists" in a tiny booklet, rather than on different scraps of paper, so that you can refer back to a previous day's activity as well as make notes for several days ahead. If you can't think of five things you need to do, you are not being serious; you will never make it through college with such an unrealistic view of your time and your responsibilities. In fact, most students will probably have more than five "To-Do's."

Lack of Curiosity

Lack of curiosity means starting the assignment with no desire to learn and no interest in the subject; it means "putting in time" and "covering the pages." The outset predicts failure because motivation is dead, progress is sluggish, and the mind is prone to wander to more exciting circumstances. The student feels like a prisoner of the assigned pages and the reading itself seems endless.

Spark an Interest • Have you ever wondered why it is that the same student who barely plods through Book A can pick up Book B, a text of equal difficulty, and become completely engrossed in the subject matter, read for hours, and later remember most of what was read? This phenomenon has probably happened to you. How can the success of Book B be applied to Book A? The student obviously finds Book B very interesting and therefore enjoyable and easy to read. How then can you generate an interest in material that has not previously seemed exciting?

Potentially dull material, like seemingly dull people, needs some background work. Ask some questions, get some ideas, and do some thinking before starting to read. If the material was assigned, it must have merit and finding it will make your job easier. Make a conscious effort to stimulate your curiosity before reading, even if in a contrived manner. Make yourself want to learn something. First look over the assigned reading for words or phrases that attract your attention, glance at the pictures, check the number of pages, and then ask yourself the following question: What do *I* want to learn about this?

With practice, this method of thinking before reading can create a spark of enthusiasm that will make the actual reading more purposeful and make concentration more direct and intense.

Time Goal • An additional trick to spark your interest is to set a time goal. Study time is not infinite and short-term goals create a self-imposed pressure to pay attention, speed up, and get the job done. After looking over the material, project the amount of time you will need to finish it. Estimate a reasonable completion time and then push yourself to meet the goal.

The following pages contain some exercises for practicing concentration techniques. The skill-development questions are designed to help you learn to apply the techniques discussed in this chapter.

• *Skill Development: Selection 1*

Directions: Before reading the first selection, take a few moments to analyze your potential for concentration and answer the following questions.

1. Look at your physical environment. Where are you and what time is it?

_____ Is this your usual study time and place or are you deviating

today for some special reason? _____

What, if any, are your external distractions?

_____

_____

_____

_____

_____

_____

2. Is anything popping into your mind that you need to remember to do? Do you feel confident that you understand the assignment and can do well? What, if any, are your internal distractions?

_____

_____

_____

_____

3. Now the big question is "Do you have any interest in what you are about to read?" The title of the selection is "Imprinting," and it is taken from a psychology book on human behavior. Do you know what "imprinting" means? Glance over the selection and see what words attract your attention. You may notice words and phrases like *critical-period hypothesis, Lorenz, goslings, baby chicks, the maternal instinct in rats, overcoming the critical period, baby geese,* and others. What do you think you would like to know about the topic? What about it is of interest to *you?*

_____

_____

_____

_____

4. Set approximate time goals for yourself. How long do you think it will take you to

read this selection? _____ minutes. Look at the compre-

hension and vocabulary questions that follow the selection. How long do you think

it will take you to answer the questions? _____ minutes.

• *Follow-Up Questions*

   When you have finished the assignment, return to this page and evaluate your reading and study time.

5. How long did it take you to read the selection? _____ minutes

How long did it take to answer the questions? _____ minutes

Did you work steadily or were you interrupted? _____

Did setting a time goal help you keep your mind on your work? _____

If you had been given the concentration pop quiz while reading this selection,

would your score have been high _____, medium _____, or low

_____?

Selection 1: Psychology

James V. McConnell, from *Understanding Human Behavior*

Imprinting*

Konrad Lorenz and goslings imprinting on him.

There is some evidence that the best time for a child to learn a given skill is at the time the child's body is just mature enough to allow mastery of the behavior in question. This belief is often called the *critical-period hypothesis*—that is, the belief that an organism must have certain experiences at a *particular time* in its developmental sequence if it is to reach its most
5   mature state.

There are many studies from animal literature supporting the critical-period hypothesis. For instance, German scientist Konrad Lorenz discovered many years ago that birds, such as ducks and geese, will follow the first moving object they see after they are hatched. Usually the first thing they see is that mother, of course, who has been sitting on the eggs when they are
10   hatched. However, Lorenz showed that if he took goose eggs away from the mother and hatched them in an incubator, the fresh-hatched *goslings* would follow him around instead.

After the goslings had waddled along behind Lorenz for a few hours, they acted as if they thought he was their mother and that they were humans, not geese. When Lorenz returned the goslings to their real mother, they ignored her. Whenever Lorenz appeared, however, they
15   became very excited and flocked to him for protection and affection. It was as if the visual image of the first object they saw moving had become so strongly *imprinted* on their consciousness that, forever after, that object was "mother."

*LEARNING STRATEGY: Even though most of this excerpt describes animal behavior, the textbook is concerned with human behavior; therefore, be alert to links between the two. Be able to define and give examples of the two major terms in this selection.

During the past 20 years or so, scientists have spent a great deal of time studying *imprinting* as it now is called. The effect occurs in many but not in all types of birds, and it also seems to occur in mammals such as sheep and seals. Whether it occurs in humans is a matter for debate. Imprinting is very strong in ducks and geese, however, and they have most often been the subjects for study.

The urge to imprint typically reaches its strongest peak 16 to 24 hours after the baby goose is hatched. During this period, the baby bird has an innate tendency to follow anything that moves, and will chase after its mother (if she is around), or a human, a bouncing football or a brightly painted tin can that the experimenter dangles in front of the gosling. The more the baby bird struggles to follow after this moving object, the more strongly the young animal becomes imprinted to the object. Once the goose has been imprinted, this very special form of learning cannot easily be reversed. For example, the geese that first followed Lorenz could not readily be trained to follow their mother instead; indeed, when these geese were grown and sexually mature, they showed no romantic interest in other geese. Instead, they attempted to court and mate with humans.

If a goose is hatched in a dark incubator and is not allowed to see the world until two or three days later, imprinting often does not occur. At first it was thought that the "critical period" had passed and hence the bird could never become imprinted to anything. Now we know differently. The innate urge to follow moving objects does appear to reach a peak in geese 24 hours after they are hatched, but it does not decline thereafter. Rather, a second innate urge—that of fearing and avoiding new objects—begins to develop, and within 48 hours after hatching typically overwhelms the prior tendency the bird has to follow after anything that moves. To use a human term, the goose's *attitude* toward strange things is controlled by its genetic blueprint—at first it is attracted to, then it becomes afraid of, new objects in its environment. As we will see in a moment, these conflicting "attitudes" may explain much of the data on "critical periods" in both animals and humans.

(*Question:* How might these two apparently conflicting behavioral tendencies help a baby goose survive in its usual or natural environment?)

In other experiments, baby chickens have been hatched and raised in the dark for the first several days of their lives. Chicks have an innate tendency to peck at small objects soon after they are hatched—an instinctive behavior pattern that helps them get food as soon as they are born. In the dark, of course, they cannot see grain lying on the ground and hence do not peck (they must be hand-fed in the dark during this period of time). Once brought into the light, these chicks do begin to peck, but they do so clumsily and ineffectively, as if their "critical period" for learning the pecking skill had passed. Birds such as robins and blue jays learn to fly at about the time their wings are mature enough to sustain flight (their parents often push them from the nest as a means of encouraging them to take off on their own). If these young birds are restrained and not allowed to fly until much later, their flight patterns are often clumsy and they do not naturally gain the necessary skills to become good fliers.

The "Maternal Instinct" in Rats Suppose we take a baby female rat from its mother at the moment of its birth and raise the rat pup "by bottle" until it is sexually mature. Since it has never seen other rats during its entire life (its eyes do not open until several days after birth), any sexual or maternal behavior that it shows will presumably be due to the natural unfolding of its genetic blueprint—and not due to learning or imitation. Now, suppose we inseminate this hand-raised female rat artificially—to make certain that she continues to have no contact with other rats. Will she build a nest for her babies before they are born, following the usual pattern of female rats, and will she clean and take care of them during and after the birth itself?

The answer to that question is yes—*if*. If, when the young female rat was growing up, there were objects such as sticks and sawdust and string and small blocks of wood in her cage, and which she played with. Then, when inseminated, the pregnant rat will use these "toys" to build a nest. If the rat grows up in a bare cage, she won't build a nest *even though we give her the*

20

25

30

35

40

45

50

55

60

65

materials to do so once she is impregnated. If this same rat is forced to wear a stiff rubber collar around her neck when she is growing up—so that she cannot clean her sex organs, as rats normally do—she will not usually lick her newborn babies clean *even though we take off*
70 *the rubber collar a day or so before she gives birth.* The genetic blueprint always operates best within a particular environmental setting. If an organism's early environment is abnormal or particularly unusual, later "innate" behavior patterns may be disrupted.

Overcoming the "Critical Period" All of these examples may appear to support the "critical-period" hypothesis—that there is one time in an organism's life when it is best-suited to learn
75 a particular skill. These studies might also seem to violate the general rule that an organism can "catch up" if its development has been delayed. However, the truth is more complicated (as always) than it might seem from the experiments we have *cited* so far.

Baby geese will normally not imprint if we restrict their visual experiences for the first 48 hours of their lives—their fear of strange objects is by then too great. However, if we give the
80 geese tranquilizing drugs to help overcome their fear, they can be imprinted a week or more after hatching. Once imprinting has taken place, it may seem to be irreversible. But we can occasionally get a bird imprinted on a human to accept a goose as its mother, if we coax it enough and give it massive rewards for approaching or following its natural mother. Chicks raised in darkness become clumsy eaters—but what do you think would happen if we gave
85 them special training in how to peck, rather than simply leaving the matter to chance? Birds restrained in the nest too long apparently learn other ways of getting along and soon come to fear heights; what do you think would happen if we gave these birds tranquilizers and rewarded each tiny approximation to flapping their wings properly?

There is not much scientific evidence that human infants have the same types of "critical
90 periods" that birds and rats do. By being born without strong innate behavior patterns (such as imprinting), we seem to be better able to adjust and survive in the wide variety of social environments human babies are born into. Like many other organisms, however, children do appear to have an inborn tendency to imitate the behavior of other organisms around them. A young rat will learn to press a lever in a Skinner box much faster if it is first allowed to
95 watch an adult rat get food by pressing the lever. This learning is even quicker if the adult rat happens to be the young animal's mother.

Different species of birds have characteristic songs or calls. A European thrush, for example, has a song pattern fairly similar to a thrush in the United States, but both sound quite different from blue jays. There are *local dialects* among songbirds, however, and these are learned
100 through imitation. If a baby thrush is isolated from its parents and exposed to blue jay calls when it is very young, the thrush will sound a little like a blue jay but a lot like other thrushes when it grows up. And parrots, of course, pick up very human-sounding speech patterns if they are raised with humans rather than with other parrots.   /1642

• *Comprehension Questions*

After reading the selection, answer the following questions with *a, b, c,* or *d.*

————————   1. The best statement of the main idea of this selection is
   a. studies show that goslings can be imprinted on humans
   b. the first few days of an animal's life are a crucial time for learning or imprinting long-lasting "natural" behavior
   c. imprinting seems to occur in mammals but is very strong in ducks and geese

    d. the "crucial period" of imprinting is important but can be overcome with drugs

_____ 2. The critical-period hypothesis is the belief that
    a. there is a "prime time" to experience and learn certain skills
    b. most learning occurs during the first few days of life
    c. fear can inhibit early learning
    d. the "maternal instinct" is not innate but is learned

_____ 3. In Lorenz's studies, after imprinting the goslings on himself, the goslings would do all of the following except
    a. follow him around
    b. flock to him for protection
    c. return to their real mother for affection
    d. become excited when Lorenz appeared

_____ 4. The author points out that in Lorenz's studies with geese, the early imprinting with humans
    a. was easily reversed with training
    b. caused the geese to be poor mothers
    c. produced later sexually abnormal behavior
    d. made it difficult for the goslings to learn to feed themselves

_____ 5. The author suggests that after 24 hours the innate urge to imprint in geese is
    a. decreased
    b. increased
    c. the same
    d. none of the above

_____ 6. In its natural environment the purpose of the innate urge to avoid new objects that develops within 48 hours of hatching might be to help a small gosling
    a. learn only the behavior of its species
    b. follow only one mother
    c. escape its genetic blueprint
    d. stay away from predators

_____ 7. The author suggests that there is a critical period for all of the following except
    a. walking
    b. pecking
    c. flying
    d. song patterns

_____ 8. The studies with rats suggest that nest building and "cleaning behavior" are
    a. totally innate behaviors
    b. totally learned behaviors
    c. a combination of innate and learned behaviors
    d. neither innate nor learned behaviors

_____ 9. Abnormal imprinting during the critical period can be overcome by using all of the following except

a. tranquilizing drugs   b. natural tendencies
c. special training   d. massive reward

_____ 10. Because humans do not seem to have strong innate behavior patterns, the author feels that humans
    a. are better able to adapt to changing environments
    b. have more difficulty learning early motor skills
    c. find adjustment to change more difficult than animals
    d. need more "mothering" than animals

Answer the following with *T* (true), *F* (false) or *CT* (can't tell).

_____ 11. Because they are easy to train, ducks and geese have been used most often in imprinting studies.
_____ 12. The author implies that a goose can be imprinted on a painted tin can.
_____ 13. In the author's opinion, studies show that organisms can catch up adequately when skill development has been delayed past the "critical period."
_____ 14. If an abandoned bird egg is hatched and raised solely by a human, the author feels that the bird will be abnormal.
_____ 15. The author suggests that the urge to imitate is innate in both humans and animals.

● *Vocabulary*

According to the way the boldface word was used in the selection, indicate *a, b, c,* or *d* for the word or phrase that gives the best definition.

____ 1. "The critical-period **hypothesis**"
    a. association
    b. theory
    c. law
    d. dilemma

____ 2. "in an **incubator**"
    a. cage
    b. electric enlarger
    c. nest
    d. artificial hatching apparatus

____ 3. "its **genetic** blueprint"
    a. sexual
    b. emotional
    c. hereditary
    d. learned

____ 4. "an **instinctive** behavior pattern"
    a. desirable
    b. natural inclination
    c. early
    d. newly acquired

____ 5. "to **sustain** flight"
    a. support
    b. imitate
    c. begin
    d. imagine

____ 6. "birds are **restrained**"
    a. pressured
    b. pushed
    c. held back
    d. attacked

_____ 7. "suppose we **inseminate**"
a. imprison
b. artificially impregnate
c. injure
d. frighten

_____ 8. "may be **disrupted**"
a. thrown into disorder
b. repeated
c. lost
d. destroyed

_____ 9. "seem to be **irreversible**"
a. temporary
b. changeable
c. frequent
d. permanent

_____ 10. "**coax** it enough"
a. encourage fondly
b. punish
c. feed
d. drill

• *Possible Essay Exam Question*

Cite examples that support and contradict the critical-period hypothesis. (Hint: First define the term and then give at least two or three examples, using different animal experiment findings, to support and refute the hypothesis.)

• *Skill Development: Selection 2*

Directions: Before reading the second selection, take a few moments to analyze your potential for concentration and answer the following questions.

1. Where are you? _____ What time is it? _____
Is this study time and place written on your weekly time schedule? What, if any, are your external distractions?

_____

_____

_____

_____

2. Is anything special on your mind at the moment? Are you ready to "attack" the material? What, if any, are your internal distractions?

_____

_____

_____

_____

_____

_____

_____

3. Do you have any interest in reading the next selection? It is called "The American Man" and comes from a sociology textbook. Do you think the role of the American man is changing? Looking over the pages, you might notice words and phrases like *masculine mystique, locker-room culture, costs and benefits of the male role, competitive syndrome,* and *machismo.* Do these phrases give you ideas you may want to explore? What ideas in particular are of interest to you?

_____

_____

_____

_____

_____

_____

4. Set approximate time goals for yourself.

How long do you think it will take you to read this selection?

_____ minutes

How long do you think it will take you to answer the questions?

_____ minutes

• *Follow-Up Questions*

When you have finished the assignment, return to this page and evaluate your reading and study time.

5. How long did it take you to read the selection? _____ minutes

How long did it take to answer the questions? _____ minutes

Did you work steadily or were you interrupted? _____

Did setting a time goal help you keep your mind on your work? _____

If you had been given the concentration pop quiz while reading this selection, would your score have been high _____, medium _____, or low _____?

Selection 2: Sociology

Donald Light, Jr. and Suzanne Keller, from *Sociology*

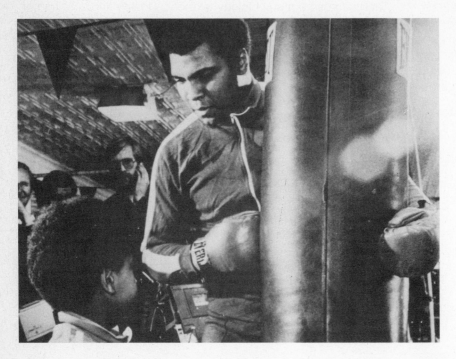

Muhammad Ali.

The American Man[*]

The male role is as deeply tied to the family as the female's, although the connections are not always so obvious. First and foremost a man is expected to be a good provider for his wife and children. Financial independence is a prerequisite for manhood in our society; respect goes to men who are reliable, hardworking, and achieving. Americans do not think it odd for a man to
5   sacrifice leisure, his time at home, even his health to a career. His accomplishments and property are a measure of his worth. Initiative, ambition, and strength are all part of the "masculine mystique." We say a man is mature if he accepts obligations for dependents, takes necessary risks, makes decisions, and provides security and protection for those in his care.

It is no wonder, then, that so many American fathers encourage their sons to excel in sports
10 (sometimes ignoring that they are not interested in or built for athletics). Sports are not an end in themselves: very few boys will go on to become professional athletes, and few fathers expect them to. But sports teach a boy to be assertive, aggressive, and competitive—all of which are thought to be essential masculine qualities, as Norman Mailer's description of boxer Muhammad Ali suggests: "Ali had shown what we all had hoped was secretly true. He was a
15 man. He could bear moral and physical torture and he could stand."

*LEARNING STRATEGY: Be able to describe the traditional male role and its demands in American society. How and why is that role changing?

Most elementary-school teachers are female and most fathers spend relatively little time at home, so contact with and acceptance by male peers may be especially important to a young boy. To a large degree boys depend on one another for information about the male role. The "locker-room culture" of adults (nights off with the boys, drinking, playing cards, going to a ball game) is reminiscent of youthful team sports. As Joseph Pleck suggests: "It seems hard to get a group of men together for very long without someone suggesting a competitive game." For many American men, realizing that it is too late to become a professional pitcher or linebacker is a sobering reminder that they are growing old.

Sports are one of many object lessons in self-reliance and stoicism. Weakness, doubt, and compromise are signs of failure for men who are raised to conceal or deny such feelings. The taboo on expressing emotions and self-doubt explains the strong silent type in American lore. The 100 percent American he-man is happiest when he is with his buddies or riding the range alone on his horse. Courteous to women, he is also detached and prefers dealing with them on a "man-to-man" basis. (Humphrey Bogart's expression of love to Ingrid Bergman in *Casablanca,* "Here's lookin' at you, kid" would hardly be considered romantic in other countries.) Impervious to pain as well as feelings, he is rugged, resourceful, and enjoys combating overwhelming odds. John Wayne, of course, is the prototype for this "ideal man."

> The on-screen John Wayne doesn't feel comfortable around women. He does like them sometimes—God knows he's not *queer.* But at the right time and in the right place— which he chooses. And always his car/horse parked directly outside, in/on which he will ride away to his more important business back in Marlboro country. (Manville, 1969, p. 111)

The ban on male emotions does not extend to sexual matters, however. Heterosexual prowess is essential to American manhood. Men are expected to have nearly unlimited appetites for sexual adventure and to enjoy sex for its own sake (unlike women, who are thought to require at least some romantic feelings). Far more stigma is attached to the effeminate boy than to the masculine girl, who can play the role of tomboy. A woman who displays little interest in heterosexual relationships may be labeled prissy or frigid; a man is assumed to be homosexual. And there is no worse insult to an American man—except perhaps the imputation that someone is "trespassing on" his woman.

Costs and Benefits of the Male Role Like the female role, the male role has mixed effects. American men have access to the pinnacles of institutional power; men (white men, that is) not women run the nation's government, churches, corporations, professions, universities, even theaters and art galleries. Men are free to exercise legal and social powers that are denied women and children. With the notable exceptions of the now defunct draft law and alimony statutes, neither law nor custom restricts or discriminates against men solely on the basis of their sex. Men have more opportunities than women to develop their talents and acquire special skills and knowledge to cope with the world. (If a family has only enough income to send one child to college, in all likelihood it will choose their son. Men are overrepresented in all professions.) In general, men earn more than women performing the same work, and are more likely to be promoted to powerful and lucrative executive positions (where they enjoy the ministrations of secretaries, who are nearly always female). The fact that men are encouraged to display initiative and independence from the time they are small must also be counted among the benefits of the male role. Finally, the pervasive myth of male supremacy cannot but buoy the male ego.

It is important to remember, however, that although these potentialities are built into the male role, they are not available to all men. Opportunities for training, economic self-support, and power are clearly more accessible to men at the top of the social pyramid than to those at the bottom. To generalize from the privileged few to the struggling many distorts the actual

65 situation for the vast majority of men, who are not in control of their lives nor anywhere near the seats of economic and political power.

The responsibilities that attach to the male role in America can be a source of great stress and anxiety as well as a source of satisfaction and pride. Being in a position to make decisions is fine if a person knows what he is doing, but it may seem less of a privilege to a man who is uncertain of himself. Complicating this is the fact that men are supposed to maintain the
70 impression of strength and courage at all times. Fear of inadequacy and failure is the dark side of the pressures on men to prove themselves.

Equally costly is the competitive syndrome that asks men to consider all other men as either inferiors or rivals and requires substantial mobilization of psychic aggression. Famed as male solidarity is, male friendships are not necessarily easy relationships.

75 When stripped of male sex role ''props,'' such as baseball scores, automobiles, and masculine sex boasting and fantasy, many men find great difficulty in relating to other men. A man in a group said, ''You know, I have a pretty good idea of what I can get in a relationship with a woman; but I just don't know what I could get from a man. I just don't know.'' (Pleck, 1972, pp. 8–9)

80 In very concrete terms, men do not live as long as women and suffer more heart attacks. It is also very revealing that they have more psychosomatic diseases, such as ulcers, spastic colons, asthma, and migraine headaches. The male suicide rate is triple the female rate, and men are fourteen times as likely to become alcoholics. Moreover, men commit 95 percent of all violent crimes and eight times as many murders as women
85 do. Men also have to fight the wars other men make.

Finally, as with the female role, a number of conflicts are built into the male role. Men are supposed to be single-minded in the pursuit of success but not neglectful of their families; they should be simultaneously interested and disinterested in women; and they must be strong and self-reliant, yet require the care of a nurturant wife.

90 As a result, masculinity is in many ways a rather vulnerable and precarious status. The male role is demanding and difficult and the rate of ''failure'' is high in the best of times. In American society, as in other industrial societies, few men can in fact achieve the wealth, power, and positions of leadership that are held out as ideals for all. *Machismo,* or compulsive masculinity, may be a last resort for men who accept the traditional masculine role
95 but cannot fill it. Machismo has two faces, an overt and a covert one. Overtly it consists of a show of strength and sexual prowess as well as the denigration, exploitation, and often brutalization of women. Covertly, this display masks fears and doubts about self-worth. As an effort to convince other men, women, and above all himself that he is truly all-male,
100 machismo is a front for insecurity, self-doubt, and worldly failure (Aramoni, 1972, pp. 69-72).

Serious doubts and anxieties about masculine identity and purpose are bound to occur as many women forego the need for male protection and successfully compete with men in spheres previously considered off-limits to them. For example, 30 percent of male undergraduates in one study experienced some conflict between the desire for female intellectual companionship
105 and the notion that as men, they should be intellectually superior (Komarovsky, 1973).

Some men have begun to see these changes in the female role as a welcome liberation. Is traditional masculinity worth the price? These men seek a new male ideal, less geared toward competition and dominance. Men will be better off, they argue, if they can learn to acknowledge their human vulnerability and limitations and escape the posturing and pretense of
110 the male role. However, others see change as a dethronement from a previously privileged status. The more they feel they have to lose, the more likely men—and women—are to resist change. The days ahead will not be easy for those who are wedded to traditional gender ideals. There is bound to be anger, conflict, misunderstandings—a tug of war as traditional roles change for both men and women.   /1476

• *Comprehension Questions*

After reading the selection, answer the following questions with *a, b, c,* or *d.*

_____ 1. The best statement of the main idea of this selection is
   a. women do not feel the pressure of society's demands as much as men
   b. the rewards of the male role far exceed the disadvantages
   c. men have been responsible for the changes in sex roles in American society
   d. men feel the pressure of living up to an impossible image in American society, but this is changing

_____ 2. In American society, according to the author, the primary male responsibility is to provide
   a. emotional stability
   b. financial security
   c. love and affection
   d. time at home with the family

_____ 3. The author believes that American fathers encourage their sons to do well in athletics because they want them
   a. to become professional athletes
   b. to be assertive, aggressive, and competitive
   c. to build healthy bodies
   d. to be able to enjoy recreational activities

_____ 4. According to the selection, to a large extent, boys learn their male role from
   a. their fathers
   b. their teachers
   c. each other
   d. the movies

_____ 5. The John Wayne stereotype of the "ideal man" is all of the following except
   a. intimately attached to his family
   b. sexually attracted to women
   c. free of emotionalism
   d. confident of his abilities

_____ 6. The author considers all of the following benefits of the male role except
   a. early training to develop initiative and independence
   b. the pressures to achieve success
   c. the ego boost from the illusion of supremacy
   d. the opportunities for professional promotion

_____ 7. This selection suggests that male friendships are difficult relationships because
   a. female relationships interfere
   b. they center around ball games and sexual prowess
   c. males are in competition with each to succeed
   d. male interest is interpreted as homosexuality

_____ 8. The author suggests that "machismo" is all of the following except
   a. a cover-up for insecurities
   b. a desirable masculine quality

c. an exploitative attitude toward women

d. a reaction brought about by failure to achieve success in the ideal male role

_____ 9. The author states that the changing female role in our society

a. offers the possibility of greater masculine freedom

b. insures an increase in the "machismo" attitude

c. is welcomed by most men and women

d. threatens the job security of men in our society

_____ 10. The author of this selection would probably agree with all of the following except

a. male roles will become less traditional in the future

b. women's lib has relieved some of the pressure of the male role

c. men sacrifice in trying to fulfill the ideal American-man image

d. men should not express emotions and self-doubt

Answer the following with _T_ (true), _F_ (false), or _CT_ (can't tell).

_____ 11. The author believes that if only one child in a family can be sent to college, the male child should go.

_____ 12. In the author's opinion, the adult male "Friday night poker game" is a result of earlier athletic team competition.

_____ 13. According to the selection, American society condemns the tomboy girl more than the effeminate boy.

_____ 14. The author believes that most men are in control of their lives and in powerful positions.

_____ 15. The female suicide rate has increased with the increase of women in responsible professional positions.

● **_Vocabulary_**

According to the way the boldface word was used in the selection, indicate _a_, _b_, _c_, or _d_ for the word or phrase that gives the best definition.

_____ 1. "a **prerequisite** for manhood"

a. burden

b. requirement beforehand

c. advantage

d. introduction

_____ 2. "of the 'masculine **mystique**' "

a. human body

b. puzzling aura

c. social status

d. genetic make-up

_____ 3. "is **reminiscent** of"

a. a mockery

b. in opposite directions

c. complimentary

d. suggestive from the past

_____ 4. "in American **lore**"

a. folk history

b. untruths

c. imagination

d. media

_____ 5. "**Impervious** to pain"

a. superior

b. welcoming

_____ 6. "Far more **stigma**"

a. importance

b. mark of disgrace

c. resistant
d. yielding

c. power
d. reward

_____ 7. "**lucrative** executive positions"
a. mobile
b. authoritative
c. profitable
d. successful

_____ 8. "**distorts** the actual situation"
a. explains
b. misrepresents
c. compares
d. simplifies

_____ 9. "**precarious** status"
a. uncertain
b. well deserved
c. unreasonable
d. newly acquired

_____ 10. "**compulsive** masculinity"
a. evil
b. spontaneous
c. destructive
d. compellingly forceful

• *Possible Essay Exam Question*

How can the changing female role be seen as a "liberation" of the traditional American man? (Hint: Describe the traditional male role and its stresses and then give examples of how a stronger female role can relieve some of these pressures for men.)

• *Skill Development: Selection 3*

Directions: The skill questions in this chapter are designed to help you develop the habit of concentration. You are sizing up the situation before getting started and taking steps to increase your chances of success. Our original questions can be condensed and should become an inherent part of your preparation to read any assignment. Answer the following boiled-down version of our original questions before starting on the next selection.

1. Is anything about the present time or place going to disrupt my thinking?

_____

2. Is anything on my mind that will distract me from my studies?

_____

3. What about this interests *me?*

_____

4. How long will it take?

_____

(after reading)
5. How did I do?

_____

Selection 3: Biology

Roy Hartenstein, from *Human Anatomy and Physiology*

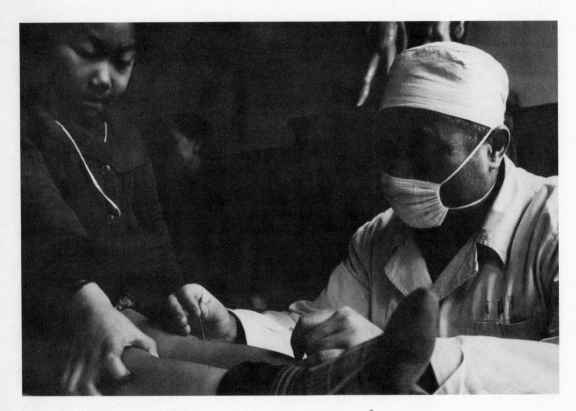

Relief of Pain by Acupuncture[*]

In recent years, much attention has been focused on acupuncture as a method of relieving pain. This ancient Chinese practice, which dates back to about 3000 B.C., involves the insertion of needles into certain spots on the body. In addition to using needles, acupuncturists may also apply heat and/or pressure to certain sites on the body.

5   Most practitioners of acupuncture, especially Chinese doctors who have not been trained in basic science, use acupuncture not only to relieve pain, but also to treat a variety of diseases, including diabetes, encephalitis, and gout. However, it should be stated that acupuncture theory and practice is based on the principle that basic organic disorders can only be given temporary relief, and that degenerated tissues cannot be treated. Thus, the "cure" of diabetes

10   by acupuncture is possible only if the insulin-producing cells of the pancreas have not degenerated and are able to respond to treatment.

Doctors who have been trained in modern Western medicine are perhaps justifiably skeptical about the curative claims of acupuncture. However, many physicians and scientists believe that it may be of value as a way of relieving pain.

*LEARNING STRATEGY: Use the subtitles in this selection to form questions to answer as you read. The title of the selection will form the overall question to be answered.

History of Acupuncture

15   The earliest known document on acupuncture is the "Yellow Emperor's Classic of Internal
Medicine," written around 300 B.C. According to legend, acupuncture treatments were
established in the course of observing that an injury or the application of pressure to one region
of the body would relieve an ongoing pain previously found elsewhere in the body. An injury
to the tip of the right index finger, for example, could relieve pain from a toothache; or
20   pressure applied to the crease between an index finger and thumb would provide some relief
from a headache. Over a period of many years, numerous observations were made, and maps
were made showing points of pain and their corresponding points of relief. Crude objects, such
as pointed sticks and stones, were used by the earliest acupuncturists to stimulate the sensitive
relief points. Later on, with the development of metals, needles were used instead.

25   Until about the end of the nineteenth century there was little communication between
Western and Chinese medicine. In 1911 the Chinese Emperor Sonbun, who had received
training in Western culture, increased the communication gap by forbidding the practice of
acupuncture. He thus implied that acupuncture was inferior to Western medicine. Because of
the value of acupuncture to the Chinese revolutionaries in 1934-35, however, Mao TseTung
30   reinstated the practice shortly after he came to power in China in 1949.

         Acupuncture was finally introduced into the United States in 1972, when American doctors
and journalists visiting China witnessed surgical operations, including chest surgery and
appendectomies, carried out without anesthesia, but under the pain-relieving effects of
acupuncture. By the mid-1970's acupuncture was legalized in more than a dozen states.

Philosophical Basis for Acupuncture

35   According to ancient Chinese theory, there are two major forces: yin and yang. These two
forces are complete opposites, but nothing is purely either yin or yang. All females, for
example, have some maleness and all males have a certain amount of femaleness.

         With regard to health, the Chinese see pain or illness as caused by an excess of either yin or
yang. Acupuncture is aimed at restoring the proper proportions of these vital forces in the body.
40   Whether Western doctors acknowledge the yin and yang philosophy is unimportant. What is
important is that the practice of acupuncture may be more beneficial to certain individuals than
some forms of Western medicine. Acupuncture is not a form of quackery. Nor is it a form of
hypnosis, because it works with infants and animals.

Practice of Acupuncture

Acupuncture therapy begins with an examination of the patient's ailment. Unlike some of the
45   sophisticated techniques used in Western medicine, however, the diagnostic techniques are
essentially the same from case to case, and no special instruments are used. Facial expressions
and voice qualities are examined, as are the nails, skin, tongue, breath, and feces. Questions
are asked about the location, date, and origin of the illness, as well as the patient's eating,
sleeping, and bowel habits. One of the most important parts of the examination is a simple but
50   subtle procedure in which six different pulse "readings" are taken from each wrist. You should
note that doctors trained in modern medicine view the pulse-reading information of
acupuncturists with deep skepticism.

         When the examination is over, a diagnosis is made, and the acupuncturist begins treatment.
Treatment consists of inserting needles into certain select spots on the skin. One or two needles
55   may be used for some illnesses and 30 or more needles for other ailments. The needles range in
thickness from about 0.3 mm to 0.5 mm and are 2 to 10 cm long. Short, thin needles are used
for certain regions, such as the face and hands, while longer, thicker needles are used for the
thighs, shoulders, and buttocks. If treatment is to be effective the needles must "take." That
is, the patient must feel a tingling sensation mixed with feelings of numbness or heaviness. The
60   needles are left in place for 10 to 30 minutes, often with periodic twirling. For certain
ailments, only one or two treatments may be necessary. For other ailments, 20 or 30 treatments
are called for.

The effectiveness of acupuncture treatment depends not only on "take" but on the location of
the needles. Depending upon the training and point of view of the acupuncturist, one or more
65   of as few as 70 points or as many as 800 points may be selected for the treatment of any kind
of pain or disease. These points run along lines that are called *meridians*. Numbering 14 in all,
these meridians are believed to carry "vital energy" from one region of the body to another and
from one internal organ to another.

There are six pairs of yin meridians, six pairs of yang meridians, a single conception
70   meridian, and a single governor meridian. The yang meridians run along the dorsal surface of
the body and head, and along the outer surfaces of the limbs. Three of them carry "vital
energy" from the fingertips to the face. The large intestine meridian, for example, begins at
the root of the index fingernail and terminates at the side of the nostril. According to basic
acupuncture theory, there are 20 points along this meridian. Pressure upon the first point, for
75   example (or the insertion of a needle), may relieve a facial pain.

The other three yang meridians run from the face to the toes. With regard to the yin
meridians, three run from the feet to the chest and three run from the chest to the fingertips.
The governor and conception meridians run along the back and front medians of the body,
respectively.

Advantages and Disadvantages of Acupuncture

80   Although modern physicians are generally skeptical about treating diseases with acupuncture,
there is a growing acceptance of this practice for the relief of pain and as a substitute for local
or general anesthesia. Acupuncture has certain advantages over the use of drugs. Allergic
reactions are not provoked, and there are no undesirable side effects, as may occur with drugs.
Also, there are no major physiological changes in the body, as in general (inhalation)
85   anesthesia, and the patient is fully conscious during surgery and is sometimes able to assist the
surgeon. In addition, the surgeons do not have to wait for the effects of anesthesia to wear off
in order to evaluate the consequences of an operation, and no complicated gas-delivering and
monitoring devices are needed.

Acupuncture also has some disadvantages and complications, however. As a substitute for
90   inhalation anesthesia, it may be only partially effective as a pain remover. Also, there is no
muscle relaxation, and this may be troublesome in certain operations. In addition,
inflammatory reactions may arise where the needles are inserted, and a nerve may be punctured
accidentally. Also, the patient may faint or enter a state of shock.   /1232

• *Comprehension Questions*

After reading the selection, answer the following questions with *a, b, c,* or *d.*

_____   1. The best statement of the main idea of this selection is that acupuncture is
   a. a method that originated in China of relieving pain by applying pressure
      to body points
   b. Chinese cure for pain
   c. the yin and yang forces at work in the body
   d. more valuable than anesthesia in relieving pain

_____   2. All of the following are used by acupuncturists to affect certain body spots
   except
   a. needles   b. heat
   c. tension   d. pressure

_____ 3. The opinion of the author seems to be that acupuncture
   a. can cure diabetes
   b. probably cannot cure diabetes
   c. can renew degenerated cells
   d. can cure cancer

_____ 4. According to the author, many Western scientists and physicians believe that acupuncture
   a. can cure diabetes, encephalitis, and gout
   b. should replace local anesthesia
   c. is a form of hypnosis
   d. can be helpful in relieving pain

_____ 5. All of the following are true about the history of acupuncture except
   a. it was used as early as 300 B.C.
   b. at one time it was forbidden in China
   c. stones and sticks were used to apply pressure
   d. most Chinese thought Western medicine was superior

_____ 6. Acupuncture has recently become popular in the United States because of
   a. Mao TseTung's leadership
   b. visits to China by doctors and journalists witnessing the technique
   c. Chinese Emperor Sonbun's training in Western culture
   d. legalization in twelve states

_____ 7. In looking at the philosophical basis for acupuncture, Chinese believe yin and yang are
   a. male and female genes
   b. life forces
   c. pressure points in the body
   d. pain and good health in a struggle

_____ 8. In acupuncture treatment, needles or pressure are applied
   a. directly on the area in pain
   b. in a region of the body away from the pain
   c. always on at least one fingertip
   d. in at least 70 points for an average treatment

_____ 9. According to the author all of the following are advantages of acupuncture over anesthesia except
   a. no allergic reactions
   b. the patient is able to assist the surgeon
   c. no muscle relaxation
   d. no physiological change in the body

_____ 10. The best statement of the author's opinion is that acupuncture
   a. should not be used in the West
   b. should be used in cases of allergy
   c. should be considered by Westerners as a pain reliever
   d. should be used in chest surgery and appendectomies

Answer the following with _T_ (true), _F_ (false), _CT_ (can't tell).

_____ 11. In order to be cured by acupuncture, the patient must believe in the philosophy of yin and yang.

_____ 12. The thickness and length of the acupuncture needles depend on the severity of the disease.

_____ 13. In the author's opinion many doctors take a dim view of diagnostic techniques of acupuncture.

_____ 14. If properly inserted, the patient should experience no feeling at all from the acupuncture needles.

_____ 15. The Chinese use acupuncture as a cure for cancer.

• *Vocabulary*

According to the way the boldface word was used in the selection, indicate *a, b, c,* or *d* for the word or phrase that gives the best definition.

____ 1. "have not **degenerated**"
a. bled
b. divided
c. deteriorated
d. renewed

____ 2. "are perhaps **justifiably** skeptical"
a. with good reason
b. cautiously
c. absolutely
d. undoubtedly

____ 3. "justifiably **skeptical**"
a. convinced
b. doubtful
c. persuaded
d. knowledgeable

____ 4. "about the **curative** claims"
a. boastful
b. assertive
c. exaggerated
d. tending to cure disease

____ 5. "a form of **quackery**"
a. the claims of a faker
b. ESP
c. the supernatural
d. management

____ 6. "of the patient's **ailment**"
a. body
b. illness
c. mind
d. background

____ 7. "may be **punctured** accidentally"
a. pierced
b. divided
c. killed
d. forgotten

____ 8. "carry '**vital** energy' "
a. renewed
b. human
c. life-sustaining
d. motor

____ 9. "a single **governor** meridian"
a. controller
b. regular
c. necessary
d. vertical

____ 10. "**terminates** at the side"
a. begins
b. extends
c. continues
d. ends

• *Possible Essay Exam Question*

Explain how acupuncture can relieve pain. (Hint: Explain the meridian theory of acupuncture practice, give examples of successful treatment, and point out the advantages of acupuncture.)

Chapter Two

Vocabulary
Vocabulary
Vocabulary
Vocabulary
Vocabulary

Vo **cab** u **lar** y

While reading, you come across the following words:

stratification   psychopathology   ultracentrifuge

What do they mean?

Should you stop reading immediately, look up each word in the dictionary, and jot down the definitions for future drill? That's ambitious, but unrealistic

Your purpose for reading is to get information and ideas from the text, not to make word lists. Stopping to look up a particular word in the dictionary may or may not improve your vacabulary, but it definitely interrupts your train of thought and detracts from your comprehension of the material. A good reader can usually employ tools other than the dictionary to get the actual meaning of a word and still not lose any understanding of the ideas in the passage.

This chapter will explain the use of three such tools: (1) context clues, (2) structural clues, and (3) glossary. It will also explain how to use the dictionary as more than a word decoder.

Context Clues

Complex scientific material has a heavy load of specialized vocabulary. Fortunately, new words are often defined as they are introduced in the text. In other words, the sentence itself explains the meaning of the word. For example, can you define the following?

erythrocytes   oxyhemoglobin

Now read a textbook sentence in which these two words appear and then indicate the correct definition for each word.

When oxygen diffuses into the blood in external respiration, most of it enters the red blood cells, or erythrocytes, and unites with the hemoglobin in these cells, forming a compound called oxyhemoglobin.

Willis H. Johnson et al., *Essentials of Biology*

erythrocytes means
(a) diffused oxygen
(b) red blood cells
(c) respiration process

oxyhemoglobin means
(a) hemoglobin without oxygen
(b) dominant oxygen cells
(c) combination of oxygen and hemoglobin

Notice that the first word is defined as a synonym in an appositive phrase, and the second is defined in the sentence.

In political science you will come across the term *gerrymander*. Keep reading and see if you can figure out the meaning from the following sentence.

Since Governor Elbridge Gerry's newly engineered electoral district "had the shape of the salamander," it quickly came to be labeled a "gerrymander," and since its wildly convoluted shape seemed to typify the widespread practice of forming districts with distorted boundaries, the usage of the term spread.

Theodore J. Lowi, *American Government: Incomplete Conquest*

gerrymander means
(a) dividing voting districts unevenly to give unfair advantage
(b) member of the salamander family
(c) voting in a new electoral district

convoluted means
(a) twisted
(b) inflated
(c) reduced

Both of these words can be figured out from restatements within the sentence.

In psychology you might frequently find a complicated word describing something you have often thought about but had not named. Read the following sentence to find out what *psychokinesis* means:

Another psychic phenomenon is *psychokinesis,* the ability to affect physical events without physical intervention. You can test your powers of psychokinesis by trying to influence the fall of dice from a mechanical shaker. Are you able to have the dice come up a certain number with a greater frequency than would occur by chance?

Douglas W. Matheson, *Introductory Psychology: The Modern View*

psychokinesis means
(a) extrasensory perception
(b) an influence on happenings without physical tampering
(c) physical intervention affecting physical change

Here the word was first defined in a complicated manner and then clarified by a simple example.

To summarize the sample exercises, three types of context clues that are frequently used in textbook material are:

1. Synonyms or direct definition
2. Restatement within the sentence
3. Clarification by example

• *Exercise 1*

How many of the following words can you define? Look down the list and check the definitions of as many as possible. Appearing in a list, the words seem difficult, but when used in sentences, they become easy. In the textbook excerpts that follow this list, each of these words has been noted in italics; read the sentences and then indicate *a, b, c,* or *d* for the current definition of each word. You are now using context clues to help you determine the meaning of unknown textbook vocabulary.

____ 1. **usurped**
a. shortened
b. acknowledged
c. aggravated
d. seized

____ 2. **derived**
a. ridiculed
b. dismayed
c. originated
d. encouraged

____ 3. **adversaries**
a. supporters
b. soldiers
c. voters
d. enemies

____ 4. **assimilationist**
a. one who adopts the habits of a larger cultural group
b. a machinist
c. typist
d. one who files correspondence

____ 5. **equalitarian**
a. horseman
b. nonauthoritarian
c. rigid
d. nonflexible

____ 6. **self-actualization**
a. imitation of self
b. reality counseling
c. achievement to fullest degree
d. evaluation of past experiences

____ 7. **proximity**
a. substitution
b. stubbornness
c. uncertainty
d. nearness

____ 8. **plausibility**
a. believability
b. spontaneity
c. amusement
d. reversibility

____ 9. **heterogeneous**
a. revolutionary
b. stagnant
c. intelligent
d. dissimilar (different)

____ 10. **gastrovascular**
a. relating to arteries of petroleum
b. explosive
c. digestive and circulatory in nature
d. cellular interaction

____ 11. **planarians**
a. meteorites
b. small worms
c. birds
d. lizards

____ 12. **anticoagulants**
a. demonstrators
b. substances against clotting
c. coal-mining disease agents
d. germs

____ 13. **ameliorated**
a. improved
b. finalized
c. united
d. exterminated

____ 14. **expropriated**
a. took from its owners
b. industrialized
c. approximated
d. increased in size

____ 15. **adherents**
a. children
b. followers
c. instigators
d. detractors

____ 16. **stimulus**
a. writing implement
b. distinguishing mark
c. something that incites action
d. result

____ 17. **debilitating**
a. weakening
b. reinforcing
c. exciting
d. enjoyable

____ 18. **autocratic**
a. automatic
b. democratic
c. self-starting
d. dictatorial

_____ 19. **incentive**
a. debt
b. sensory agent
c. encouragement
d. suggestion

_____ 20. **disseminated**
a. dissolved
b. spread
c. destroyed
d. originated

1. Henry, to the end of his life, thought of himself as a pious and orthodox Catholic who had restored the independent authority of the Church of England *usurped* centuries before by the Bishop of Rome.

Shepard B. Clough et al., A History of the Western World

2,3. But his own income was *derived* largely from other sources. He regained much of the royal domain and its revenues that had previously passed out of the crown's hand and added to it by confiscating the estates of his *adversaries*.

ibid.

4. When members of a minority group wish to give up what is distinctive about them and become just like the majority, they take an *assimilationist* position. An example is the Urban League.

Reece McGee et al., Sociology: An Introduction

5. The goal argument should also hold for organizations of the same general type. For example, if we see that some elementary schools are organized in an authoritarian way, giving students and teachers little independence and flexibility, while others are democratic and *equalitarian* then we are led to suspect goal differences as well.

ibid.

6. Rogers believes that everyone has a tendency toward *'self-actualization'*, the realization of one's potentials, and stresses that the human need for acceptance and approval is essential if self-actualization is to occur.

ibid.

7,8,9. However, the United States has lived in rather close *proximity* to its own Constitution and can by virtue of that fact at least claim, with some *plausibility*, that as a country we have managed to maintain conquest over an immensely *heterogeneous* society without falling prey to tyranny.

Theodore J. Lowi, American Government: Incomplete Conquest

10. The gut is essentially an elaborate *gastrovascular* cavity.

Willis H. Johnson et al., Essentials of Biology

11. Locomotion ranges from the generally nonmotile tapeworms to freely moving flatworms such as *planarians*, that glide on a slime they secrete by ciliary action of their epidermal cells and generalized muscular contractions of the body.

ibid.

12. The body can produce some natural *anticoagulants* such as heparin or dicumarol, which are formed in the liver. Also, some animals that depend on blood for nutrition—such as fleas and leeches—secrete substances to inhibit clotting.

ibid.

13. If France's sharp regional differences in development and prosperity are to be *ameliorated*, the Southeast and the West must be encouraged to grow more rapidly.

Jesse H. Wheeler, Jr., J. Trenton Kostbade and Richard S. Thoman, Regional Geography of the World

14. Under a decree of September 1952, the government *expropriated* several hundred thousand acres from large landholders and redistributed this land among the peasants.

ibid.

15. One of the fundamental features of Hinduism has been the division of its *adherents* into the most elaborate caste system ever known.

ibid.

16. While we are sleeping, for example, we are hardly aware of what is happening around us, but we are aware to some degree. Any loud noise or other abrupt *stimulus* will almost certainly awaken us.

Gardner Lindzey, Calvin Hall and Richard F. Thompson, *Psychology*

17. However, anyone who has passed through several time zones while flying east or west knows how difficult it can be to change from one sleep schedule to another. This "jet lag" can be so *debilitating* that many corporations will not allow their executives to enter negotiations for at least two days after such a trip.

ibid.

18. *Autocratic* leadership can be extremely effective if the people wielding it have enough power to enforce their decisions and if their followers know that they have it. It is especially useful in military situations where speed of decision is critical. Among its disadvantages are the lack of objectivity and the disregard for opinions of subordinates.

David J. Rachman and Michael Mescon, *Business Today*

19. Many social critics decry profits as an *incentive* but have proposed no practical alternative in a free society. The only other incentive that has worked is the one used most often in communist countries: severe punishment for nonproductive persons.

ibid.

20. Disseminated Magmatic Deposits are the simplest of the magmatic deposits. The valuable mineral is *disseminated* or scattered throughout the igneous body. In the diamond deposits of South Africa, for example, the diamonds are disseminated in unusual rock, somewhat similar to peridotite.

Robert J. Foster, *Physical Geology*

Structure

What is the longest word in the English language and what does it mean? Maxwell Nurnberg and Morris Rosenblum in *How to Build a Better Vocabulary* (Prentice-Hall, Inc. 1949) say that in 1939 the longest word in Webster's *New International Dictionary* was

pneumonoultramicroscopicsilicovolcanokoniosis

Look at the word again and notice the smaller and more familiar word parts. Do you know enough of the smaller parts to figure out the meaning of the word? Nurnberg and Rosenblum unlock the meaning as follows:

pneumono: pertaining to the lungs, as in *pneumo*nia
ultra: beyond, as in *ultra*violet rays
micro: small, as in *micro*scope
scopic: from the root of Greek verb *skopein,* to view or look at
silico: from the element *silicon,* found in quartz, flint, and sand
volcano: the meaning of this is obvious
koni: the principal root, from a Greek word for dust
osis: a suffix indicating illness, as in trichin*osis*

Now, putting the parts together again, we deduce that *pneumonoultramicroscopicsili-covolcanokoniosis* is a disease of the lungs caused by extremely small particles of volcanic ash and dust.

This dramatic example demonstrates how an extremely long and technical word can become more manageable by breaking it into smaller parts.

Often you can apply what you know about one word to unlock the meaning of another. Like people, words have families and, in some cases, an abundance of close relations. Clusters, or what might be called "word families," are comprised of words with the same base or root. For example, the root word *vert* means "to turn." By adding prefixes, suffixes, or a combination of the two to *vert,* the one base word expands into many family members.

• *Exercise 2*

For each of the following, supply the "family member."

1. to change one's beliefs: _____vert

2. to go back to old ways again: _____vert

3. a car with a removable top: _____ vert _____

4. to change the direction of a stream: _____vert

5. activities intended to undermine or destroy: _____vers_____

6. an outgoing, gregarious person: _____vert

7. a quiet, introspective, shy person: _____vert

8. conditions that are turned against you; misfortune: _____vers_____

9. one who deviates from normal behavior, especially sexual: _____vert

10. the side of a coin bearing the main design: _____verse

In several of the *vert* examples, the letters change slightly to accommodate language sounds. *Vert* becomes *vers* or *verse*. Such variations of a letter or two are typical when working with word parts. Letters are often dropped or added to maintain the rhythm of the language, but the meaning of the word part remains the same regardless of the change in spelling. For example, the prefix *con* means "with" or "together" as in *conduct.* This same prefix is used with variations in many other words:

cooperate   **col**lection   **cor**relate   **com**municate

Thus, *con, co, col, cor, com* are all forms of the prefix that means "with" or "together."

A thorough knowledge of word parts will help you unlock the meaning of literally thousands of words. The most effective way to remember the meaning of a root, prefix, or suffix is to relate the part to words that you already know. *Port,* for example, means "to carry." Thinking of words like *import, export, transport,* and *portable* helps to fix the definition in your mind.

Now what does *deportation* mean? What are the parts?

_____   _____   _____

The following is a list of the most frequently used word parts. Some authorities say that if you know these parts, you can unlock the meaning of as many as 14,000 words. Study this list and make up additional example words from your own vocabulary. Learn the meaning of each of these parts and use them to expand your vocabulary.

Word Part	Meaning	Example	Your example
1. ad	to, toward	advance	_____
2. com, con, co, col, cor	with, together	comrade	_____
3. in, im, il, ir	not	incomplete	_____
4. de	down, from, away from	debark	_____
5. ab	away from	abstain	_____
6. dis	not, opposite of	disinfect	_____
7. ex	out of	exit	_____
8. re	back, again	retread	_____
9. ob, op	against	obliterate	_____
10. in, im, en, em	into	ingrown	_____
11. port	carry	portable	_____
12. mit, miss	send	transmit	_____
13. duct, duce	lead	conduct	_____
14. vers, vert	turn	revert	_____
15. ten, tent	hold	content	_____
16. spec, spect	to look at	spectacle	_____
17. cap, cept, cep	take, receive	intercept	_____
18. fac, fact, fic, fec	make, do	manufacture	_____
19. ven, vent, veni	come	advent	_____
20. fid, fide, feder, feal	faith, trust	confidence	_____

21. er, or, ant, ist	person who	actor	_____
22. ation, ition, ion	act of	violation	_____
23. able, ible	capable of	enjoyable	_____
24. ful	full of	careful	_____
25. ology	study of	climatology	_____
26. al	relating to	natural	_____
27. ify, fy	make or cause to be	exemplify	_____
28. tude	quality of	solitude	_____
29. ism	doctrine of	romanticism	_____
30. age	act of, condition of	salvage	_____

• *Exercise 3*

Using the word part from the corresponding number of the word-part list, write a word to match the definition in each blank.

1. one who has a habit for something _____

2. infectious or catching _____

3. not possible _____

4. to jump from the tracks _____

5. away from the normal _____

6. to get off a horse _____

7. to breathe out _____

8. to patch up or fix _____

9. the reverse of something _____

10. to blow air into _____

11. to trade or carry goods out of the country _____

12. a duty one is sent to perform _____

13. an artificial channel for bringing water _____

14. usable on both sides _____

15. one who leases an apartment, occupant _____

16. one who looks on, an observer _____

17. the party for receiving guests after a wedding _____

18. the plant where products are made   _____

19. a meeting for people of similar interest   _____

20. to trust a friend with a secret   _____

21. one who has a specialty   _____

22. the act of making pure   _____

23. that which you are able to see   _____

24. being full of thanks   _____

25. study of bacteria   _____

26. relating to the mouth, spoken   _____

27. to make larger in size   _____

28. state of thankfulness   _____

29. doctrine concerned with reality and facts   _____

30. act of storing   _____

Glossary

The first shock in a new subject area, like sociology or geology, is the vocabulary. Each subject seems to have a language or jargon of its own. Words like *sociocultural,* or *socioeconomic* crop up again and again in a sociology text. In truth, these words are somewhat unique to the subject-matter area—they are "made-up words" to describe sociological phenomena. The best explanation of such words and their relation to the subject area can usually be found in the textbook itself rather than in the dictionary. Often, textbooks have definitions inserted in a corner or at the bottom of a page, or more frequently, texts will include a glossary of terms at the end of the book. The glossary defines the words as they are used in the textbook. Examples of two different glossary pages follow, one from a psychology and another from a biology textbook.

• **Exercise 4**

By referring to the glossary page from *Introductory Psychology,* answer the following with *T* (true) or *F* (false).

_____ 1. A person with neurosis should not be encouraged to hold a full-time job.

_____ 2. An Oedipus complex is associated with a female child.

_____ 3. An obsessive-compulsive neurotic does not have complete control over his own life.

_____ 4. Neurons are an integral part of the nervous system.

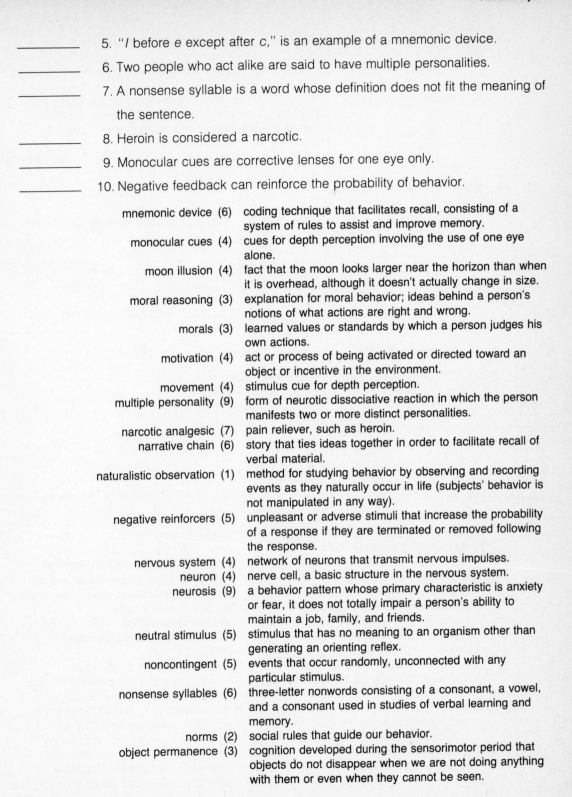

_____ 5. "*I* before *e* except after *c*," is an example of a mnemonic device.

_____ 6. Two people who act alike are said to have multiple personalities.

_____ 7. A nonsense syllable is a word whose definition does not fit the meaning of the sentence.

_____ 8. Heroin is considered a narcotic.

_____ 9. Monocular cues are corrective lenses for one eye only.

_____ 10. Negative feedback can reinforce the probability of behavior.

mnemonic device (6)	coding technique that facilitates recall, consisting of a system of rules to assist and improve memory.
monocular cues (4)	cues for depth perception involving the use of one eye alone.
moon illusion (4)	fact that the moon looks larger near the horizon than when it is overhead, although it doesn't actually change in size.
moral reasoning (3)	explanation for moral behavior; ideas behind a person's notions of what actions are right and wrong.
morals (3)	learned values or standards by which a person judges his own actions.
motivation (4)	act or process of being activated or directed toward an object or incentive in the environment.
movement (4)	stimulus cue for depth perception.
multiple personality (9)	form of neurotic dissociative reaction in which the person manifests two or more distinct personalities.
narcotic analgesic (7)	pain reliever, such as heroin.
narrative chain (6)	story that ties ideas together in order to facilitate recall of verbal material.
naturalistic observation (1)	method for studying behavior by observing and recording events as they naturally occur in life (subjects' behavior is not manipulated in any way).
negative reinforcers (5)	unpleasant or adverse stimuli that increase the probability of a response if they are terminated or removed following the response.
nervous system (4)	network of neurons that transmit nervous impulses.
neuron (4)	nerve cell, a basic structure in the nervous system.
neurosis (9)	a behavior pattern whose primary characteristic is anxiety or fear, it does not totally impair a person's ability to maintain a job, family, and friends.
neutral stimulus (5)	stimulus that has no meaning to an organism other than generating an orienting reflex.
noncontingent (5)	events that occur randomly, unconnected with any particular stimulus.
nonsense syllables (6)	three-letter nonwords consisting of a consonant, a vowel, and a consonant used in studies of verbal learning and memory.
norms (2)	social rules that guide our behavior.
object permanence (3)	cognition developed during the sensorimotor period that objects do not disappear when we are not doing anything with them or even when they cannot be seen.

obsessions (9)   persistent thoughts that a person may recognize as irrational but still cannot stop thinking.

obsessive-compulsive neurotic (9)   person who has repetitive thoughts or impulses that rule his life.

Oedipus complex (3)   according to Freud, sexual attachment which a boy has to his mother. (A girl's attachment to her father is usually called an Electra complex and doesn't seem to occur as often as the Oedipus complex.)

Douglas W. Matheson, *Introductory Psychology: The Modern View*

• *Exercise 5*

By referring to the glossary page from *Essentials of Biology,* answer the following with *T* (true) or *F* (false).

_____   1. A pollen grain and a pollen tube are the same.

_____   2. Plankton denotes both plant and animal organisms.

_____   3. The placenta is a region for the exchange of nutrients between a mother and an embryo.

_____   4. Photoperiodism includes both a plant and animal response.

_____   5. Chemical waste can be considered pollution.

_____   6. Platelets help stop bleeding.

_____   7. Phototropism is the intensity of light on a plant.

_____   8. The pistil is not part of the flower.

_____   9. A phylum is organized in a random order.

_____   10. An animal, such as man, with one life form in a life cycle is polymorphic.

Phenylketonuria   A metabolic disease characterized by faulty phenylalanine metabolism and mental retardation.

Pheromone   Substances secreted by one individual which elicit a physiological, developmental, or behavioral response from an individual of the same species; an insect sex attractant.

Phloem   A conducting tissue, functioning chiefly in food conduction. Sieve tubes and sieve cells are the important units of conduction.

Phosphoglyceric acid   A three-carbon compound that is the first intermediate to appear in photosynthesis; also metabolite in glycolysis.

Photon   A light quantum.

Photoperiodism   Response of plants in growth and development to differing lengths of exposure to light; refers to vegetative organ responses as well as to flowering response; also response of animals to light duration.

Photophosphorylation   ATP production from ADP and P_i under the direct influence of light.

Photoreactivation   Recovery of microorganisms from ultraviolet damage under the influence of white light.

Photosynthesis   The manufacture of a simple carbohydrate from CO_2 and water in the presence of chlorophyll, with light as a source of energy and with electrons released. Oxygen is generally the electron acceptor.

Phototropism   Movement toward or away from light.

Phylogeny   The evolutionary history of a group of organisms.

Phylum   A taxonomic category; subdivision of a kingdom; a group of next higher rank than a class.

Phytochrome   Pigment that exists in green plants in two forms, one absorbs red light and one far-red light; involved in such processes as flowering, dormancy, leaf formation, and seed germination.

Pinocytosis   The intake of fluid droplets by a cell.

Pistil   The ovule-bearing part of the flower, composed of one to several carpels (megasphorophylls).

Pith   The central area of parenchyma cells in a shoot axis.

Placenta   In plants, a central part of some fruits, such as tomatoes, and to which the seeds are attached. In animals, the combination of extraembryonic membranes of the embryo and the wall of the uterus of the mother. It is a region for exchanges of nutrients, gases and wastes between the mother and the embryo.

Plankton   Free-floating microscopic aquatic organisms, both plant and animal.

Plaque method   Determination of the number of bacterial viruses in a sample by counting the clear zones of viral lysis in a layer of bacteria.

Plasma   Fluid fraction of blood in which corpuscles are suspended.

Plasmagel   The outer region of the endoplasm; stiff and jellylike.

Plasma membrane   The very thin membrane that surrounds and differentiates from the cytoplasm of the cell.

Plasmasol   The inner part of the endoplasm; fluid in nature.

Plasmodesma   Fine thread that leads from the cytoplasm of one plant cell through the wall to the cytoplasm of an adjacent cell.

Plasmolysis   Shrinkage of the cytoplasm of a plant cell away from the wall when placed in hypertonic solution due to loss of water.

Platelets   Formed elements in the blood that participate in clotting of blood.

Polar body   The very small nonfunctioning cells that are produced in the maturation of an egg cell.

Polar nuclei   In plants, two nuclei of the endosperm which will triple-fuse with a sperm nucleus.

Pollen grain   Young male gametophyte of seed plants.

Pollen sacs   Areas in the anthers derived from microsporangia and laden with pollen.

Pollen tube   An outgrowth of a germinated pollen grain.

Pollination   Mechanical transfer of pollen from where it is formed to where it will germinate.

Pollution   Defilement of the environment with solid waste, heat, trash, chemicals, sewage, and so forth.

Polymer   A large molecule composed of many similar units; for example, polysaccharides, proteins, and nucleic acids.

Polymorphism   The occurrence of more than one body form in the life cycle of an animal.

Polypeptide   Many amino acids linked together from amino end to carboxyl end.

Polyploid   Containing one or more extra sets of chromosomes.

Polytene   The duplication of chromosomes in the absence of cell division. Usually there are many duplications, thereby giving rise to large chromosomes.

Population   A group of organisms of the same species that interbreed with one another in a particular geographical area.

Position effect   The phenomenon of varying phenotype with the different arrangement of the same number of genes on the chromosomes; for example, bar eye in the fruit fly.

Primary block   A metabolic blockage due to a genetically inactivated enzyme.

Primary endosperm nuclei   The single triploid nucleus in the ovule of higher plants that is the product of triple fusion.

Willis H. Johnson et al., *Essentials of Biology*

Dictionary

The dictionary obviously contains the definitions of words, but, in fact, it goes far beyond that. It also provides pronunciations, preferred spellings, origins, grammar, history, sample usage, and sometimes visual examples.

• *Exercise 6*

To illustrate the value of the dictionary as a reference tool, answer the following questions, using page 691 from Webster's *New Collegiate Dictionary*, with *T* (true), *F* (false) or *CT* (can't tell).

_____ 1. If *Mamluk* is spelled *Mameluke,* it is pronounced differently.

_____ 2. The food supplied to the Israelites in the Bible is called *mana.*

_____ 3. The tusks of ancient mammoths have been found in the United States by geologists.

_____ 4. The three words, *man, about,* and *town* can be used as a single hyphenated word to denote worldliness.

_____ 5. When *man* means "brace" it is being used as a verb.

_____ 6. *Manage* is derived from the French word *maneggiare* meaning *hand.*

_____ 7. The bite of a black mamba often kills its victim.

_____ 8. The first *n* in *mañana* is pronounced the same as the second.

_____ 9. The past tense of manacle is *manaclled.*

_____ 10. Manitoba (Man.) is a province in Canada.

691

malvoisie ● Manchu

mal·voi·sie \ˌmalv-wə-'zē\ *n* [F, fr. MF *malvesie,* fr. *Malvesie* Monemvasia]: MALMSEY

ma·ma *or* **mam·ma** \'mäm-ə, *chiefly Brit* mə-'má\ *n* [baby talk] **1** : MOTHER **2** *slang* : WIFE, WOMAN

mam·ba \'mäm-bə, 'mam-\ *n* [Zulu im-amba]: any of several tropical and southern African venomous snakes (genus *Dendraspis*) related to the cobras but with no hood; *esp* : an aggressive southern African snake (*D. angusticeps*) that grows to a length of 12 feet, has a light or olive green phase and a black phase, and readily inflicts its often fatal bite

mam·bo \'mäm-(ˌ)bō\ *n, pl* **mambos** [AmerSp] : a ballroom dance of Cuban origin that resembles the rumba and the cha-cha; *also* : the music for this dance — **mambo** *vi*

Mam·luk \'mam-ˌlük\ *or* **Mam·e·luke** \'mam-ə-ˌlük\ *n* [Ar *mamlūk,* lit., slave] **1** : a member of a politically powerful Egyptian military class occupying the sultanate from 1250 to 1517 **2** *usu* **Mameluke,** often not *cap* : a Caucasian or oriental slave in Muslim countries

mam·ma \'mam-ə\ *n, pl* **mam·mae** \'mam-ˌē, -ˌī\ [L, mother, breast, of baby-talk origin] : a mammary gland and its accessory parts — **mam·mate** \'mam-ˌāt\ *adj*

pound idea of infinite Spirit : the spiritual image and likeness of God : the full representation of Mind **6** *often cap* : POLICE ⟨when I heard the siren, I knew it was the *Man* —Amer. Speech⟩ **7** *often cap* : the white establishment : white society ⟨surprise that any black ... should take on so about The *Man* —Peter Goldman⟩ — **man·less** \'man-ləs\ *adj* — **man·like** \-ˌlīk\ *adj* — **as one man** : with the agreement and consent of all : UNANIMOUSLY — **one's own man** : free from interference or control : INDEPENDENT — **to a man** : without exception

²man *vt* **manned; man·ning 1 a** : to supply with men ⟨~ a fleet⟩ **b** : to station members of a ship's crew at ⟨~ the capstan⟩ **c** : to serve in the force or complement of ⟨workers who ~ the production lines⟩ **2** : to furnish with strength or powers of resistance : BRACE

³man *abbr* manual

Man *abbr* Manitoba

ma·na \'män-ə\ *n* [of Melanesian & Polynesian origin; akin to Hawaiian & Maori *mana*] **1** : the power of the elemental forces of nature embodied in an object or person **2** : moral authority : PRESTIGE

mam·mal \'mam-əl\ *n* [deriv. of LL *mammalis* of the breast, fr. L *mamma* breast] : any of a class (Mammalia) of higher vertebrates comprising man and all other animals that nourish their young with milk secreted by mammary glands and have the skin usu. more or less covered with hair — **mam·ma·li·an** \mə-'mā-lē-ən, ma-\ *adj or n*

mam·mal·o·gy \mə-'mal-ə-jē, ma-'mal-, -'māl-\ *n* [ISV, blend of *mammal* and *-logy*] : a branch of zoology dealing with mammals — **mam·mal·o·gist** \-jəst\ *n*

mam·ma·ry \'mam-ə-rē\ *adj* : of, relating to, lying near, or affecting the mammae

mammary gland *n* : one of the large compound modified sebaceous glands that in female mammals are modified to secrete milk, are situated ventrally in pairs, and usu. terminate in a nipple

mam·ma·to·cu·mu·lus \ma-,māt-ō-'kyü-myə-ləs\ *n* [NL, fr. L *mammatus* having breasts, (fr. *mamma*) + NL *cumulus*] : a cumulus or cumulostratus storm cloud having breast-shaped protuberances below

mam·mer *vi* [ME *mameren* to stammer, of imit. origin] *obs* : WAVER, HESITATE

mam·mil·la·ry \'mam-ə,ler-ē, ma-'mil-ə-rē\ *adj* [L *mammilla* breast, nipple, dim. of *mamma*] **1** : of, relating to, or resembling the breasts **2** : studded with breast-shaped protuberances

mam·mil·lat·ed \'mam-ə-,lāt-əd\ *adj* [LL *mammillatus*, fr. L *mammilla*] **1** : having nipples or small protuberances **2** : having the form of a bluntly rounded protuberance

¹mam·mock \'mam-ək\ *n* [origin unknown] *chiefly dial* : a broken piece : SCRAP

²mammock *vt, chiefly dial* : to tear into fragments : MANGLE

mam·mo·gram \'mam-ə-,gram\ *n* [L *mamma* + -o- + -gram] : a photograph of the breasts made by X rays

mam·mog·ra·phy \ma-'mäg-rə-fē\ *n* : X-ray examination of the breasts for early detection of cancer

mam·mon \'mam-ən\ *n, often cap* [LL *mammona*, fr. Gk *mamōna*, fr. Aram *māmōnā* riches] : material wealth or possessions esp. as having a debasing influence ⟨you cannot serve God and ~ —Mt 6:24 (RSV)⟩ — **mam·mon·ism** \-ə-,niz-əm\ *n*

mam·mon·ist \-ə-nəst\ *n, archaic* : one devoted to the ideal or pursuit of wealth

mam·mon·ite \-ə-,nīt\ *n, archaic* : MAMMONIST

¹mam·moth \'mam-əth\ *n* [Russ *mamont, mamot*] **1** : any of numerous extinct Pleistocene elephants distinguished from recent elephants by molars with cementum filling the spaces between the ridges of enamel and by large size, very long tusks that curve upward, and well-developed body hair **2** : something immense of its kind : GIANT ⟨a company that is a ~ of the industry⟩

²mammoth *adj* : of very great size : GIGANTIC **syn** see HUGE

mam·my \'mam-ē\ *n, pl* **mammies** [alter. of *mamma*] **1** : MAMA **2** : a Negro woman serving as a nurse to white children esp. formerly in the southern U.S.

mammoth 1

mammy wagon *n* : a small open-sided bus or light truck used to transport passengers or goods in West Africa

¹man \'man, *in compounds* ,man *or* mən\ *n, pl* **men** \'men, *in compounds* ,men *or* mən\ [ME, fr. OE; akin to OHG *man* man, Skt *manu*] **1 a** (1) : a human being; *esp* : an adult male human (2) : a man belonging to a particular category (as by birth, residence, membership, or occupation) — usu. used in combination ⟨councilman⟩ (3) : HUSBAND **b** : the human race : MANKIND **c** : a bipedal primate mammal (*Homo sapiens*) that is anatomically related to the great apes but distinguished esp. by notable development of the brain with a resultant capacity for articulate speech and abstract reasoning, is usu. considered to form a variable number of freely interbreeding races, and is the sole representative of a natural family (Hominidae); *broadly* : any living or extinct member of this family **d** (1) : one possessing in high degree the qualities considered distinctive of manhood (2) *obs* : the quality or state of being manly : MANLINESS **e** : FELLOW, CHAP ⟨come, come, my good ~⟩ **f** — used interjectionally to express intensity of feeling ⟨~, what a game⟩ **2 a** : a feudal tenant : VASSAL **b** : an adult male servant **c** *pl* : the working force as distinguished from the employer and usu. the management **3** : INDIVIDUAL, PERSON ⟨a ~ could get killed there⟩ **4** : one of the distinctive objects moved by each player in various board games **5** *Christian Science* : the com-

man–about–town \,man-ə-,baut-'taun\ *n, pl* **men–about–town** \,men-\ : a worldly and socially active man

¹man·a·cle \'man-i-kəl\ *n* [ME *manicle*, fr. MF, fr. L *manicula*, dim. of *manus* hand — more at MANUAL] **1** : a shackle for the hand or wrist : HANDCUFF **2** : something used as a restraint

²manacle *vt* **man·a·cled; man·a·cling** \-k(ə-)liŋ\ **1** : to confine (the hands) with manacles **2** : to make fast or secure : BIND; *broadly* : to restrain from movement, progress, or action **syn** see HAMPER

¹man·age \'man-ij\ *vb* **man·aged; man·ag·ing** [It *maneggiare*, fr. *mano* hand, fr. L *manus*] *vt* **1** : to handle or direct with a degree of skill or address: as **a** : to make and keep submissive ⟨my mother . . . was the only one that ever could ~ him —George Macdonald †1905⟩ **b** : to treat with care : HUSBAND ⟨managed his resources carefully⟩ **2** : to alter by manipulation **3** : to succeed in accomplishing : CONTRIVE ~ *vi* **1 a** : to direct or carry on business or affairs **b** : to admit of being carried on **2** : to achieve one's purpose **syn** see CONDUCT

²manage *n* [It *maneggio* management, training of a horse, fr. *maneggiare*] **1 a** : the action and paces of a trained riding horse **b** : the schooling or handling of a horse **c** : a riding school : MANEGE **2** *obs* : MANAGEMENT

man·age·able \'man-ij-ə-bəl\ *adj* : capable of being managed : TRACTABLE — **man·age·abil·i·ty** \,man-ij-ə-'bil-ət-ē\ *n* — **man·age·able·ness** \'man-ij-ə-bəl-nəs\ *n* — **man·age·ably** \-blē\ *adv*

man·age·ment \'man-ij-mənt\ *n* **1** : the act or art of managing : the conducting or supervising of something (as a business) **2** : judicious use of means to accomplish an end **3** : capacity for managing : executive skill **4** : the collective body of those who manage or direct an enterprise — **man·age·men·tal** \,man-ij-'ment-ᵊl\ *adj*

man·ag·er \'man-ij-ər\ *n* : one that manages: as **a** : one who conducts business or household affairs **b** : a person whose work or profession is management **c** (1) : a person who directs a team or athlete **c** (2) : a student who in scholastic or collegiate sports supervises equipment and records under the direction of a coach — **man·ag·er·ess** \-ə-rəs\ *n* — **man·a·ge·ri·al** \,man-ə-'jir-ē-əl\ *adj* — **man·a·ge·ri·al·ly** \-ē-ə-lē\ *adv* — **man·ag·er·ship** \'man-ij-ər-,ship\ *n*

managing editor *n* : an editor in executive and supervisory charge of all editorial activities of a publication (as a newspaper)

¹ma·ña·na \mən-'yän-ə\ *adv* [Sp, lit., tomorrow, fr. earlier *cras mañana* early tomorrow, fr. *cras* tomorrow (fr. L) + *mañana* early, fr. L *mane* early in the morning] : at an indefinite time in the future

²mañana *n* : an indefinite time in the future

man ape *n* **1** : GREAT APE **2** : any of various fossil primates intermediate in characters between recent man and the great apes

Ma·nas·seh \mə-'nas-ə\ *n* [Heb *Měnashsheh*] **1** : a son of Joseph and the traditional eponymous ancestor of one of the tribes of Israel **2** : a king of Judah reigning in the 7th century B.C. and noted for his attempt to establish polytheism

man–at–arms \,man-ət-'ärmz\ *n, pl* **men–at–arms** \,men-\ : SOLDIER; *esp* : a heavily armed and usu. mounted soldier

man·a·tee \'man-ə-,tē\ *n* [Sp *manatí*] : any of several chiefly tropical aquatic herbivorous mammals (genus *Trichechus*) that differ from the related dugong esp. in having the tail broad and rounded

manatee

Man·ches·ter terrier \'man-,ches-tər, -,chə-stər-\ *n* [*Manchester*, England] : any of a breed of small slightly built short-haired black-and-tan terriers developed in England by interbreeding local rat-catching dogs with whippets

man·chet \'man-chət\ *n* [ME] *archaic* : a loaf or roll of fine wheat bread

man·chi·neel \,man-chə-'nē(ə)l\ *n* [F *mancenille*, fr. Sp *manzanilla*, fr. dim. of *manzana* apple] : a poisonous tropical American tree (*Hippomane mancinella*) of the spurge family having a blistering milky juice and apple-shaped fruit

Man·chu \'man-(,)chü, man-\ *n, pl* **Manchu** *or* **Manchus** **1** : a member of the native Mongolian race of Manchuria that is related

ə abut	ˢ kitten	ər further	a back	ā bake	ä cot, cart
au̇ out	ch chin	e less	ē easy	g gift	i trip	ī life
j joke	ŋ sing	ō flow	ȯ flaw	ȯi coin	th thin	t̲h̲ this
ü loot	u̇ foot	y yet	yü few	yu̇ furious	zh vision	

Chapter Three

Overviewing

Mindless reading is minus thinking and is a complete waste of time. Calling words is not really reading; reading takes energy. Reading involves anticipation, synthesis, and memory; it is an active rather than a passive process and requires that thinking occur before, during, and after the act.

Because of the purpose, textbook reading demands a more organized approach than recreational reading. Reading a murder mystery might be an escape into intrigue and adventure, whereas, the purpose of textbook reading is to learn and remember a body of information. Each chapter, and even each page, contains a heavy load for the reader. To be successful, the techniques must differ.

Research studies show that overviewing techniques increase understanding and retention of textbook material. These techniques involve organizational thinking both before and after reading and are called (1) previewing and (2) recalling.

Previewing

Experiment A: The Harvard Experiment

As an experiment, Dr. William Perry, director of a reading course at Harvard, presented 1500 freshmen with a complete chapter from a history book to read. He told them to read and study the chapter in any way they thought best to enable them to answer brief questions and write a short essay.

Twenty-two minutes later he stopped them, and to find out the methods of study they had used, he gave a multiple-choice test on the details. The entire class scored high. Then he asked them to write a short statement on what the chapter was all about. Only fifteen of "1500 of the finest freshmen readers in the country" were able to do so. These were the only ones who had "the moral courage" to pull themselves out of the details of the chapter to first skim through the pages and read the headings and subheadings, and to read the last paragraph clearly marked "Summary." In this particular chapter, the summary was unusually clear and well-organized. Half a minute's study of this summary paragraph would have given the reader a clear overview of the entire chapter.

Walter Pauk, *How to Study in College*

Only one percent of the students in this experiment really knew what they had read. They took the time initially to size up the situation rather than start with the first sentence and move to the next and then the next. The 15 students who previewed the material demonstrated superior reading comprehension over the 1485 who did not; they understood what the assignment was about as opposed to simply recalling details.

What Is Previewing?

Previewing is a method of "getting your act together" before starting to read by deciding what the material is about, what needs to be done, and how to go about doing it. It is formulating a reading strategy and then reading to meet those goals. Even though it may take a few extra minutes in the beginning, the results are worth the time, as demonstrated by the Harvard study. Previewing is the easy way to approach a text.

How to Preview?

What to Ask? • To preview, look over the material, think, and ask questions. The process is similar to the concentration technique of sparking an interest before reading, except that in previewing, the questions are more directly related to purpose. The focus is "What do I need to know and how do I go about finding it out?"

More specifically, ask the following questions before beginning to read:

1. What is *my purpose* for reading?
   What is it about? What do I already know about it? What will I need to know when I finish it?
2. How is the material *organized*?
   What is the general outline or framework of the material? Is the author listing reasons, explaining a process, or comparing a trend?
3. What will be my *plan* of attack?
   What parts seem most important? Do I need to read everything with equal care? Can I skim some parts? Can I skip some sections completely?

What to Read? • A public speaking "rule" says, "Tell them what you are going to tell them, tell them, and then tell them you told them." This same organizational pattern frequently applies to textbook material. An author begins with a brief introduction to overview the topic, the ideas are then developed in paragraphs or chapters, and concluding statements at the end summarize the important points the author wants remembered. Although this pattern is not true in every case, it can serve as a guide in determining what to read when previewing textbook material.

The following chart illustrates the previewing pattern:

Previewing: What to Read?

for a Book	for a Chapter or an Article
in beginning material	
Study the table of contents.	Read italicized introductory material.
Skim the first chapter.	Read the first paragraph.
in developmental material	
Skim the introductions to each chapter.	Read subheadings and boldface print.
Skim summary chapters (locate from table of contents).	Read the first sentence of some paragraphs.
in concluding material	
Skim the final chapter.	Read the last paragraph.
Stop and summarize your thoughts.	Stop and summarize your thoughts.

Previewing a Table of Contents

The table of contents outlines what is contained in the book and highlights issues that the author feels are most important. Previewing the table of contents can help you get a general idea of the book and how it is organized, predict possible exam questions, and locate the sections that are most important for a particular type of assignment.

• *Exercise 1*

Following is the table of contents of a sociology textbook. Glance over the chapter titles and think about the book as a whole. Anticipate what the book will probably cover, what will be left out, and what are the main concerns of the author. *Think* and then answer the questions that follow.

Table of Contents

Part 1:   Beginnings

      1. Life Designs: Concepts and Approaches
      2. The Acquisition of Gender Identities and Roles

Part 2:   Partner Selection in Adolescence and Young Adulthood
      3. From Childhood to Adolescence: Sources and Contexts of Change
      4. Pathways to Partners: Sociocultural Dimensions of Partner Selection
      5. Experiments in Choice: Partner and Mate Selection in Contemporary United States
      6. Living Together Before Marriage
      7. Pregnancy Before Marriage: Contraception, Abortion, and Out-Of-Marriage Births

Part 3:   Marriage and Families: Their Internal Designs
      8. The Beginnings of Marriage
      9. The Psychosocial Interior
      10. Marital Sexuality
      11. Fertility and the Family Life Cycle

Part 4:   Marriage and Families: Their External Connections
      12. Men and Women in the Labor Force
      13. The Labor of the Household
      14. The Ties of Kinship and Friendship
      15. Intimate and Erotic Relations Outside Marriage

Part 5:   Marriages and Families: Complexities and Crises
      16. The Impact of Change and Crisis
      17. Ending Marriages

Part 6:   The Multiple Worlds of the Nonmarried
      18. After Divorce and Death
      19. The Single Alternative

Epilogue: Continuity and Change in Life Designs

J. Gagnon and C. Greenblat, *Life Designs*

1. The book is divided into how many major sections?_____

2. The book follows the individual in society from gender identity in childhood to _____
_____.

3. A majority of the chapters in this book focus on what aspect of a person's life in society? _____

4. Which chapter seems to be most summary in nature?_____

5. What do chapters 6, 7, and 15 suggest about the authors' approach to the subject?_____

6. Suggest an essay exam question for Part 2. _____
_____

7. Suggest an essay exam question that would cover the information in parts 3, 4, and 5. _____
_____

8. If you were doing a research paper on widows in society, what chapter would you read? _____

9. If you were researching how people react in crowds, what chapter would your read? _____

10. If you were researching sex before marriage, what chapters would you read? _____

Previewing a Chapter

Rather than use a complete chapter as a practice exercise, the first paragraph, the subheadings, and the last paragraph of a chapter from a criminal justice textbook are included in the exercise below.

• *Exercise 2*

To preview, notice the title and read the first paragraph, the subheadings, and the summary. Think about the chapter as a whole, and then answer the questions that follow.

American Police Forces

As we saw in Chapter 3, the passage of laws is the responsibility of the legislative branches of federal, state, and local governments. When a law has been passed by a legislature, it must then be enforced. In modern societies, enforcing the law is the responsibility of policing agencies.

In this chapter we will briefly discuss the development of police forces and the ways in which American police forces are organized. We will then look at the diverse activities involved in the enforcement of law and end with a consideration of the people who make law enforcement a career.

History of American Police Forces
    European Origins
    The Development of Police Forces in the United States
Structure of American Police Forces
    Types of Policing Agencies
    Types of Department Organization
Police Activities
    Field Operations
        Patrol duties
        Effectiveness of patrol
        Domestic services
        Detective duties
        Special operations
        Juvenile units
        Apprehension of suspects
    Administration
    Technical Services
    Inspectional Services
The Police Personality
    Motivations for Entering Police Work
    Public Image and Private Sentiments

Summary

The origins of the American police system can be traced back to preindustrial England, where policing was a community effort, but the nature of the American experience and the settlement patterns on the North American continent created unique situations that shaped the development of police forces in this country. Most American metropolitan police forces evolved from systems employing a handful of men who were ill-trained and often had questionable credentials to professionalized forces employing hundreds or even thousands of officers who have specialized functions and who use sophisticated technical equipment.

Most law enforcement officers are employed by local police departments. There are also state, federal, and private policing agencies. The most common form of departmental organization is the traditional model, characterized by division into four bureaus: field operations, administrative services, technical services, and inspection. The modified plan, or team policing, is used in some large departments.

Traditionally the most important aspect of field operations, in terms of the resources allotted it, has been patrol work. The effectiveness of patrol in today's cities has come under serious questioning. Field operations also include domestic services, detective duties, traffic responsibilities, special operations, juvenile units, and apprehension of suspects.

Activities performed in the administrative services bureau include the formulation of policy decisions. This bureau is organized in a quasi-military, hierarchical manner characterized by division of labor, unity of command, chain of command, and span of control.

The technical services bureau provides record keeping and analyzing services. It also takes charge of the lockup or jail and of vehicles and other police equipment.

The functions of the inspectional services bureau revolve around inspecting police officers and investigating possible misconduct. Such bureaus also engage in a variety of intelligence-gathering activities.

There are many reasons that individuals give for wanting to become police officers; the major one seems to be job security. Some police officers may have authoritarian personality structures, possibly because of the nature of the job. There is hope that better training will help prepare officers for the demands of the job and create more professional police forces.

Peter C. Kratcoski and Donald B. Walker, *Criminal Justice in America*

1. This chapter is divided into how many major sections? _____

2. The purpose of this chapter is to describe

   a. _____

   b. _____

   c. _____

   d. _____

3. Chapter Three of *Criminal Justice in America* is primarily concerned with

_____

_____

4. How many police activities are categorized under field operations? _____

_____

5. Suggest an essay exam question concerning the history of the police force.

_____

_____

_____

6. Suggest an essay exam question concerning police activities. _____

_____

_____

7. What is the major motivation for entering police work? _____

8. Where is the most money spent in the police force? _____

9. If you were researching police personality structure, what section would you read? _____

10. If you were researching the chain of command in the police department, what section would you read? _____

How Does Skimming Differ from Previewing?

Skimming might be called a more intensive form of previewing; the difference is determined by purpose. Previewing gives background before the actual reading occurs and skimming can be done when a complete reading is not necessary. For example, if you are writing a research paper and need to use the ideas of several different authors, a thorough reading of each book or article probably is not needed. Instead, skim for the main ideas and the points relevant to your research, use what you need, and move on to other material.

Perhaps you have heard the advice, "To skim, read the first and last paragraphs and the first sentence of every other paragraph." Sometimes this will work, sometimes not. When a selection begins with an introduction and ends with a summary, the first part of the "rule of thumb" works. The following graphic design will help you visualize the pattern:

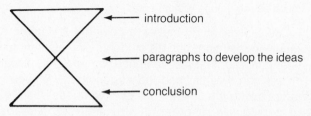

Frequently in textbook material the first sentence of the paragraph will state the topic covered in the paragraph. If so, reading the first sentence will give you an overview. Visualize the paragraph in the following manner:

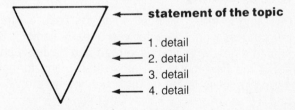

The problem in following this pattern, however, is that even though the first sentence frequently states the topic, it does not necessarily follow that all paragraphs must be constructed in this manner. In reality, you will also find topics stated in the middle, at the end, or sometimes not stated at all. Therefore, when you skim, remain flexible. Read the first sentence of a paragraph if it seems to have import. If not, skip to the next paragraph. Try the "rule of thumb" as long as you are not rigid and realize that it will not work every time. Skimming, like previewing, requires more thinking than reading.

• *Skimming Exercises*

The instructor's guide describes numerous skimming exercises that can be done using selections throughout this textbook.

Recalling

Experiment B: The Classic Spitzer Study

Herbert Spitzer ("Studies in Retention," *Journal of Educational Psychology* 30 [1939]: 641–659) investigated the effects of recall on retention with 3600 Iowa students. He divided the students into ten groups and gave each group the same article to read. Immediately after reading the article, Groups I and II recalled the important points of what they had read. The other eight groups, however, did not engage in any immediate recall activities.

To measure retention of the articles, tests were given to each group. The time of testing varied; some groups were tested one day after reading the article, some after seven days, and some after 14, 21, 28, and 63 days. Spitzer analyzed the data and found that "more is forgotten on one day without recall than is forgotten in sixty-three days with the aid of recall." In some cases, the recall groups remembered over twice as much as the groups without recall.

The Spitzer study makes a powerful statement about the positive effects of recall on retention, but still students are reluctant to take the time to do it. At the final period of that last sentence, do you stop, breathe a sign of relief, and say, "Hallelujah, I've finished the assignment!" Do you immediately close the book, never taking the time to mull over what has been read and put it into some type of perspective or order? If you are such a reader, much of what you have learned will be lost because you have given yourself no reminder of what's important, of what you should remember.

What Is Recalling?

Recalling is telling yourself what you have learned, what you wish to remember, and relating it to what you already know. It is taking those few extra minutes to digest what you have read and having a short conversation with yourself about the new material. Rather than being formal, long, and involved, the recalling process is the natural overviewing step that follows the "Hallelujah Period."

Why Recall? • Engaging in recall immediately after reading forces the reader to (1) select the most important points, (2) relate the supporting information, and (3) repeat what has been learned. These three elements form the basis of a good memory.

1. *Select the most important points.*

   The poor student wants to remember everything—facts have equal importance and thus no priorities are set. In short, no decisions have been made and the student has failed to sift through the reading and pull out the important issues.

2. *Relate the information.*

   Facts are difficult to learn in isolation. Memory experts use a technique of linking one item with another and through a series of associations are able to recall an exhaustive amount of seemingly unrelated trivia. To borrow from this technique, students must set up a linking system for each subject-matter area. New facts can then be placed into an overall skeleton of information and be more easily remembered. For example, many students have difficulty with history courses because they have no framework or skeleton into which to fit information. Events are isolated happenings rather than results of previous occurrences or parts of ongoing trends.

3. *Repeat what has been learned.*

How many times did you sing "Twinkle, Twinkle, Little Star" and how well do you know it right now? The rhythm and repetition help you remember the words without much effort. Perhaps this is an exaggerated example of overlearning, yet it represents an important element in memory. That element is repetition. For example, a new word is difficult to incorporate into your vocabulary unless you have the opportunity to use it, see it in print, or hear others use it. The same is true with facts; a review of the information makes it easier to remember. Beyond just pulling the facts into perspective, a review reinforces and cements the ideas in your mind.

How to Recall? • To recall, simply take a few minutes after the "Hallelujah Period" to recap what you have learned. This can be done in your head or it can be done on paper. To visualize the main points graphically, make a recall diagram. On a straight line state briefly the main point of the selection and underneath it, state the significant supporting details. The following is an example of the recall diagram:

What is it mainly about?

significant supporting examples
(or) significant related facts
(or) significant clarifying phrases

• *Exercise 3*

Read the following passages and record the main point and the significant supporting details on each of the recall diagrams.

Many talented people grew up in families that were headed by talented parents. Johann Sebastian Bach, for instance, did not simply "discover" his musical ability; his father was a court musician and probably taught his son to think in musical terms from an early age. The *situational* factor is thought to be important in developing creativity. Today teachers and parents in western cultures may ask children to "do things their own way" and express themselves as individuals rather than follow the conventional rules. For instance, it has been shown that pupils in "open classrooms" (where they are allowed to choose their own activities and proceed at their own pace) do more productive and original classroom work than pupils who learn on a prearranged or structured schedule (Parnes, 1967). Some freedom to experiment, to develop one's own approach to problems, seems more likely to result in creative and meaningful solutions. If students are always given the answers, they do not need to find answers for themselves.

An important factor in creativity is thought to be *motivation.* To be creative you need an incentive. In experimental situations it has been shown that incentives can come from either some outside reward or from a desire for self-expression and doing something that is personally satisfying.

David Dempsey and Philip Zimbardo, *Psychology and You*

A number of factors were responsible for the post-Civil War industrial boom. The United States possessed bountiful raw materials, and the government was willing to turn them over to industry for little or no money. Coupled with the abundance of natural resources was a home market steadily expanding through immigration and a high birth rate. Both capital and labor were plentiful. The increase in trade and manufacturing in the Northeast in the years before the war produced an accumulation of savings, while additional millions of dollars came from European investors. Unbroken waves of European immigration provided American industry with workers as well as with customers. From 1860 to 1900 about 14 million immigrants came to the United States, most of whom settled in cities and became industrial workers.

Carl N. Degler et al., *The Democratic Experience*

Hormones have no uniform structure. They may be proteins, peptides, amino acids or their derivatives, or steroids and fatty acids. Of interest is how slight variations in the structure of some hormones can cause them to have different functions. Two quite similar steroids of the adrenal cortex, for instance, differ notably in their functions. Hydroxycortisone stimulates the synthesis and storage of glycogen while aldosterone regulates sodium and potassium metabolism. Also, oxytocin and vasopressin, hormones produced in the hypothalamus of the brain and stored in the posterior pituitary, differ by only two amino acids, but their functions are quite different. Oxytocin stimulates uterine muscle contraction and release of milk, whereas vasopressin stimulates smooth muscle contraction and promotes water resorption in the kidney. The first and second messenger hypothesis helps to account for the differences in behavior of such similar molecules. The hormones are presumed to have specific receptor sites that only accommodate the hormone of a precise molecular configuration. This interaction, through the action of adenyl cyclase, causes the cyclic AMP to stimulate a specific response in the cell activated by the hormone.

Willis H. Johnson et al., *Essentials of Biology*

• *Previewing Exercise: Selection 1*

Before reading the next selection, preview to (1) establish a purpose, (2) size up how the material is organized, and (3) plan an attack. Read any introductory material, the first paragraph, the subheadings, the boldface and italicized print, the first sentence of some paragraphs (if it seems important), and the last paragraph. Think about the selection as a whole and answer the following questions:

1. This selection seems to be mainly about _____

_____

2. What major question should you seek to answer while reading this? _____

_____

_____

3. What are some terms that you should be able to define after reading this?

_____

_____

4. How does this selection seem to be organized? _____

_____

5. If you were researching diaper pricing, what section would you read? _____

_____

Selection 1: Marketing

Louis E. Boone and David L. Kurtz, from *Contemporary Business*

An early retail market, c. 1898.

New Product Pricing*

Pampers, the paper baby diaper, failed in its original market test because of pricing. Later, it became Proctor & Gamble's second best-selling brand (the detergent Tide is first). When it was first introduced, Pampers sold for about ten cents each. This was more than the per use cost of buying a cloth diaper and washing it. When Pampers bombed in the marketplace, Procter &
5 Gamble reduced production costs to the point where Pampers could be priced at six cents each, and the product became a household word in families with infants.

Procter & Gamble's experience with Pampers shows how difficult it is to select a price for a new product line. All such pricing decisions are risky; it is usually best to field test possible alternative prices with a sample group of consumers. Once the product is actually launched, it
10 is difficult to modify its price during the introductory period.

*LEARNING STRATEGY: During the previewing step, you are formulating your learning strategy. Be able to explain the different factors to be considered in the pricing of products.

New product pricing can take one of two alternative strategies. One is to *price the new product relatively high compared to substitute goods, and then gradually lower it.* Du Pont, which offers many specialty items, has traditionally followed such a pattern. Du Pont's polyester fiber, Dacron, was sold at $2.25 a pound in 1953. It now goes for about 40¢.

15 Similarly, the price of Quiana, a synthetic silklike fiber, has fallen 35 percent in 5 years. This alternative is known as a **skimming price policy,** and is used where the market is segmented on a price basis. In other words, some may buy an item at $10; another, larger group will buy if it is priced at $7.50; and a still larger group will buy if the item sells for $6.00. Color television and electronic calculators are examples of where this policy has been used effectively.

20 Today's best-selling ballpoint pen sells for 25¢, but when this product was first introduced after World War II it sold for about $20. A skimming price policy allows the firm to recover its costs rapidly by maximizing the revenue it receives. But the policy has a disadvantage in that early profits tend to attract competition, and this puts eventual pressure on prices.

Soaps and toothpastes are often introduced using a **penetration price policy.** This means *the*
25 *new product is priced low relative to substitute items in order to secure wide market acceptance.* Later it is hoped that brand acceptance will allow the firm to raise prices. Dow Chemical, which sells many commodity products, tends to be a penetration pricer. Dow attempts to build its market share with lower prices, and then stay in a certain market for a long time.

30 Penetration pricing discourages competition because of its low profits. It can also provide competitive opportunities against users of a skimming price policy. Wella-Balsam hair conditioner was introduced at $1.98 (compared to $1.19 for regular cream rinses). Alberto-Culver Company countered with Alberto-Balsam at $1.49 and an advertising budget ten times the size of the one supporting Wella-Balsam. The Alberto-Culver product overtook Wella-
35 Balsam in ten months, and now accounts for about 55—60 percent of hair conditioner sales.

Price Lining

Price lining occurs when *a seller decides to offer merchandise at a limited number of prices, rather than pricing each item individually.* For instance, a boutique might offer lines of women's sportswear priced at $60, $90, and $110. Price lining is a common marketing practice among retailers. The original five-and-ten-cent stores were an example of its early use.

40 As a pricing strategy the concept of price lining prevents the confusion common to situations where all items are priced individually. The pricing function is more easily managed. But marketers must clearly identify the market segments to which they are appealing. Three ''high price'' lines might not be appropriate to a store located in an area of young married couples.

A disadvantage of price lining is that it is sometimes difficult to alter the price ranges once
45 they are set. This may be a crucial factor during a period of inflation when the firm must either raise the price of the line or reduce its quality. Consumers may resist either of these decisions. Price lining can be useful, but its implementation must be considered carefully.

Price-Quality Relationships

Numerous research studies have shown that the consumers' perception of product quality is related closely to the item's price. The higher the price of the product, the better the consumer
50 perceives its quality. One study asked four hundred respondents what terms they associated with the word *expensive.* Two-thirds of the replies referred to high quality—such as *best* or *superior.*

Most marketers believe that the price-quality relationship exists over a relatively wide range of prices. It also appears that there are extreme prices that can be viewed as either *too*
55 *expensive* or *too cheap.* Marketing managers need to study and experiment with prices for their own particular products. The price-quality relationship can be of key importance to a firm's pricing strategy.

Psychological Pricing

Many marketers feel that certain prices are more appealing to buyers than others. Psychological pricing is widely used by industry throughout the world. The image pricing goals mentioned earlier are an example of psychological pricing.

60

Have you ever wondered why retailers use prices like $39.95, $18.98, or $9.99? Why don't the stores use $40, $19, or $10 instead? Years ago **odd pricing** (as this practice is called) was employed to force clerks to make change. This was before the age of cash registers, so odd pricing served as a cash control technique for retailers. It is now a common technique in retail pricing. Many retailers believe that odd prices are more attractive to consumers than even ones. In fact, some stores have now begun to use prices ending in 2, 3, 4, or 7 to avoid the look of ordinary prices like $5.95, $10.98, and $19.99. The "new" prices are more likely to be $2.22, $6.53, or $10.94.   /959

65

● *Recall Diagram*

Reflect on what you have read and then record on this diagram the main point and the significant supporting details.

● *Comprehension Questions*

After reading the selection, answer the following questions with *a, b, c,* or *d.*

_____   1. The best statement of the main idea of this selection is
   a. new product pricing is based on the value of the product
   b. the psychological needs of the consumer as well as eventual company profit must be considered in new product pricing
   c. the psychology of the consumer determines the market price of a new product
   d. the price of a new product depends on whether the company wants a short- or long-range return of its investment

_____   2. The final success of Pampers depended on all of the following except
a. changing the price
b. reducing production cost
c. a skimming price policy
d. a penetration price policy

_____   3. In selecting the price for a new product, the authors recommend
a. initial high pricing to gain early profits
b. lower prices to develop a market
c. expensive prices to imply quality
d. testing several prices on selected consumers

_____   4. The skimming price policy includes all of the following except
a. a unique product for which the consumer will pay a high price
b. early profits to recover research costs
c. a market that is segmented on a price basis
d. a tendency toward attracting competition

_____   5. The major reason for a penetration pricing policy is
a. initial market acceptance
b. raising prices later
c. initial advertising costs
d. the value of the product

_____   6. The authors consider an advantage of price lining to be
a. lower costs to the consumer
b. easy management
c. a tendency to guard against inflation
d. the ease of entering higher price markets

_____   7. The idea of price-quality relationships is based on
a. consumer perception
b. production cost
c. only expensive items
d. early development cost recovery

_____   8. Odd pricing was first used as a cash control technique to
a. increase the product price
b. force the sale to be registered
c. create a psychologically attractive price
d. lower the product price

_____   9. When introducing a new product, the best pricing technique to discourage competition is
a. a skimming price policy
b. a penetration price policy
c. price lining
d. odd pricing

_____   10. It would seem that the greatest initial benefit to the consumer would come from
a. a skimming price policy
b. a penetration price policy
c. price lining
d. odd pricing

Answer the following with *T* (true), *F* (false), or *CT* (can't tell).

_____ 11. The author implies that an item can be too cheap for a consumer to buy.
_____ 12. Many lower-priced substitutes for Quiana have now been marketed.
_____ 13. The author implies that odd pricing was initiated to keep clerks honest.
_____ 14. Even without the advertising, Alberto-Balsam still would have overtaken Wella-Balsam in market sales.
_____ 15. The author implies that the gradual demise of the five-and-ten-cent store is an example of the impact of inflation on price lining.

● *Vocabulary*

According to the way the boldface word was used in the selection, indicate *a*, *b*, *c*, or *d* for the word or phrase that gives the best definition.

____ 1. "When Pampers **bombed**"
a. destroyed
b. exploded
c. entered
d. failed

____ 2. "is actually **launched**"
a. started off
b. withdrawn
c. submerged
d. designated

____ 3. "is difficult to **modify**"
a. solidify
b. change
c. argue
d. overlook

____ 4. "**relatively** high"
a. comparatively
b. favorably
c. slowly
d. outrageously

____ 5. "many **commodity** products"
a. unnecessary
b. luxury
c. convenience
d. expensive

____ 6. "a **penetration** pricer"
a. retraction
b. act of cutting through
c. approximation
d. agreeable

____ 7. "a **crucial** factor"
a. informative
b. enjoyable
c. logical
d. decisive

____ 8. "its **implementation** must"
a. act of carrying out
b. renewal
c. motivation
d. release

____ 9. "the consumer **perceives**"
a. buys
b. becomes aware
c. directs
d. acquires

____ 10. "four hundred **respondents**"
a. customers
b. workers
c. persons who answer
d. managers

● *Possible Essay Exam Question*

If you had just manufactured a new baseball bat, what factors would you consider in pricing it for sale in your store? (Hint: Explain and relate each pricing factor to your situation.)

- ## *Word Parts*

Study the meaning of the word parts and supply an additional example from your own vocabulary. In the second set of items, use the corresponding part to write the word that best fits the definition.

Word Part	Meaning	Example	Your Example
1. contra	against	contraband	_____
2. du, di	two	dual	_____
3. rog	question	abrogate	_____
4. lum, luc	light	lucid	_____
5. vis, vid	see	visualize	_____
6. scribe	write	describe	_____
7. super	over, above	supervise	_____
8. ness	state or condition of	goodness	_____
9. ward	in a direction	forward	_____
10. ant, ent	quality of	reliant	_____

1. to speak against another's statement _____

2. marriage dissolution _____

3. to question _____

4. to light up _____

5. not able to be seen _____

6. engraved words _____

7. forces other than nature _____

8. state of being happy _____

9. the direction of the wagon trains _____

10. demanding _____

- ### *Previewing Exercise: Selection 2*

Before reading the next selection, preview to (1) establish a purpose, (2) size up how the material is organized, and (3) plan an attack. Read any introductory material, the first paragraph, the subheadings, the boldface and italicized print, the first sentence of some paragraphs (if it seems important), and the last paragraph. Think about the selection as a whole and answer the following questions:

1. This selection seems to be mainly about _____
_____

2. What major question should you seek to answer while reading this?
_____

3. What are some terms that you should be able to define after reading this?
_____

4. How does this selection seem to be organized? _____
_____

5. If you were researching whale songs, what section would you read? _____
_____

___

Selection 2: Biology

William T. Keeton, from *Biological Science*

Communication by Sound[*]

Being vocal animals ourselves, we are very familiar with the use of sound as a medium of communication. No other species has a sound language that even approaches the complexity and refinement of human spoken languages. But many other species can communicate an amazing amount of information via sound, information upon which both the life of the individual and the continued existence of the species may depend.

Sound Communication in Insects. We have already mentioned two examples of sound communication: Male *Aedes* mosquitoes are attracted by the buzzing sound produced by the female's wings during flight (or by devices such as tuning forks that emit sounds of a similar pitch), and hen chickens respond in a characteristic fashion to the distress calls of their chicks. Let us return to the first of these examples. The head of a male mosquito bears two antennae, each covered with long hairs. When sound waves of certain frequencies strike the antennae,

5

10

*LEARNING STRATEGY: From the examples given, be able to explain how and why each uses sound to communicate.

these are caused to vibrate in unison. The vibrations stimulate sensory cells packed tightly into a small segment at the base of each antenna. The male responds to such stimulation by homing in on the source of the sound, thus locating the female and copulating with her. A striking

15 demonstration of the adaptiveness of this communication system is that during the first 24 hours of the adult life of the male, when he is not yet sexually competent, the antennal hairs lie close to the shaft . . . and thus make him nearly deaf. Only after he becomes fully developed sexually do the hairs stand erect . . ., enabling the antennae to receive sound stimuli from the female. Thus the male does not waste energy responding to females before he is sexually

20 competent, but once he becomes competent he has a built-in system for locating a mate without random searching. Furthermore, his built-in receptor system is species-specific; it is stimulated by sounds of the frequency characteristic of females of his own species, not by the frequencies characteristic of other species of mosquitoes. Hence the sound produced by the female's wings functions both as mating call and species recognition signal.

25 Many other insects utilize sound in a similar way. For example, male crickets utilize calls produced by rasping together specialized parts of their wings. These calls function in species recognition, in attracting females and stimulating their reproductive behavior, and in warning away other males. So species-specific are the calls of crickets that in several cases closely related species can best be told apart by human beings on the basis of the calls; the species

30 may be almost indistinguishable on an anatomical basis, but have distinctively different calls.

Sound Communication in Frogs. The calls of frogs serve functions similar to those of cricket calls, and like these they are very species-specific. The male frogs attract females to their territory by calling. In one experiment, C. M. Bogert of the American Museum of Natural History recorded the call of male toads. He then captured 24 female toads and released them in

35 the dark in the vicinity of a loudspeaker over which he was playing the recorded male call. Thirty minutes later, he turned on the lights and determined the position of each female. Nineteen of the females had moved nearer the loudspeaker, four had moved farther away, and one had escaped. Eighteen of the nineteen females that had moved toward the speaker were physiologically ready to lay eggs; of the four females that moved away from the speaker, three

40 had already laid their eggs and the other was not yet of reproductive age. In a control experiment, Bogert showed that 24 females released in the dark near a silent speaker had scattered randomly in all directions by the time the lights were turned on 30 minutes later. This

45   demonstration that females ready for mating are strongly attracted by the male's vocalizations while other females are not serves to emphasize the effectiveness of a releasing stimulus depends, among other things, on the condition of the recipient of the stimulus; the call of the male frog is an effective releaser for movement by the female toward the male only if the female's reproductive drive is high, largely as a result of a high level of sex hormones.

50   **Bird Songs.** Of all the familiar animal sounds—the buzzing of mosquitoes, the calling of crickets and frogs, the barking, roaring, purring, grunting, etc. of various mammals—perhaps none, with the exception of human speech, has received so much attention as the singing of birds. It has been celebrated in poetry, copied in musical compositions, mimicked by whistlers, adored by lovers, and enthusiastically welcomed by those impatient for spring. The popular "explanation" for bird song is simple: The bird is happy and sings with joy, welcoming the morning and the spring and expressing love for his mate. Probably few other

55   biological phenomena have been so enshrouded in anthropomorphic fancies. But biologists must cast a skeptical eye on such admittedly appealing interpretations. Objective investigation has demonstrated that bird song functions primarily as a species recognition signal, as a display that attracts females to the male and contributes to the synchronization of the reproductive drives (increasing sexual motivation and decreasing attack and escape motivations), and as a display

60   important in defense of territory. In its defensive function, a bird's singing is certainly no indication of "happiness" or "joy"; if such human-oriented concepts could properly be applied to birds, which they cannot, the singing would more accurately be taken as an indication of combativeness.

The role of singing in the establishment and defense of territories is an especially interesting

65   one. A territory may be defined as an area defended by one member of a species against intrusion by other members of the same species (and occasionally against members of other species). A male bird chooses an unoccupied area and begins to sing vigorously within it, thus warning away other males. The boundaries between the territories of two males are regularly patrolled, and the two may sing loudly at each other across the border. Although during early

70   spring there is often much shifting of boundaries as more and more males arrive and begin competing for territories, later in the season the boundaries usually become fairly well stabilized and each male knows where they are. During the period when the boundaries are being established, it is often the males that can sing loudest and most vigorously that successfully retain large territories or even expand their territories at the expense of other males

75   that sing less loudly and vigorously.

Sound Communication by Whales. Recent research on whales by Roger Payne of Rockefeller University has revealed that many species sing amazingly elaborate songs. In some cases, a single song may last over half an hour before repetition begins. Because the frequencies of the sounds are ones that can be transmitted over very long distances in water, Payne thinks it is

80   possible that singing whales may be heard by other whales hundreds (or perhaps even thousands) of miles away. The eerie beauty of whale songs, as recorded by Payne, has inspired several new musical compositions in the last few years.

There is evidence that the small whales called dolphins can produce a great variety of sounds that convey many types of information. One investigator even believes that dolphins have an

85   intelligence approaching that of human beings and that they have a language far more extensive and advanced than that of any other animal except man. Though this is a minority view, there is no denying the desirability of more intensive research on dolphin communication.   /1268

● ***Recall Diagram***

Reflect on what you have read and then record on this diagram the main point and the significant supporting details.

● ***Comprehension Questions***

After reading the selection, answer the following questions with *a, b, c,* or *d.*

_____ 1. The best statement of the main idea of this selection is
   a. insects and frogs use sound communication in species-specific mating
   b. sound vibrations are used to attract mates and express attitudes
   c. many different species use sound to communicate information relevant to the survival of the individual and the species
   d. man's sound communication is superior to that of other species

_____ 2. The female *Aedes* mosquito sexually attracts by
   a. a buzz from its antennae   c. hairs on the wings that stand erect
   b. a device similar to a tuning fork   d. a sound from its wings in flight

_____ 3. In responding to the mating call of the female, the male *Aedes* mosquito experiences all of the following except
   a. vibrating antennae
   b. stimulation of cells at the base of the antennae
   c. a buzzing from his wings
   d. erect hairs on the antennae

_____ 4. "Species-specific" behavior refers to a natural attraction for
   a. members of related species
   b. members of the same limited species group
   c. sexually competent mates
   d. specific individuals within a species

_____ 5. The main purpose of Bogert's experiment was to show that a female frog will respond to the male mating call only if she is
   a. ready to reproduce at that time   c. old enough to reproduce
   b. species-specific   d. experienced in reproduction

_____ 6. The primary reason Bogert used the control experiment with the silent speaker was to show that
   a. female frogs react to darkness
   b. with no sound, thirty minutes is not long enough for a reaction
   c. frogs not yet of reproduction age would not respond
   d. his first results were not accidental

_____ 7. The author believes that the melodious song of a bird is most likely
   a. a welcoming of spring
   b. a sign of love
   c. an expression of happiness and joy
   d. a declaration of ownership

_____ 8. According to the selection, in order to keep competition out of territorial boundaries, a bird must
   a. arrive early in the spring
   b. sing more forcefully than competing birds
   c. engage in physical combat with competing birds
   d. attract more female birds than the competition

_____ 9. All of the following are characteristics of the song of a whale except that it
   a. is repetitious
   b. can be transmitted over long distances
   c. can last for over a half an hour
   d. has a beauty that has inspired musicians

_____ 10. The author feels that the most complex of all the sound communications mentioned is that of
   a. mosquitoes
   b. frogs
   c. birds
   d. whales

Answer the following with _T_ (true), _F_ (false), or _CT_ (can't tell).

_____ 11. The author implies that territorial boundaries are species-specific.
_____ 12. A male _Aedes_ mosquito with damaged antennae cannot mate.
_____ 13. The call of the cricket is a vocal sound.
_____ 14. In describing the results of his first experiment, Bogert fails to account for the behavior of one of the frogs.
_____ 15. The author implies that female birds do not establish territorial boundaries.

• _Vocabulary_

According to the way the boldface word was used in the selection, indicate _a_, _b_, _c_, or _d_ for the word or phrase that gives the best definition.

____ 1. "not yet sexually **competent**"
   a. older
   b. complete
   c. capable
   d. proven

____ 2. "to vibrate in **unison**"
   a. perfect agreement
   b. opposite directions
   c. total isolation
   d. lower frequencies

_____ 3. "insects **utilize** sound"
a. buzz
b. ignore
c. use
d. sting

_____ 4. "in the **vicinity** of"
a. only in front of
b. same time period
c. only to the right of
d. surrounding region

_____ 5. "the **recipient** of the stimulus"
a. sender
b. evaluator
c. receiver
d. originator

_____ 6. "**mimicked** by whistlers"
a. beloved
b. imitated
c. recognized
d. sought after

_____ 7. "few other biological **phenomena**"
a. mistakes
b. laws
c. experiments
d. extraordinary events

_____ 8. "have been so **enshrouded**"
a. interested
b. substituted
c. veiled
d. unlucky

_____ 9. "cast a **skeptical** eye"
a. approving
b. doubting
c. knowledgeable
d. welcoming

_____ 10. "an indication of **combativeness**"
a. readiness to fight
b. cooperation
c. insecurity
d. anxiety

• *Possible Essay Exam Question*

Explain the importance of sound communication in mating behavior. (Hint: Make a general statement and give specific examples from the species listed.)

• *Word Parts*

Study the meaning of the word parts and supply an additional example from your own vocabulary. In the second set of items, use the corresponding part to write the word that best fits the definition.

Word Part	Meaning	Example	Your Example
1. bio	life	biology	_____
2. zoo	animals	zoology	_____
3. aud	hear	audible	_____
4. sect, seg	cut	dissect	_____
5. mut, mutat	change	mutation	_____
6. phag	eat	esophagus	_____
7. cata	down, downward	catalyst	_____
8. orgy, ary, ery	place for	granary	_____

| 9. osis | state or condition of | diagnosis | _____ |
| 10. oid | in the form of, resembling | asteroid | _____ |

1. story of a person's life _____

2. an animal that is a parasite _____

3. an assembly of listeners _____

4. to cut in half _____

5. to maim or destroy _____

6. to eat animals _____

7. underground galleries for burial _____

8. cloister for monks _____

9. induced state resembling sleep _____

10. a newspaper half ordinary size _____

• *Previewing Exercise: Selection 3*

Before reading the next selection, preview to (1) establish a purpose, (2) size up how the material is organized, and (3) plan an attack. Read any introductory material, the first paragraph, the subheadings, the boldface and italicized print, the first sentence of some paragraphs, and the last paragraph. Think about the selection as a whole and answer the following questions:

1. This selection seems to be mainly about _____

_____

2. What major question should you seek to answer while reading this? _____

_____

3. What are some terms that you should be able to define after reading this? __

_____

4. How does this selection seem to be organized? _____

5. If you were researching rules that guide everyday behavior, what section

would you read? _____

Selection 3: Sociology

Donald Light, Jr. and Suzanne Keller, from *Sociology*

Unity in Diversity[*]

What is more basic, more "natural" than love between a man and woman? Eskimo men offer their wives to guests and friends as a gesture of hospitality; both husband and wife feel extremely offended if the guest declines (Ruesch, 1951, pp. 87-88). The Banaro of New Guinea believe it would be disastrous for a woman to conceive her first child by her husband
5   and not by one of her father's close friends, as is their custom.

> The real father is a close friend of the bride's father. . . . Nevertheless the first born child inherits the name and possessions of the husband. An American would deem such a custom immoral, but the Banaro tribesmen would be equally shocked to discover that the first born child of an American couple is the offspring of the husband. (Haring,
10   1949, p. 33)

    The Yanomamö of northern Brazil, whom anthropologist Napoleon A. Chagnon (1968) named "the fierce people," encourage what we would consider extreme disrespect. Small boys are applauded for striking their mothers and fathers in the face. Yanomamö parents would laugh at our efforts to curb aggression in children, much as they laughed at Chagnon's naïveté when
15   he first came to live with them.
    The variations among cultures are startling, yet all peoples have customs and beliefs about marriage, the bearing and raising of children, sex, and hospitality—to name just a few of the

[*]LEARNING STRATEGY: How do the examples explain the different principles and the overall idea of cultural unity?

universals anthropologists have discovered in their cross-cultural explorations. But the *details* of cultures do indeed vary: in this country, not so many years ago, when a girl was serious about
20   a boy and he about her, she wore his fraternity pin over her heart; in the Fiji Islands, girls put hibiscus flowers behind their ears when they are in love. The specific gestures are different but the impulse to symbolize feelings, to dress courtship in ceremonies, is the same. How do we explain this unity in diversity?

Cultural Universals

Cultural universals are all of the behavior patterns and institutions that have been found in all
25   known cultures. Anthropologist George Peter Murdock identified over sixty cultural universals, including a system of social status, marriage, body adornments, dancing, myths and legends, cooking, incest taboos, inheritance rules, puberty customs, and religious rituals (Murdock, 1945, p. 124).

The universals of culture may derive from the fact that all societies must perform the same
30   essential functions if they are to survive—including organization, motivation, communication, protection, the socialization of new members, and the replacement of those who die. In meeting these prerequisites for group life, people inevitably design similar—though not identical—patterns for living. As Clyde Kluckhohn wrote, "All cultures constitute somewhat distinct answers to essentially the same questions posed by human biology and by the
35   generalities of the human situation" (1962, p. 317).

The way in which a people articulate cultural universals depends in large part on their physical and social environment—that is, on the climate in which they live, the materials they have at hand, and the peoples with whom they establish contact. For example, the wheel has long been considered one of the humankind's greatest inventions, and anthropologists were
40   baffled for a long time by the fact that the great civilizations of South America never discovered it. Then researchers uncovered a number of toys with wheels. Apparently the Aztecs and their neighbors did know about wheels; they simply didn't find them useful in their mountainous environment.

Adaptation, Relativity, and Ethnocentrism

Taken out of context, almost any custom will seem bizarre, perhaps cruel, or just plain
45   ridiculous. To understand why the Yanomamö encourage aggressive behavior in their sons, for example, you have to try to see things through their eyes. The Yanomamö live in a state of chronic warfare; they spend much of their time planning for and defending against raids with neighboring tribes. If Yanomamö parents did *not* encourage aggression in a boy, he would be ill equipped for life in their society. Socializing boys to be aggressive is *adaptive* for the
50   Yanomamö because it enhances their capacity for survival. "In general, culture is . . . adaptive because it often provides people with a means of adjusting to the physiological needs of their own bodies, to their physical-geographical environment and to their social environments as well" (Ember and Ember, 1973, p. 30).

In many tropical societies, there are strong taboos against a mother having sexual intercourse
55   with a man until her child is at least two years old. As a Hausa woman explains,

> A mother should not go to her husband while she has a child she is sucking . . . if she only sleeps with her husband and does not become pregnant, it will not hurt her child, it will not spoil her milk. But if another child enters in, her milk will make the first one ill. (Smith, in Whiting, 1969, p. 518)

60   Undoubtedly, people would smirk at a woman who nursed a two-year-old child in our society and abstained from having sex with her husband. Why do Hausa women behave in a way that seems so overprotective and overindulgent to us? In tropical climates protein is scarce. If a mother were to nurse more than one child at a time, or if she were to wean a child before it reached the age of two, the youngster would be prone to *kwashiorkor,* an often fatal disease

65 resulting from protein deficiency. Thus, long postpartum sex taboos are adaptive. In a tropical environment a postpartum sex taboo and a long period of breast-feeding solve a serious problem (Whiting, in Goodenough, 1969, pp. 511-24).

No custom is good or bad, right or wrong in itself; each one must be examined in light of the culture as a whole and evaluated in terms of how it works in the context of the entire
70 culture. Anthropologists and sociologists call this *cultural relativity*. Although this way of thinking about culture may seem self-evident today, it is a lesson that anthropologists and the missionaries who often preceded them to remote areas learned the hard way, by observing the effects their best intentions had on peoples whose way of life was quite different from their own. In an article on the pitfalls of trying to "uplift" peoples whose ways seem backward and
75 inefficient, Don Adams quotes an old Oriental story:

> Once upon a time there was a great flood, and involved in this flood were two creatures, a monkey and a fish. The monkey, being agile and experienced, was lucky enough to scramble up a tree and escape the raging waters. As he looked down from his safe perch, he saw the poor fish struggling against the swift current. With the very best intentions,
80 > he reached down and lifted the fish from the water. The result was inevitable.
> (1960, p. 22)

Ethnocentrism is the tendency to see one's own way of life, including behaviors, beliefs, values, and norms as the only right way of living. Robin Fox points out that "any human group is ever ready to consign another recognizably different human group to the other side of the
85 boundary. It is not enough to possess culture to be fully human, you have to possess *our* culture" (1970, p. 31).

Values and Norms

The Tangu, who live in a remote part of New Guinea, play a game called *taketak,* which in many ways resembles bowling. The game is played with a top that has been fashioned from a dried fruit and with two groups of coconut stakes that are driven into the ground (more or less
90 like bowling pins). The players divide into two teams. Members of the first team take turns throwing the top into the batch of stakes; every stake the top hits is removed. Then the second team steps to the line and tosses the top into their batch of stakes. The object of the game, surprisingly, is not to knock over as many stakes as possible. Rather, the game continues until both teams have removed the *same* number of stakes. Winning is completely irrelevant
95 (Burridge, 1957, pp. 88-89).

In a sense games are practice for "real life"; they reflect the values of the culture in which they are played. *Values* are the criteria people use in assessing their daily lives, arranging their priorities, measuring their pleasures and pains, choosing between alternative courses of action. The Tangu value equivalence: the idea of one individual or group winning and another losing
100 bothers them, for they believe winning generates ill-will. In fact, when Europeans brought soccer to the Tangu, they altered the rules so that the object of the game was for two teams to score the same number of goals. Sometimes their soccer games went on for days! American games, in contrast, are highly competitive; there are *always* winners and losers. Many rule books include provisions for overtime and "sudden death" to prevent ties, which leave
105 Americans dissatisfied. World Series, Superbowls, championships in basketball and hockey, Olympic Gold Medals are front page news in this country. In the words of the late football coach Vince Lombardi, "Winning isn't everything, it's the only thing."

Norms, the rules that guide behavior in everyday situations, are derived from values, but norms and values can conflict, as we indicated in chapter 3. You may recall a news item that
110 appeared in American newspapers in December 1972, describing the discovery of survivors of a plane crash 12,000 feet in the Andes. The crash had occurred on October 13; sixteen of the passengers (a rugby team and their supporters) managed to survive for sixty-nine days in near-zero temperatures. The story made headlines because, to stay alive, the survivors had eaten

115 parts of their dead companions. Officials, speaking for the group, stressed how valiantly the survivors had tried to save the lives of the injured people and how they had held religious services regularly. The survivors' explanations are quite interesting, for they reveal how important it is to people to justify their actions, to resolve conflicts in norms and values (here, the positive value of survival vs. the taboo against cannibalism). Some of the survivors compared their action to a heart transplant, using parts of a dead person's body to save another

120 person's life. Others equated their act with the sacrament of communion. In the words of one religious survivor, "If we would have died, it would have been suicide, which is condemned by the Roman Catholic faith" (Read, 1974).   /1708

• Recall Diagram

Reflect on what you have read and then record on this diagram the main point and the significant supporting details.

• Comprehension Questions

After reading the selection answer the following questions with *a, b, c,* or *d.*

_____   1. The best statement of the main idea of this selection is
   a. the variety of practices and customs in society show few threads of cultural unity
   b. the unusual variations in societies gain acceptability because of the cultural universals in all known societies
   c. a variety of cultural universals provides adaptive choices for specific societies
   d. cultural universals are found in all known societies even though the details of the cultures may vary widely

_____   2. The author believes that the primary cultural universal addressed in the Eskimo custom of offering wives to guests is

      a. bearing and raising of children
      b. social status
      c. hospitality
      d. incest taboos

_____ 3. The custom of striking practiced by the Yanomamö serves the adaptive function of
      a. developing fierce warriors
      b. binding parent and child closer together
      c. developing physical respect for parents
      d. encouraging early independence from parental care

_____ 4. Cultural universals might be defined as
      a. each culture in the universe
      b. similar basic living patterns
      c. the ability for cultures to live together in harmony
      d. the differences among cultures

_____ 5. The author implies that universals of culture exist because of
      a. a social desire to be more alike
      b. the differences in cultural behavior patterns
      c. the competition among societies
      d. the needs of survival in group life

_____ 6. The author suggests that the wheel was not a part of the ancient Aztec civilization because the Aztecs
      a. did not need wheels
      b. were not intelligent enough to invent wheels
      c. were baffled by inventions
      d. did not have the materials for development

_____ 7. The underlying reason for the postpartum sexual taboo of the Hausa tribe is
      a. sexual
      b. nutritional
      c. moral
      d. religious

_____ 8. The term cultural relativity explains why a custom can be considered
      a. right or wrong regardless of culture
      b. right or wrong according to the number of people practicing it
      c. right in one culture and wrong in another
      d. wrong if in conflict with cultural universals

_____ 9. The author relates Don Adams' Oriental story to show that missionaries working with tribesmen
      a. should be sent back home
      b. can do more harm than good
      c. purposefully harm tribal culture to seek selfish ends
      d. usually do not have a genuine concern for the tribal people

_____ 10. The tendency of enthnocentrism would lead an American to view the Eskimo practice of wife sharing as
      a. right
      b. wrong
      c. right for Eskimos but wrong for Americans
      d. a custom about which an outsider should have no opinion

Answer the following questions with *T* (true), *F* (false) or *CT* (can't tell).

_____ 11. An American's acceptance of the Banaro tribal custom of fathering the first born is an example of an understanding by cultural relativity.

_____ 12. The author feels that the need to symbolize feelings in courtship is a cultural universal.

_____ 13. The author feels that culture is not affected by climate.

_____ 14. Among the Harisa, there is a tribal taboo against eating beef.

_____ 15. The Yanomamö are forced to raid neighboring villages because they cannot grow enough food to support their own tribe.

• *Vocabulary*

According to the way the boldface word was used in the selection, indicate *a, b, c,* or *d* for the word or phrase that gives the best definition.

____1. "efforts to **curb** aggression"
a. stabilize
b. release
c. promote
d. restrain

____2. "at Chagnon's **naiveté**"
a. lack of knowledge
b. gentle manner
c. jolly nature
d. clumsiness

____3. "body **adornments**"
a. ailments
b. treatments
c. scars
d. decorations

____4. "**articulate** cultural universals"
a. remember
b. design
c. express clearly
d. substitute

____5. "will seem **bizarre**"
a. phony
b. unjust
c. grotesque
d. unnecessary

____6. "**smirk** at a woman"
a. refuse to tolerate
b. smile conceitedly
c. lash out
d. acknowledge approvingly

____7. "**abstained** from having sex"
a. matured
b. regained
c. refrained
d. reluctantly returned

____8. long **postpartum** sex taboos
a. after childbirth
b. awaited
c. subcultural
d. complicated

____9. "being **agile** and experienced"
a. eager
b. nimble
c. young
d. knowledgeable

____10. "ready to **consign**"
a. assign
b. remove
c. reorganize
d. overlook

• *Possible Essay Exam Question*

Identify elements of unity among diverse cultures of the world. (Hint: Discuss the common needs of group life and illustrate how the cultural concepts listed by the author are found in diverse cultures as well as our own.)

• *Word Parts*

Study the meaning of the word parts and supply an additional example from your own vocabulary. In the second set of items use the corresponding part to write the word that best fits the definition.

Word Part	Meaning	Example	Your Example
1. frater	brother	fraternity	_____
2. andr, andro	man	androgynous	_____
3. col, cult	inhabit	colonization	_____
4. be	thoroughly	bedeck	_____
5. pel, puls	drive, push, throw	impulsive	_____
6. ridi, rise, ri	laughter	derision	_____
7. ploy	action, doing	deploy	_____
8. crea	create	procreate	_____
9. ette, let	little, insignificant	starlet	_____
10. dom	state or condition of	stardom	_____

1. to kill a brother   _____

2. having many husbands   _____

3. youthful mores against society   _____

4. promise to marry   _____

5. to push forward or drive   _____

6. to mock or make fun   _____

7. to hire   _____

8. rest and refreshment after work   _____

9. small dining area   _____

10. condition of great knowledge   _____

Chapter Four

Sentence Unraveling

Unraveling

Unraveling

Unraveling

How are the following sentences alike?

1. I see her.
2. As the office workers crowd the sidewalks and John and I patiently begin our ten-minute wait at the corner for the last afternoon bus home, I always see her resting on the post-office steps selling bouquets of roses to passersby.

Can you spot the similarity? The first sentence has three words and the second has forty, yet both sentences have the same subject, the same action, and the same receiver of the action. The three-word core, "I see her," forms the heart of both sentences—the other thirty-seven words in the second sentence merely describe the situation more vividly. By adding extra padding, descriptive words and phrases can sometimes transform a simple sentence into a tangled jungle of verbiage.

Have you ever read a sentence that was so long that you had forgotten how it started by the time you got to the end? Have you ever read a lengthy paragraph that was made up of just one long sentence? Have you ever read a poem in which one sentence meandered through three or four verses? Have you ever read a sentence that was so complicated that you couldn't figure out the meaning?

Surely, the answer to all four questions is "yes." Even for the best readers, some sentences can be monstrosities to unravel. Essential elements lie hidden amid a maze of clauses, phrases, commas, and semicolons. Think of a sentence as having only a few vital parts. Find them, and then relate the remaining words and phrases to those core parts. In other words, find the skeleton of the sentence, and then worry about the "hangers-on."

To unravel the meaning of a sentence, ask the following questions:

1. Who or what is the sentence about? (Who or what is doing the acting? Who or what is the subject or chief topic of the sentence?)
2. What is being said about the who or what? (What is happening in the sentence? What is the action?)

Sentence Types

Because sentences vary widely in structure, answers to these questions are not always readily pinpointed. Study the following classifications of sentence types and use them as guidelines in unraveling sentence meaning.

Simple Action Sentences

A woman made the first and most lasting trouble for Jackson.

Samuel E. Morison, Henry S. Commager and William E. Leuchtenburg,
A Concise History of the American Republic

1. Who or what is the sentence about? *a woman*
2. What is the action of the woman? *made the first and most lasting trouble for Jackson* or the core action is *made*
3. What was it that the woman made? *trouble*
4. "The first and most lasting" describes what? *trouble*
5. "For Jackson" describes what? *trouble*

Simple Linking Sentences

A very important step toward forming an opposition party was an understanding between Virginia malcontents and those of New York.

Morison, Commager and Leuchtenburg, *A Concise History of the American Republic*

1. Who or what is the sentence about? *A very important step toward forming an opposition party* or the core subject is *step*
2. What is being said about the step? *was an understanding between Virginia malcontents and those of New York* or the core is *was*
3. "A very important" describes what? *step*
4. "toward forming an opposition party" describes what? *step*
5. "understanding" renames what? *step*
6. "between Virginia malcontents and those in New York" describes what? *step*
7. "those" refers to whom? *malcontents*

Simple Sentences with Multiple Subjects or Actions

Single-celled animals occupy both fresh and salt water, are found on and in other organisms, and live in a range of environments including the chill and dark of the seas, the digestive tracts, body cavities, and circulatory systems of other animals.

Willis H. Johnson et al., *Essentials of Biology*

1. Who or what is the sentence about? *single-celled animals*
2. What are the core actions of the subject? *occupy, are found, live*
3. What do they occupy? *both fresh and salt water*
4. "on and in other organisms" tells what? *where they are found*
5. "in a range of environments" tells what? *where they live*
6. "circulatory systems of other animals" describes what? *range of environments*

Equal Sentences Combined

Rather than write several short, choppy statements, the author will frequently join together two or more sentences to add rhythm and style. Words used to link equal sentences together are *and, but, or, either–or, neither–nor,* and a semicolon (;).

The Confederacy was tightly pinched along its waistline; but the blood could still circulate.

Morison, Commager and Leuchtenburg, A Concise History of the American Republic

1. Who or what is the first part of the sentence (before the semicolon) about? *the Confederacy*
2. What is being said (core) about the Confederacy? *was pinched*
3. "along its waistline" describes what? *where it was pinched*
4. Who or what is the second part of the sentence about? *the blood*
5. What is the core action of the blood? *could circulate*

Unequal Sentence Parts Added to Sentences

Modifying parts with their own separate subjects and actions may be attached to simple sentences as descriptive material, but still not be part of the core. Parts like this are clauses which depend on the rest of the sentence for a complete meaning and thus cannot stand alone. Such modifying parts are joined to the sentence by *as, if, because, since, when, that, which, who,* etc.

Probably because the Persian fleet still ruled the Aegean Sea and so presented a constant danger behind him, Alexander marched southward taking all the port cities of the Syrian coast on the way.

Shepard B. Clough et al., A History of the Western World

1. Who or what is the sentence about? *Alexander*
2. What (core) did Alexander do? *marched*
3. "Probably because the Persian fleet still ruled the Aegean Sea and so presented a constant danger behind him" tells what? *why he marched*
4. "taking all the port cities of the Syrian coast on the way" tells what? *how he marched*

   Read the following sentences and write in the blanks the answers to the questions about the relationships of the sentence parts.

• *Exercise 1*

Deprived of all but the most trivial and fleeting human contact, these extremely neglected children have only their genetic resources to draw upon in order to become human.

Society Today

1. Who or what is this sentence about? _____

2. "Deprived of all but the most trivial and fleeting human contact" describes

_____

3. "most trivial and fleeting" describes _____

4. What is the only thing the children have? _____

● *Exercise 2*

If Homer had tried reading the *Iliad* to the gods on Olympus, they would either have started to fidget and presently asked if he hadn't got something a little lighter, or, taking it as a comic poem, would have roared with laughter or possibly, even, reacting like ourselves to a tear-jerking movie, have poured pleasing tears.

W. H. Auden, The Dyer's Hand

1. Who would "have started to fidget"? _____

2. Who "would have roared with laughter"? _____

3. Who would "have poured"? _____

4. "he" takes the place of _____

● *Exercise 3*

Earthquakes result from sudden movement by faulting; but apparently the actual movements within the earth are slow, and rupture only occurs when the forces have built up to the point that they exceed the strength of the rocks.

Robert J. Foster, Physical Geology

1. What is the core action of "earthquakes"? _____

2. What "are slow"? _____

3. When do ruptures occur? _____

4. "within the earth are slow" describes _____

● *Exercise 4*

If Sam Fathers had been his mentor and the backyard rabbits and squirrels his kindergarten, then the wilderness the old bear ran was his college and the old male bear itself, so long unwifed and childless as to have become its own ungendered progenitor, was his alma mater.

William Faulkner, "The Bear"

1. What was his alma mater? _____

2. "the old bear ran" describes _____

3. What was his kindergarten? _____

4. "so long unwifed and childless as to have become its own ungendered progenitor" describes _____

• *Exercise 5*

Mudflows, or debris flows, which are similar to mudflows but contain much material coarser than mud, are common and are the most devastating type of activity at Mt. Ranier.

Robert J. Foster, Physical Geology

1. Even though this sentence expresses only one complete thought, what two things is it about? _____
2. "common" describes _____
3. "the most devastating type of activity at Mt. Ranier" describes _____
4. "which are similar to mudflows" describes _____

• *Exercise 6*

Within the body water the chemical interactions of molecules which contain the element carbon are the key to both the structure of the body and its various physiological activities.

John Raynor, Anatomy and Physiology

1. What is the sentence about? _____
2. "which contain the element carbon" describes _____
3. "key" renames _____
4. "of the body" describes what? _____

• *Exercise 7*

When it occurs to a man that nature does not regard him as important, and that she feels she would maim the universe by disposing of him, he at first wishes to throw bricks at the temple, and he hates deeply the fact that there are no bricks and no temples.

Stephen Crane, The Open Boat

1. Who wishes and hates? _____
2. What does a man want to do that he can't? _____

3. "she" refers to _____

4. How does nature feel about man? _____

• *Exercise 8*

When they are crowded together or pulled apart by irresistible forces in the crust, rocks may break and the separate portions move past each other along the line of fracture.

Jesse H. Wheeler, J. Trenton Kostbade and Richard S. Thoman, *Regional Geography of the World*

1. What breaks? _____

2. What moves? _____

3. What does "they" refer to? _____

4. "When they are crowded together or pulled apart by irresistible forces in

the crust" tells when what occurs? _____

• *Exercise 9*

He lifted his head from his drinking, as cattle do,
And looked at me vaguely, as drinking cattle do,
And flickered his two-forked tongue from his lips, and
    mused a moment,
And stooped and drank a little more,
Being earth brown, earth golden from the burning
    burning bowels of the earth
On the day of Sicilian July, with Etna smoking.

D. H. Lawrence, from "Snake"

1. Who is the sentence about? _____

2. The subject engages in six different actions. Name them. _____

_____

3. "Being earth brown" describes _____

4. When was "Etna smoking"? _____

• *Exercise 10*

Hamilton wished to concentrate power; Jefferson, to diffuse it.

Morison, Commager and Leuchtenburg, *A Concise History of the American Republic*

1. This sentence has two parts. Who is the first part (before the semicolon) about? _____

2. What action does he exhibit? _____

3. In the second part of the sentence a word has been left out. What is it? ____
_____

4. Who is the second part of the sentence about? _____

• Exercise 11

As the depression deepened, as some Americans approached a second winter without employment, as charities and states ran out of funds for relief, as newspapers reported that people were foraging in dumps and garbage heaps, and as malnutrition and exposure came to public attention, Herbert Hoover became the nation's scapegoat.

Henry F. Bedford and Trevor Calbourn, The Americans

1. Who is the sentence about? _____

2. What was Hoover renamed? _____

3. "As the depression deepened" tells which of the following: how? when? where? why? _____

4. "as malnutrition and exposure came to public attention" tells which of the following: how? where? when? why? _____

• Exercise 12

In a sudden and startling break with the worship of Amon, the divine father of the pharaohs of the XVIIIth dynasty, and with all the other gods dear to the tradition of Egyptian polytheism, Akhenaten gave his entire allegiance to a single, all-powerful, and merciful creator, the sun disk or Aten whose rays brought blessings to the earth.

Shepard B. Clough et al., A History of the Western World

1. Who is the sentence about? _____

2. What did Akhenaten do? _____

3. "the divine father of the pharoahs of the XVIIIth dynasty" renames _____

4. "the sun disk or Aten whose rays brought blessings to the earth" renames
_____

• *Exercise 13*

> Under yonder beech-tree single on the green sward,
> Couched with her arms behind her golden head,
> Knees and tresses folded to slip and ripple idly,
> Lies my young love sleeping in the shade.
> Had I heart to slide an arm beneath her,
> Press her parting lips as her waist I gather slow,
> Waking in amazement she could but embrace me
> Then would she hold me and never let me go?
>
> George Meredith, "Love in the Valley"

1. Who is the sentence about? _____

2. Where is the girl? _____

3. "Couched with her arms behind her golden head" describes _____

_____

4. "sleeping in the shade" describes _____

• *Exercise 14*

More than secure economically as well, Franklin no longer practiced the frugality he still recommended to his fellow Americans through *Poor Richard's Almanac,* a sort of handbook and guide to mercantilist economic theory he had devised for the common man.

Lloyd C. Gardner and William L. O'Neill, *Looking Backward*

1. Who is the sentence about? _____

2. What has he stopped? _____

3. "he still recommended to his fellow Americans through *Poor Richard's*

Almanac" describes _____

4. "a sort of handbook and guide to mercantilist economic theory he had

devised for the common man" renames _____

• *Exercise 15*

At the end of that year Hamilton presented to Congress his Report on Manufacturers.

Morison, Commager and Leuchtenburg, *A Concise History of the American Republic*

1. Who is the sentence about? _____

2. What did he do? _____

3. What object received the direct action? _____

4. "on Manufacturers" describes _____

• *Exercise 16*

General Jackson, a tall, lean figure dressed in black, with the hawk-like frontier face under a splendid crest of thick white hair, walked from Gadsby's Hotel up Pennsylvania Avenue, unescorted save by a few friends, to the Capitol.

ibid.

1. Who is the sentence about? _____

2. What did he do? _____

3. "with the hawk-like frontier face under a splendid crest of thick white hair" describes _____

4. "unescorted save by a few friends" describes _____

• *Exercise 17*

Up to the farmhouse to dinner through the teeming, dusty field, the road under our sneakers was only a two-track road.

E. B. White, from "Once More on the Lake"

1. What is the sentence about? _____

2. "teeming" describes what? _____

3. Where did the road go? _____

4. "under our sneakers" describes _____

• *Exercise 18*

Upon my entrance, Usher arose from a sofa on which he had been lying at full length, and greeted me with a vivacious warmth which had much in it, I at first thought, of an overdone cordiality—of the constrained effort of the ennuyé man of the world.

Edgar Allan Poe, *The Fall of the House of Usher*

1. Who is the sentence about? _____

2. What are the two actions of the subject? _____

3. "on which he had been lying at full length" describes _____

_____

4. "which had much in it" describes _____

- ## *Exercise 19*

A wealthy man, addicted to his pleasure and to his profits, finds religion to be a traffic so entangled, and of so many piddling accounts, that of all mysteries he cannot skill to keep a stock going upon that trade. What should he do?

John Milton, Areopagitica

1. Who is the sentence about? _____

2. What is the core action of the subject? _____

3. "addicted to his pleasure and to his profits" describes _____

4. "to be a traffic so entangled" describes _____

- ## *Exercise 20*

The sun, above the mountain's head,
A freshening luster mellow
Through all the long green fields, has spread,
His first sweet evening yellow.

William Wordsworth, from "The Tables Turned"

1. What is the sentence about? _____

2. What is the core action of the subject? _____

3. What was spread in the fields? _____

4. "above the mountain's head" describes _____

Selection 1: History

Shepard B. Clough et al., from *A History of the Western World*

Elizabeth of England[*]

The ruler who was Mary Stuart's embarrassed hostess for eighteen years had come to the throne at age twenty-five after the death of her half sister Mary Tudor. In part, Elizabeth owed her accession and her very life to the influence of her brother-in-law Philip of Spain. During the English Mary's reign an attempted rising against the queen had been put afoot without
5   Elizabeth's knowledge but in her name. The result was that Mary, who had been tenderly kind to Elizabeth during her young girlhood, had turned against Elizabeth, banished her from court and later committed her to the awesome fortress of the Tower of London. It had seemed highly likely that Elizabeth's candle would be snuffed out as had been that of her studious young cousin, Lady Jane Grey, who had been executed in the Tower a few weeks earlier for having

[*]LEARNING STRATEGY: History views events as causes or effects of other occurrences. As you read, relate one circumstance to another and seek to understand how Elizabeth became a great queen of England.

Portrait of Queen Elizabeth I, 1588.

10 been the unwitting focus of another plot against Mary and whose blood is said to have still stained the rushes about the headsman's block when Elizabeth was taken by boat to the Tower.

After the marriage of Mary Tudor and Philip of Spain, however, the Spanish prince came to realize that his wife would probably not live long and that if Elizabeth were despatched, the next in line for the throne of England would be Mary of Scotland who was also, at that time,
15 queen of France. Because of Mary Stuart's French connection her accession to the English throne would have been far less than ideal from the Spanish point of view. Combined under one ruler, France and England could easily have driven the Spanish out of the Netherlands and would have seriously threatened the power of Spain in the European world. In short the union of the two kingdoms would represent a strategic and diplomatic disaster for Spain. Moreover,
20 Philip did not fail to remark the obvious popularity among the English people of the young princess who was so much her father's daughter. He realized that Elizabeth would probably make an effective ruler, that he would do well to be on good terms with her, and that Mary would only injure herself by persecuting Elizabeth. Accordingly, Philip advised his bride to reconcile herself with Elizabeth. He also cautioned Mary regarding the wisdom of burning quite
25 so many heretics.

And so it was that one of the most intelligent and best educated persons of her time survived and came to rule over an English people, the majority of whom were overwhelmingly delighted with these facts. Elizabeth was not only bright and well educated; she was also rigorously trained in the hard school of English royal fortunes. The execution of her mother for adultery,

30 her step-mother's death as a result of childbirth, and the execution of another step-mother (the beautiful and wanton Catherine Howard) for adultery could not have failed to impress her young mind. Moreover Elizabeth, too, had cringed nearly in the shadow of the executioner's blade. One result of this series of macabre girlhood experiences was that Elizabeth, who was endowed with the lively imagination that usually accompanies a sensitive intelligence,

35 developed a certain ambivalence regarding the subject of love and marriage. Throughout her reign, her great, continuing and abiding love affair was with the English people upon whom she lavished her womanly wiles, always in touch and sympathy. As time went on, the English people came more and more to appreciate their queen who so artfully sought to amuse them and so sturdily defended their interests.

40 The quality of a ruler can often best be measured by the quality of his advisors. From the beginning, Elizabeth surrounded herself with extraordinarily able men, most of them of humble origins. William Cecil, Francis Walsingham, and Christopher Hatton served steadily and sometimes magnificently in the Privy Council. Aristocrats like Robert Dudley, Earl of Leicester, gave less useful service. Often these men were at odds with each other, but they

45 were always ready to join ranks whenever danger threatened their queen.

The situation immediately upon Elizabeth's succession was one of severe crisis. The honor of the crown had been sacrificed to the Spanish alliance. Religious divisions rent the realm: internal peace had vanished as Protestants and Roman Catholics had fought one another during the reign of Edward (1547-1553) and as Mary (r. 1553-1558) had burnt hundreds of victims at

50 the stake. The currency was depreciated; the royal treasury stood empty and economic activity was at a low level. The sorry internal condition of the country was matched by its external situation. Calais had been lost to the French; the fleet had been neglected; and England stood almost defenseless against the real danger of foreign intrusion.

The tasks that lay before Elizabeth and her councilors were fourfold: (1) economic

55 development, (2) religious settlement, (3) re-establishment of the prestige of the crown, (4) diplomatic maneuvering of the most delicate sort until such time as English internal health and external defenses were sufficient to maintain the security of the realm. These were great tasks; and the remarkable fact is that Elizabeth and her servants managed to perform all of them during her reign.   /846

• *Skill Development*

Read the following sentences from the selection and write in the blanks the answers to the questions about the relationships of the sentence parts.

I. "The result was that Mary, who had been tenderly kind to Elizabeth during her young girlhood, had turned against Elizabeth, banished her from court and later committed her to the awesome fortress of the Tower of London."

1. What is the subject of the sentence? _____

2. "who had been tenderly kind to Elizabeth during her young girlhood"

describes whom? _____

3. Who "banished her from court"? _____

4. Who "committed her to the. . . Tower"? _____

II. "It had seemed highly likely that Elizabeth's candle would be snuffed out as had been that of her studious young cousin, Lady Jane Grey, who had been executed in the Tower a few weeks earlier for having been the unwitting focus of another plot against Mary and whose blood is said to have still stained the rushes about the headsman's block when Elizabeth was taken by boat to the Tower."

1. What "would be snuffed out"? _____

2. Who was "executed in the Tower"? _____

3. Whose blood is said to have left a stain? _____

4. What did the blood stain? _____

III. "After the marriage of Mary Tudor and Philip of Spain, however, the Spanish prince came to realize that his wife would probably not live long and that if Elizabeth were despatched, the next in line for the throne of England would be Mary of Scotland who was also, at that time, queen of France."

1. Who is the subject of the sentence? _____

2. "After the marriage of Mary Tudor and Philip of Spain," tells how?

when? where? or why? _____

3. Who was "his wife"? _____

4. Who was "queen of France"? _____

IV. "The execution of her mother for adultery, her step-mother's death as a result of childbirth, and the execution of another step-mother (the beautiful and wanton Catherine Howard) for adultery could not have failed to impress her young mind."

1. What is this sentence about? _____

2. What is the action of the subjects? _____

3. "as a result of childbirth" describes _____

4. "for adultery" in both cases describes what word? _____

V. "Throughout her reign, her great, continuing and abiding love affair was with the English people upon whom she lavished her womanly wiles, always in touch and sympathy."

1. What is this sentence about? _____

2. "her great, continuing" describes what? _____

3. "upon whom she lavished her womanly wiles" describes _____

4. "always in touch and sympathy" tells where? how? or when? _____

● **Comprehension Questions**

After reading the selection, answer the following questions with *a, b, c,* or *d.*

_____ 1. The best statement of the main idea of this selection is
   a. the schemes of Mary Tudor were not clever enough to keep Elizabeth from the throne of England
   b. Elizabeth was able to solve the country's problems because she surrounded herself with capable advisors
   c. Elizabeth survived the intrigues of the English court to become an extremely capable, effective, and beloved queen of England
   d. Elizabeth's early life made her adept in the political maneuvering required to reestablish England's economic stability

_____ 2. Mary Tudor turned against Elizabeth because
   a. Elizabeth joined forces with Lady Jane Grey
   b. Elizabeth was thought to be plotting against Mary Tudor
   c. Philip was too fond of Elizabeth
   d. Elizabeth had a very unpleasing personality

_____ 3. According to the selection, Mary Tudor ordered all of the following except
   a. the execution of Lady Jane Grey
   b. imprisonment of Elizabeth
   c. the burning of heretics
   d. the execution of Catherine Howard

_____ 4. The author implies that Philip's positive interest in the welfare of Elizabeth was primarily motivated by his
   a. concern for Spain
   b. affection for Elizabeth
   c. love for Mary
   d. desire for effective English rule

_____ 5. According to the selection, Philip did not favor Mary Stuart's accession to the English throne because she
   a. was queen of Scotland
   b. was queen of France
   c. had lived in England for eighteen years
   d. wished to own the Netherlands

_____ 6. The author implies that the experiences involving violent death in Elizabeth's childhood background had a great influence on her
   a. never marrying
   b. choosing able advisors
   c. relationship with Philip
   d. resistance to foreign intrusion

_____ 7. According to the article, Elizabeth's real mother was
  a. Mary Tudor's sister
  b. involved in a political plot
  c. executed for romantic affairs
  d. stricken dead during childbirth

_____ 8. In seeking advisors the author implies that Elizabeth
  a. wanted none of greater intellect than herself
  b. would not consider the counsel of aristocrats
  c. prefered lords of title, wealth, and experience
  d. focused on capability and overlooked background

_____ 9. When Elizabeth became queen of England, she was faced with all of the following problems except
  a. an Italian threat to English security
  b. religious division between Protestants and Roman Catholics
  c. weak military defenses
  d. economic instability

_____ 10. The author feels that Elizabeth owes the greatest debt for her survival to
  a. Mary Tudor
  b. Lady Jane Grey
  c. Philip of Spain
  d. Mary Stuart

Answer the following questions with *T* (true), *F* (false), or *CT* (can't tell).

_____ 11. Mary Stuart was also called Mary Tudor.
_____ 12. Elizabeth left the Tower of London by boat.
_____ 13. The author suggests that Elizabeth courted the English people as she would a lover.
_____ 14. Elizabeth was crowned queen of England at 25 years of age.
_____ 15. Mary Tudor resented the efforts of Philip of Spain.

• *Vocabulary*

According to the way the boldface word was used in the selection, indicate *a, b, c,* or *d* for the word or phrase that gives the best definition.

____ 1. "**banished** her from court"
  a. exiled
  b. invited
  c. encouraged
  d. released

____ 2. "to the **awesome** fortress"
  a. sturdy
  b. ancient
  c. beautiful
  d. inspiring dread

____ 3. "her **studious** young cousin"
  a. foolish
  b. fond of study
  c. sensitive
  d. disobedient

____ 4. "if Elizabeth were **despatched**"
  a. crowned
  b. courted
  c. entertained
  d. killed

_____ 5. "to **reconcile** herself with
Elizabeth"
a. settle arguments with
b. break away from
c. show superiority
d. sign a treaty

_____ 6. "burning quite so many **heretics**"
a. murderers
b. churchmen opposing official
doctrines
c. robbers
d. revolutionaries against the country

_____ 7. "**macabre** girlhood experiences"
a. gruesome
b. early
c. manufactured
d. fanciful

_____ 8. "developed a certain
ambivalence"
a. negative
b. feeling both love and hate
c. shyness
d. religious fervor

_____ 9. "her womanly **wiles**"
a. fantasies
b. intellectual achievement
c. fashions
d. beguiling trickery

_____ 10. "currency was **depreciated**"
a. lost
b. rejected
c. lessened in value
d. melted

• *Possible Essay Exam Question*

What factors contributed to Elizabeth's survival to become a great queen? (Hint:
Briefly explain how she remained alive to become queen and the effects of
events on her personality.)

• *Word Parts*

Study the meaning of the word parts and supply an additional example from
your own vocabulary. In the second set of items, use the corresponding part to
write the word that best fits the definition.

Word Part	Meaning	Example	Your Example
1. capit, capt	head	captain	_____
2. hier	power, holy	hieroglyphic	_____
3. uni	one	universe	_____
4. vice	in place of	viceroy	_____
5. poly	many	polygon	_____
6. nom, nomy	law, study of	autonomy	_____
7. acer, acid, acri	bitter, sour	acrimony	_____
8. archy	rule	monarchy	_____
9. gamy	marriage	bigamy	_____
10. drome	run	syndrome	_____

1. behead   _____

2. a ranked series of importance   _____

3. mythical animal with one horn   _____

4. next to serve in place of the president   _____

5. worship of many gods   _____

6. study of the stars   _____

7. quality of sour taste   _____

8. state of no rule and disorder   _____

9. having more than one spouse at a
   time   _____

10. arena for horse racing   _____

Selection 2: Poetry

William Wordsworth, "Lucy Gray"

Lucy Gray[*]

OR SOLITUDE

Oft I had heard of Lucy Gray:
And, when I crossed the wild,
I chanced to see at break of day
The solitary child.

5   No mate, no comrade Lucy knew;
She dwelt on a wide moor,
—The sweetest thing that ever grew
Beside a human door!

You yet may spy the fawn at play,
10   The hare upon the green;
But the sweet face of Lucy Gray
Will never more be seen.

*LEARNING STRATEGY: Visualize the hills, the snow, and the small child and try to feel the emotions of the parents and the townspeople.

"Tonight will be a stormy night—
You to the town must go;
15   And take a lantern, Child, to light
Your mother through the snow."

"That, Father! will I gladly do:
'Tis scarcely afternoon—
The minster clock has just struck two,
20   And yonder is the moon!"

At this the Father raised his hook,
And snapped a faggot band;
He plied his work—and Lucy took
The lantern in her hand.

25   Not blither is the mountain roe;
With many a wanton stroke
Her feet disperse the powdery snow,
That rises up like smoke.

The storm came on before its time;
30   She wandered up and down;
And many a hill did Lucy climb,
But never reached the town.

The wretched parents all that night
Went shouting far and wide;
35   But there was neither sound nor sight
To serve them for a guide.

At daybreak on a hill they stood
That overlooked the moor;
And thence they saw the bridge of wood,
40   A furlong from their door.

They wept—and, turning homeward, cried,
"In heaven we all shall meet";
—When in the snow the mother spied
The print of Lucy's feet.

45   Then downwards from the steep hill's
        edge
They tracked the footmarks small;
And through the broken hawthorn hedge,
And by the long stone wall;

And then an open field they crossed:
50   The marks were still the same;
They tracked them on, nor ever lost;
And to the bridge they came.

They followed from the snowy bank
Those footmarks, one by one,
55   Into the middle of the plank;
And further there were none!

—Yet some maintain that to this day
She is a living child;
That you may see sweet Lucy Gray
60   Upon the lonesome wild.

O'er rough and smooth she trips along,
And never looks behind;
And sings a solitary song
That whistles in the wind.   /377

- ## *Skill Development*

Read the following sentences from the selection and write in the blanks the answers to the questions about the relationships of the sentence parts.

I. "You yet may spy the fawn at play,
The hare upon the green;
But the sweet face of Lucy Gray
Will never more be seen."

1. What is the action of "you" in the first part of the sentence? _____

2. What are the two things you may spy? _____

3. "at play" describes _____

4. What "will never more be seen"? _____

II. "Not blither is the mountain roe;
With many a wanton stroke
Her feet disperse the powdery snow,
That rises up like smoke."

1. What does "with many a wanton stroke" describe? _____

2. What does "disperse" describe? _____

3. What is dispersed? _____

4. "That rises up like smoke" describes what? _____

III. "At daybreak on a hill they stood
That overlooked the moor;
And thence they saw the bridge of wood,
A furlong from their door."

1. Whom does the "they" stand for? _____

2. Where did they stand? _____

3. "That overlooked the moor" describes what? _____

4. "from their door" describes what? _____

IV. "They followed from the snowy bank.
Those footmarks, one by one,
Into the middle of the plank;
And further there were none!"

1. What did they follow? _____

2. Does "one-by-one" tell how? when? or why? _____

3. Where did the footprints stop? _____

4. "of the plank" describes what? _____

    V. "O'er rough and smooth she trips along,
       And never looks behind;
       And sings a solitary song
       That whistles in the wind."

1. What are the three core actions of the subject? _____

_____

_____

2. "O'er rough and smooth" describes what? _____

3. What does she sing? _____

4. "That whistles in the wind" describes what? _____

- ## *Comprehension Questions*

  After reading the selection, answer the following questions with *a, b, c,* or *d.*

_____ 1. The best statement of the main idea of this selection is
    a. Lucy Gray's parents were remiss in sending a child out in the snow
    b. Lucy Gray has found a better life than the one she lived on earth
    c. the mystery and tragedy of Lucy Gray's disappearance in a snowstorm has become a legend of the town
    d. the death of Lucy Gray could have been avoided if more precautions had been taken

_____ 2. The "I" who speaks at the beginning of the poem is
    a. Lucy Gray
    b. the father
    c. the mother
    d. the author

_____ 3. The reason Lucy Gray went into the town was
    a. to buy a lantern
    b. to accompany her mother
    c. to help her mother get back home
    d. to get more wood for fuel

_____ 4. The author implies that the father did not go into town because
    a. he was busy collecting wood for the fire
    b. he wanted to teach Lucy responsibility

     c. the mother expected Lucy
     d. the father was lazy and unwilling to make the effort

_____ 5. The poem implies that Lucy Gray actually met her death by
     a. falling into water
     b. being taken away by evil spirits
     c. overexposure from huddling in the snow
     d. wandering to another town

_____ 6. The poem implies that the body of Lucy Gray was
     a. buried in the snow
     b. found on the bridge
     c. buried by her parents
     d. never found

_____ 7. The time that Lucy left home to go into town was
     a. noon
     b. early afternoon
     c. late afternoon
     d. early evening

_____ 8. The reason Lucy's parents did not find her footprints earlier is that
     a. they were looking in the wrong place
     b. the tracks were covered with snow
     c. there were none
     d. it was dark

_____ 9. After the title the author inserted "or Solitude" to emphasize primarily
     a. the emptiness of the grieved parents
     b. the lonely wanderings of a friendless child
     c. the open expanse of snow
     d. the isolation of country life

_____ 10. The townspeople have probably made Lucy Gray into a legend because of all of the following except
     a. the mystery surrounding her disappearance
     b. the hostility of life on the moor
     c. her parent's desire to keep her alive
     d. the sweetness of the child and the purpose of her mission

Answer the following questions with *T* (true), *F* (false), or *CT* (can't tell).

_____ 11. The author feels that Lucy Gray was wrong in wanting to assist her mother.

_____ 12. Lucy Gray's father was unemployed.

———— 13. Lucy Gray's mother came home with somebody else.

———— 14. Lucy Gray's parents died from grief shortly after her disappearance.

———— 15. The wooden planks on the bridge were decaying and dangerous.

- ## *Vocabulary*

According to the way the boldface word was used in the selection, indicate *a*, *b*, *c*, or *d* for the word or phrase that gives the best definition.

———— 1. "The **solitary** child"
a. disobedient
b. heartbroken
c. lonely
d. lost

———— 2. "no **comrade** Lucy knew"
a. friend
b. enemy
c. family
d. leader

———— 3. "on a wide **moor**"
a. island
b. mountain
c. open wasteland
d. valley

———— 4. "the **fawn** at play"
a. child
b. young deer
c. spirit
d. angel

———— 5. "**plied** his work"
a. kept busy at
b. neglected
c. forgot
d. regretted

———— 6. "Not **blither** is"
a. younger
b. more beautiful
c. sweeter
d. happier

———— 7. "the mountain **roe**"
a. range
b. deer
c. flower
d. road

———— 8. "a **wanton** stroke"
a. hidden
b. awkward
c. playful
d. heavy

———— 9. "Her feet **disperse**"
a. scatter
b. flatten
c. darken
d. repel

———— 10. "The **wretched** parents"
a. guilty
b. miserable
c. unwholesome
d. delinquent

- ## *Possible Essay Exam Question*

Why do "some maintain that to this day she is a living child"? (Hint: Relate to this poem the emotional needs of people and legends that grow out of them.)

• *Word Parts*

Study the meaning of the word parts and supply an additional example from your own vocabulary. In the second set of items, use the corresponding part to write the word that best fits the definition.

Word Part	Meaning	Example	Your Example
1. eu	well, good	euphoria	_____
2. mort, mors, more	death	immortal	_____
3. dia	through	diameter	_____
4. climax	high point	climactical	_____
5. ante	before	antecedent	_____
6. viv, vita	alive, life	vitamin	_____
7. glot, gloss	tongue	glottis	_____
8. log, logue	speak	dialogue	_____
9. epi	upon, beside	epitaph	_____
10. sign, signi	sign, mark	significance	_____

1. speech praising a dead person _____

2. undertaker _____

3. determination of weaknesses through

   examination _____

4. disappointing descent in excitement _____

5. room before the main room _____

6. to give life; animate _____

7. speaker of many languages _____

8. a soliloquy _____

9. outer layer of skin _____

10. to appoint or select _____

Selection 3: Geology

Robert J. Foster, from *Physical Geology*

Geologic Work of Ice—Glaciers[*]

Although glaciers are much less important than rivers in overall erosion, they have shaped many of the landforms of northern North America and Eurasia. In addition, most of the high mountain ranges of the world have been greatly modified by mountain glaciers.

A glacier is a mass of moving ice. Glaciers form as a result of accumulation of snow in areas
5   where more snow falls than melts in most years. This can occur at sea level at the poles to about 20,000 feet near the equator. The accumulation of snow must, however, become thick enough so that it recrystallizes to ice. The recrystallization process depends on the pressure of the overlying snow, which transforms the light, loosely packed snow into small ice crystals; with increased pressure, the small crystals become larger. The process is quite similar to the
10   metamorphism of sandstone into quartzite and of limestone into marble. The tendency of snow to recrystallize and form larger crystals is well known to anyone who skis or who has lived in snowy areas. Falling snowflakes are generally small and light, but after a few sunny days, or in the spring, they are much larger at the surface; digging will reveal even larger crystals. When the amount of ice formed in this way becomes large enough that it flows under its own
15   weight, a glacier is born. Ice, as we see it, is a brittle substance, so the fact that a glacier flows under its own weight, much like tar, may seem strange; however, a mass of ice a few hundred feet thick behaves as a very viscous liquid.

Glaciers are of two main types: the alpine or mountain glacier, and the much larger continental or icecap glacier. Present-day continental glaciers occur only near the poles, but
20   mountain glaciers occur at all latitudes where high enough mountains exist.

*LEARNING STRATEGY: Follow and be able to explain the process of glacier formation and the characteristics of the glacial movement.

Mountain Glaciers

Mountain glaciers develop in previously formed stream valleys, which, because they are lower than the surrounding country, become accumulation sites for snow. When enough ice has formed, the glacier begins to move down the valley. How far down the valley it extends will depend on how much new ice is formed and how much melting occurs each year. As the
25 glacier extends further down the valley, the amount of melting each year will increase until a point is reached at which it equals the amount of new ice added. Such a glacier is in equilibrium. If the amount of snowfall increases or the summers become cooler, it will advance further; and if the snowfall decreases or the summers become warmer, it will melt back. However, it generally takes a number of years for the more- or less-than-normal snowfall of a
30 single year, or group of years, to become ice and to reach the snout of the glacier. This means that although a glacier is sensitive to climate changes, it tends to average snowfall and temperature changes over a number of years. Hence, the advance or the retreat of glaciers gives some information on long-term climatic changes. Study of old photographs and maps shows, for instance, that the glaciers in Glacier National Park—and elsewhere—have retreated in the
35 last few decades. Glaciers reached maximum advances about 1825, 1855, and 1895. In general, they have been receding since the turn of the century although with some minor advances. One point needs emphasis: the glacial ice is always moving down-valley, even if the snout of the glacier is retreating because of melting.

The movement of glacial ice can be measured by driving a series of accurately located stakes
40 into the glacier and surveying them periodically. As would be expected, because of friction, the sides of the glacier move more slowly than the center. The upper 100 to 200 feet of the glacial ice behaves brittlely so that the different rates of flow at the surface open large cracks, called *crevasses*, in this brittle zone. The movement of mountain glaciers varies from less than an inch a day to over 50 feet a day.

45 Erosion by mountain glaciers produces such spectacular mountain scenery as Yosemite Valley in the Sierra Nevada of California. Glaciers erode by plucking large blocks of bedrock and by abrasion. Plucking is accomplished by melt-water that flows into joints in the bedrock and later freezes to the main mass of ice which, on advancing, pulls out the blocks of loosened bedrock. These blocks arm the moving ice with rasp-like teeth that grind the sides and bottom of the
50 glacial valley. Glacial erosion greatly modifies the shape of the stream valley occupied by the glacier. Most of the erosion is probably done by plucking, and abrasion generally smooths and even polishes the resulting form.   /783

• *Skill Development*

Read the following sentences from the selection and write in the blanks the answers to the questions about the relationships of the sentence parts.

I. "Mountain glaciers develop in previously formed stream valleys, which, because they are lower than the surrounding country, become accumulation sites for snow."

1. What is the sentence about? _____

2. What is the action of the subject? _____

3. "in previously formed stream valleys" describes _____

4. "which, because they are lower than the surrounding country, become

accumulation sites for snow" describes _____

II. "As the glacier extends further down the valley, the amount of melting each year will increase until a point is reached at which it equals the amount of new ice added."

1. What is the sentence about? _____

2. What is the action of the subject? _____

3. "As the glacier extends further down the valley" describes _____

4. "until a point is reached at which it equals the amount of new ice

added" tells where? why? or how much? _____

III. "If the amount of snowfall increases or the summers become cooler, it will advance further; and if the snowfall decreases or the summers become warmer, it will melt back."

1. This sentence consists of two complete thoughts joined by a semicolon.

In the first core part, what is the sentence about?_____

2. What is the action of the first core part? _____

3. What is the second core part about? _____

4. What is the action of the second core part? _____

IV. "The upper 100 to 200 feet of the glacial ice behaves brittlely so that the different rates of flow at the surface open large cracks, called *crevasses,* in this brittle zone."

1. What is the sentence about? _____

2. What is the subject doing? _____

3. "so that the different rates of flow at the surface open large cracks,

called *crevasses,* in this brittle zone" tells what? where? or why? _____

4. "in this brittle zone" describes _____

V. "Plucking is accomplished by melt-water that flows into joints in the bedrock and later freezes to the main mass of ice, which, on advancing, pulls out the blocks of loosened bedrock."

1. What is the sentence about? _____

2. What is the action of the subject? _____

3. "that flows into joints in the bedrock" describes _____

4. "which, on advancing, pulls out the blocks of loosened bedrock"

describes _____

- ## Comprehension Questions

After reading the selection, answer the following questions with *a, b, c,* or *d.*

_____ 1. The best statement of the main idea of this selection is
a. rivers are a more important and more prevalent cause of erosion than glaciers
b. the rugged terrain of the California mountains was carved by the movement of glaciers
c. a glacier is a river of ice that erodes the landscape and thus modifies the terrain as it moves downward
d. in order to move, the snow accumulated in a mountain glacier must recrystallize into ice

_____ 2. The formation of glaciers is based on
a. the yearly average snowfall for an area
b. the amount of snow that does not melt yearly
c. the distance from the equator
d. the altitude

_____ 3. The immediate result of weight or pressure of new-fallen snow on a glacier is
a. recrystallization of older snow
b. the new-fallen snow turns to ice
c. the metamorphism of sandstone
d. a state of equilibrium

_____ 4. The author implies that mountain glaciers were
a. the first glaciers
b. once more prevalent than they are today
c. never a cause of erosion in North America or Eurasia
d. restricted to the poles

_____ 5. Mountain glaciers form in stream valleys because
a. the ice from the stream can provide a base for the glacier
b. the melting stream pushes the glacier downward
c. the natural funnel encourages snow accumulation
d. the temperature is colder in the deeper valleys

_____ 6. The distance the mountain glacier moves down the valley depends on all of the following except
a. altitude
b. pressure
c. temperature
d. recrystallization

_____ 7. In order for a glacier to retreat, the amount of melting must
a. equal the amount of new ice added
b. be greater than the amount of new ice added over a five-year average
c. be less than the amount of new ice added
d. be less than the amount of new snow accumulation over a five-year average

_____ 8. Glacier cracks or crevasses are caused by all of the following except
a. brittle surface ice

b. downward movement

c. varying rates of surface flow

d. the texture of glacial ice below 200 feet

_____ 9. Plucking is an erosion process that demonstrates the superior force of

a. melted water

b. ice

c. bedrock

d. joints

_____ 10. The smoothing and polishing effect caused by the abrasive force of a glacier is mainly due to

a. the speed of the glacier

b. snow accumulation

c. broken bedrock within the ice

d. crevasses in the glacier

Answer the following questions with *T* (true), *F* (false), or *CT* (can't tell).

_____ 11. Since the turn of the century, Glacier National Park must have had less snow or higher temperatures than in previous years.

_____ 12. When retreating, the glacial ice is moving in an upward direction.

_____ 13. Today the number of mountain glaciers is greater than that of continental glaciers.

_____ 14. The melting ice of mountain glaciers empties primarily into lakes.

_____ 15. Some degree of melting is a prerequisite for plucking.

• *Vocabulary*

According to the way the boldface word was used in the selection, indicate *a, b, c,* or *d* for the word or phrase that gives the best definition.

____ 1. "**accumulation** of snow"

a. continuous falling

b. drifts

c. piling up

d. packing

____ 2. "small ice **crystals**"

a. pieces of glass

b. definite solidified forms

c. sheets

d. snowballs

____ 3. "**metamorphism** of sandstone"

a. substitution

b. decomposition

c. reorganization

d. transformation

____ 4. "a **brittle** substance"

a. easily broken

b. low temperature

c. skinny

d. heavy

____ 5. "very **viscous** liquid"

a. cold

b. sirupy

c. fierce

d. lumpy

____ 6. "**alpine** or mountain glacier"

a. high altitudes

b. dense forest

c. river bed

d. low land

____7. "**continental** glacier"
a. distant
b. large land mass
c. European
d. ancient

____8. "is in **equilibrium**"
a. stagnation
b. final growth
c. a state of balance
d. no return

____9. "the **snout** of the glacier"
a. prolongation of the head
b. source
c. surface
d. tail

____10. "**abrasion** generally smooths"
a. rapid movement
b. wearing away by scraping
c. solid ice
d. melting action

• *Possible Essay Exam Question*

Explain how glaciers form and how they move. (Hint: Summarize the formation process and the highlights of glacial movement.)

• *Word Parts*

Study the meaning of the word parts and supply an additional example from your own vocabulary. In the second set of items, use the corresponding part to write the word that best fits the definition.

Word Part	Meaning	Example	Your Example
1. geo	earth	geocentric	_____
2. pyr	fire	pyrotechnical	_____
3. thermo	heat	thermonuclear	_____
4. cosmo	universe, order	cosmic	_____
5. aster, astro	star	astrology	_____
6. tele	far, distant	telephone	_____
7. tact, tang	touch	tangible	_____
8. meter	measure	thermometer	_____
9. ics	art, science	mathematics	_____
10. grav, gravito	heavy, weighty	gravitation	_____

1. earth study as recorded in rocks   _____

2. glass dishes for cooking   _____

3. flask to keep liquid warm   _____

4. sophisticated; belonging to the world   _____

5. star used in writing to note something   _____

6. communication between minds   _____

7. catching, as a disease   _____

8. instrument to measure heat   _____

9. study of the action of electrons   _____

10. weighty; serious   _____

Chapter Five

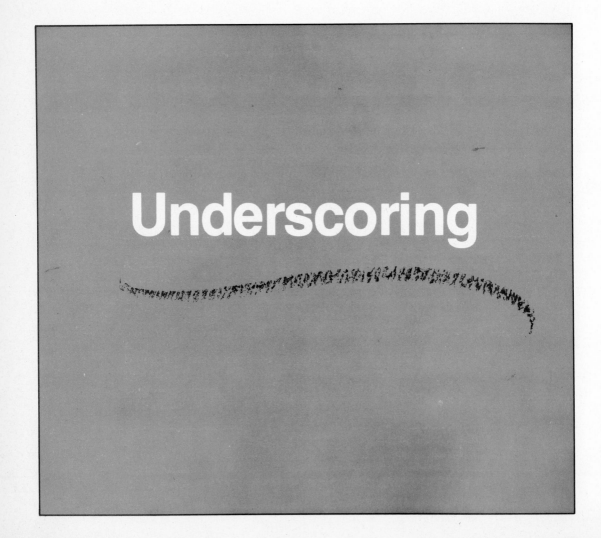

Underscoring

Which of the following would seem to indicate the most effective use of the textbook as a learning tool?

1. A text without a single mark—not even the owner's name has spoiled the sacred pages
2. A text ablaze with color—almost every line is adorned with a red, blue, yellow, and/or green magic marker
3. A text with a scattered variety of markings—underlines, numbers, and stars are interspersed with circles, arrows, and short, written notes

Naturally number three is the best, but unfortunately the first two are not just silly examples; they are commonplace in every classroom. The student's rationale for the first is probably for resale of the book at the end of the course. The reason for the second is procrastination in decision making which is a result of reading without thinking. In other words, the student underlines everything and relies on coming back later to figure out what is *really* important and worth remembering. Both of these extremes are inefficient and ineffective methods of using a college textbook.

Why Underscore?

The textbook is a learning tool and should be used as such; it should not be preserved as a treasure. A college professor requires a particular text because it contains information vital to your understanding of the course. The text places a vast body of knowledge in your hands, much more material than the professor could possibly give in class. It then becomes your job to wade through this information, to make some sense out of it, and to select the important points that need to be remembered.

Underscoring is a method of highlighting these important points. By using a system of symbols and notations, you mark the text during the first reading so that a complete rereading will not be necessary in order to review the information. The markings indicate the most important issues, the significant supporting material, and the relationship of one part to another.

Marking in the textbook itself is faster than writing notes or making an outline in a separate notebook and is probably more effective. All your material is in one place and can be viewed at a glance for later study; the textbook has become a workbook.

Just like overmarking, failure to mark robs you of a valuable learning tool. With no personal indications of prior thinking, there are no clues for quick review. A textbook that remains pure and clean is a handicap.

When to Underscore

Underscoring the words as they are first read is a mistake. The underscoring should be done after a unit of thought has been presented and the information can be viewed as a whole. This may mean marking after only one paragraph or after three pages; marking varies with the material. When you are first reading, every sentence seems of major importance as each new idea unfolds, and the tendency is to underline too much. This serves no useful purpose and is a waste of both reading and review time. However, if you wait until a complete thought has been developed, the significant points will emerge from a background of lesser details. You will then have all the facts and can make decisions about what you want to remember later. At the end of the course your textbook should have that worn, but well-organized look.

How to Underscore

Develop a System of Notations

Highlighting material is not just underlining; it is circling and starring and numbering and generally making an effort to visually put the material into perspective. Notations vary with the individual, and each student develops a number of original creations. Anything that makes sense to you is a correct notation. The following are examples of a marking system:

_____	Main idea
_____	Supporting material
☆	Major trend or possible essay exam question
✓	Important smaller point to know for multiple-choice item
⬭	Word that you must be able to define
▭	Label of a key issue to remember
{ }	Section of material to reread for review
(1), (2), (3)	Numbering of important details under a major issue
?	Didn't understand and must seek advice
Def or C-C or C+E	Notes in the margin
⌇	Indicating relationships

Be Alert to Organizational Patterns

Anticipating the order in which the material will be presented helps you put the facts into perspective and see how the parts fit into the whole. For example, if the selection begins by indicating that there are four important components of management, you are alert to look for four key phrases to mark and remember. Likewise, if a comparison is suggested, you want to mark the points that are similar in nature. For material that shows cause and effect, you need to anticipate the linkage and note the relationship.

The importance of these patterns is that they signal how the proceeding facts will be presented. They are blueprints for you to use in marking and remembering. In textbook reading the number of details can be overwhelming. The mind responds to a logical pattern; relating the small parts to the whole simplifies complexities of the material and makes remembering easier.

Although key signal words help in identifying the particular type of pattern, a single paragraph can be a mixture of different patterns. Your aim is to anticipate the overall pattern and thus place the facts into a broad perspective.

The following examples are the patterns of organization that are most frequently found in textbooks. Each passage has been underscored to demonstrate how a notation system works.

Simple Listing • Items are randomly listed in a series of supporting facts or details. These supporting elements are of equal value, and the order in which they are presented is of no importance. Changing the order of the items does not change the meaning of the paragraph.*

Signal words often used for simple listing: *in addition, also, another, several, for example, a number of*

List of 5

The year 1879 isn't as famous as many other dates in history, but a number of notable things did occur during that year. ① Thomas A. Edison invented the incandescent lamp; F. W. ② Woolworth opened the first five- and ten-cent store ③ the state of California prohibited employers from hiring Chinese people; W. C. Fields first saw the light of day; and the science of psychology was born. For it was in the year 1879 that a scientist named ④ Wilhelm Wundt set up the world's first psychology laboratory in Leipzig, Germany. (p. 3)

(a) Definition

Frequently in textbook reading an entire paragraph is devoted to defining a complex term or idea. The concept is initially defined and then further expanded with examples and restatements. This explanation is actually a form of simple listing but because of its prominence in textbook material deserves special consideration.

def.

Ex.

The preoperational phase is often referred to as the symbolic period, for this is the time of appearance for communicative language, which uses a shared set of symbols. It is at this age also that children most enjoy symbolic play, or make-believe. You can probably think of many preschoolers who spend hours playing house, pretending they are mommy or daddy, or talking on a nonexistent telephone. This is also the time in which

*All examples are from Douglas W. Matheson, *Introductory Psychology: The Modern View* (Hinsdale, Illinois: The Dryden Press, 1975).

deferred imitation first appears. By this Piaget means the child's mimicking of a series of actions he has observed earlier, such as another child's temper tantrum or a song from a TV show. In order to mimic, the child must be able to remember and then recreate what he has previously experienced. (p. 103)

(b) Description

Description also falls into the category of simple listing, but may be more difficult to recognize as such. The characteristics that make up a description are no more than a simple listing of details.

Watch a baby explore the world from his crib. When a moving object is dangled above him, he will follow it with his eyes. If he can reach, he will touch it with his hands. If the object makes a noise when he shakes it, he will shake it again. Finally, he will try to put it in his mouth, which he uses to explore everything in his world. The baby is actively seeking information about his environment; he is getting to know the things around him. Seeing, hearing, tasting, smelling, body position, and touching are basic to all behavior. (p. 135)

Time Order or Sequence • Items are listed in the order in which they occurred or in a specifically planned order in which they must develop. In this case, the order is important and changing it would change the meaning.

Signal words often used for time order or sequence: *first, second, third, after, before, when, until, at last, next, later*

Three insurance salesmen were discussing the merits of their policies. The first man stated that his policy was the best available. He said, "This policy is so good it lasts from the basket to the casket!" Not to be outdone, the second salesman replied, "In my twenty-two years as an insurance salesman, I have never seen a better policy than mine. This policy covers you from the womb to the tomb!" The third salesman smiled and said, "Those policies sound great, but my policy tops both of yours. It covers you from the sperm to the worm!" (p. 79)

Comparison-Contrast • Items are presented according to similarities and differences. They are related according to the comparisons and the contrasts that exist.

Signal words often used for comparison-contrast: *different, similar, on the other hand, but, however, bigger than, in the same way, parallels*

It does not take much thinking to come up with real life parallels to the Milgram experiment. Images of Nazi Germany and My Lai massacre in Vietnam immediately come to mind. Indeed Milgram showed in another experiment (5) that normal, healthy American men will give severe shocks to a kindly old man at the command of the experimenter. Even though subjects complained vigorously to the experimenter, sweated, trembled, and bit their lips, most continued to shock the learner. Evidently the pressures of either the group or an authority figure (the experimenter) can overcome the subjects' sense of morality. In fact, many of the subjects felt no guilt or responsibility for their actions. In their minds, it was not they themselves who were delivering the shocks, even though they actually pushed the button. They viewed themselves as the tools of others and explained their actions in words highly reminiscent of the Nuremberg war trials: "I was only following orders." (p. 42)

Cause and Effect • In this pattern, one item is showed as having produced another element. One is the *cause* or the "happening" that stimulated the particular result or *effect.*

Signal words often used for cause and effect: *for this reason, consequently, on that account, hence, because, made*

Groups demand conformity because deviance threatens their social consensus about beliefs and opinions and their ability to obtain desired goals. As we pointed out earlier, people validate their opinions through social consensus. However, deviants threaten this consensus by holding conflicting views; this destroys the other group members' sense of confidence in the group's "official ideology." Since people find it uncomfortable to be unsure of what is right and wrong, they tend to react with hostility toward anyone who threatens the consensus. Also, particular norms are needed to ensure that the group can obtain its goals. Obviously, if each person on a basketball team came and left practice whenever he felt like it, the team would not be very effective. (pp. 38–39)   } Example

- ## *Exercise 1*

Pretend that each of the following sentences begins a passage that you are about to read in a textbook. Indicate the letter that best describes the pattern of organization that you would anticipate.
a. Simple Listing
b. Definition
c. Description
d. Time Order or Sequence
e. Comparison–Contrast
f. Cause and Effect

_____ 1. One great contrast between the United States and the Soviet Union lies in the lack of automobiles, good highways, and service facilities in the USSR.
Wheeler, Kostbade and Thoman, *Regional Geography of the World*

_____ 2. The nail itself is made of layers of flattened, keratinized cells that have lost their organelles, much like the horny layer of the epidermis.
Roy Hartenstein, *Human Anatomy and Physiology*

_____ 3. Between 1929 and 1933 about two-thirds of all peasant households in the Soviet Union were collectivized. By 1940 this figure had risen 97 percent. Today the number of independent peasant cultivators is insignificant.
Wheeler, Kostbade and Thoman, *Regional Geography of the World*

*All examples are from Douglas W. Matheson, *Introductory Psychology: The Modern View* (Hinsdale, Illinois: The Dryden Press, 1975).

_____ 4. These great business leaders were notable for taking what they could by any means at hand. The Erie Railroad war was a classic example of their contempt for law and custom.

Lloyd C. Gardner and William O'Neill, *Looking Backward*

_____ 5. As the Enlightenment flowered, Philadelphia replaced Boston as the colonies' intellectual capital.

ibid.

_____ 6. This old town of Salem—my native place though I have dwelt much away from it both in boyhood and maturer years—possesses, or did possess, a hold on my affection, the force of which I have never realized during my seasons of actual residence here.

Nathaniel Hawthorne, *The Scarlet Letter*

_____ 7. This movement resulted in three types of anti-Chinese legislation. The first restricted or excluded Chinese immigration to the United States.

Reece McGee et al., *Sociology: An Introduction*

_____ 8. Thomas Jefferson's election in 1800 broke the Federalist party's grip on the presidency and initiated a quarter century of Republican government. Three Virginia patricians—Jefferson, James Madison, and James Monroe—successively occupied the White House during those years and gave the nation dignified and occasionally distinguished direction.

Henry F. Bedford and Trevor Calbourn, *The Americans*

_____ 9. The American colonists had a split image of the Indians. On the one side was the picture of the noble savage. The French philosopher Jean-Jacques Rousseau popularized the idea of the noble savage, and Benjamin Franklin and others took it up in America.

Leonard Pitt, *We Americans*

_____ 10. Three states of matter are distinguished depending on how freely molecules can move. In a *solid* the molecules are bound quite strongly to each other.

John Raynor, *Anatomy and Physiology*

_____ 11. Many different types of epileptic seizures exist. The particular type of seizure depends on the area of the brain that is electrically stimulated and whether the stimulation is restricted to a small area or spreads throughout the brain.

Gerard J. Tottora and Nicholas P. Anagnostakos, *Principles of Anatomy and Physiology*

_____ 12. The *memory,* or storage unit, is the heart of the total computer system. This is where information is stored. The memory element of the computer serves as its filing cabinet, where it stores both information for solving a problem and instructions on how to use the information that is stored there.

Louis E. Boone and David Kurtz, *Contemporary Business*

_____ 13. Although the terms Gemeinschaft and Gesellschaft were originally intended to describe the social organization of entire communities, these concepts have been adopted to describe different types of smaller groups. The primary group is analogous to Gemeinschaft and the secondary to Gesellschaft.

Donald Light, Jr. and Suzanne Keller, *Sociology*

_____ 14. Feminism, which gained strength as a social movement in the early 1970's, has a long and often overlooked history. As early as 1872 an English feminist named Mary Wollstonecraft was protesting women's frivolous existence and "slavish obedience" to men.

ibid.

_____ 15. The fifth or sixth or tenth time this pattern is repeated, a very strange event often occurs. The pigeon behaves as if it has experienced a flash of insight into what is happening.

James V. McConnell, *Understanding Human Behavior*

• *Exercise 2*

For each of the following passages, indicate the overall organizational pattern and underscore the passage as if you were preparing for a quiz on the material.

> On June 1, 1812, President Madison asked Congress to declare war on Great Britain, listing the catalog of British offenses over the past years, none of major importance but adding up to an intolerable total. On June 18 Congress responded with a declaration of war. The vote was close in the Senate—19 to 13—and not overwhelming in the House, 79 to 49, with New England and the Middle Atlantic states against, the South and West for. Ironically, unknown to Madison, Parliament had already on June 16 revoked the orders restricting neutral trade with France— orders which had so stirred American resentment—and there were signs that the British might be willing to negotiate differences further.

Carl N. Degler et al., *The Democratic Experience*

1. The organizational pattern is _____.

> Sometimes eggs can develop into adults without ever having been fertilized. This sort of asexual (or monosexual) reproduction is called **parthenogenesis.** A certain species of desert lizard consists only of females. These lizards lay eggs which, unfertilized, develop into adult females. Laboratory experiments with the eggs of rabbits, frogs, and turkeys have resulted in a very few cases of parthenogenetic development. When pricked with a needle or bathed in certain chemicals, these unfertilized eggs will occasionally develop into normal-seeming adults.
>
> Parthenogenesis is not uncommon among some arthropod species, such as honeybees, water fleas, aphids, and wasps. In spring and summer, female water fleas lay diploid eggs that develop, unfertilized, into female adults. In the fall, however, they lay some eggs that develop into male fleas. The males then fertilize a few haploid eggs laid by the females. These fertilized eggs remain dormant until spring, and then the parthenogenetic female generation begins anew. Honeybees, too, usually alternate a parthenogenetic generation with a sexually produced one.

Victor A. Greulach and Vincent J. Chiappetta, *Biology: The Science of Life*

2. The organizational pattern is _____.

Carl Jung, a Swiss psychiatrist, coined the terms *extravert* and *introvert* to explain two contrasting types of personalities. An extravert is an "outer-directed" individual who likes people, participates in many activities, and seems to need a high level of outside stimulation. Introverts tend to keep to themselves, seek tranquil surroundings, and be less sociable and confident when dealing with people. According to Jung, one or the other of these qualities predominates to some degree in everyone.

More recently, experiments suggest that these personality differences can be measured by the way the individual responds to stimulation. Psychologist William Revelle and his colleagues typed 101 graduate students along an extraversion-introversion scale (and included ambiversion for those who were intermediate between the extremes). He then gave them a standard sixty-question test involving analogies, antonyms, and sentence completions. All the students took the test under three sets of conditions: (1) a ten-minute time limit and 200 milligrams of caffeine (equivalent to about two cups of coffee); (2) a ten-minute time limit but no caffeine; and (3) unlimited time and no caffeine.

The results showed that introverts did better when relaxed than when under the stress of the deadline or when stimulated by caffeine. Extraverts, however, did better when keyed up by the caffeine and poorly without it, regardless of the amount of time they had. For ambiverts the caffeine made no difference but having a deadline did: their performance went down when they were given all the time they wanted.

Revelle concludes that one important difference between extraverts and introverts is in their response to situations that arouse or stimulate the brain. To function most comfortably and effectively, extraverts seek more outside stimulation, introverts less. When the test situation was reversed—caffeine for the introverts and none for the extraverts—the performance of both groups declined. Revelle suspects that this phenomenon holds for most intellectual activities, not just formal tests (Revelle, Amaral, & Turriff, 1976).

If you think of yourself as an introvert, then, coffee won't help you on intellectual tasks. Plenty of time, and a relaxed attitude, however, can make you more effective.

David Dempsey and Philip C. Zimbardo, *Psychology and You*

3. The organizational pattern is _____.

Dick Tuck, widely regarded as a Democratic "prankster" in the 1960s, is sometimes blamed for triggering the Republican "dirty tricks" revenge of the 1970s. Tuck, dressed as a railroad trainman, once signaled a train to pull out just before a Republican candidate was to make a speech from its rear platform. On another occasion, at a "Chinatown" campaign appearance, he stuffed the fortune cookies with questions embarrassing to the candidate.

When Richard Nixon, the prime target of this mischief, was running for reelection in 1972, the Republicans hired Donald Segretti to strike back. Segretti was convicted for sending out a letter over the phony signature of Senator Henry Jackson (D–Wash.). The letter falsely accused two other candidates, Senators Hubert Humphrey (D–Minn.) and Edmund Muskie (D–Maine), of extramarital sexual activity. More significantly, E. Howard Hunt and G. Gordon Liddy organized the burglary at the Watergate headquarters of the Democratic National Committee. The burglary was supposedly to determine whether any relationship existed between the Democratic candidates and foreign agents.

Charles P. Sohner, *American Government and Politics Today*

4. Even though the passage lists examples, the relationship the author wants the reader to see is _____.

Selection 1: Economics

Marilu Hurt McCarty, from *Dollars and Sense*

Skill Development: Underscore the following selection as if you were preparing for an examination.

Inflation*

It has been said that if you ask five economists for their opinion on a subject, you will get six opinions—one can't make up his (or her) mind.

This is particularly true of the subject of inflation. Because the sources of inflation are difficult to pinpoint, it is often hard to choose the proper policy for correcting the problem. 5 Before policy alternatives can be evaluated, the problem must be carefully analyzed and the process by which it travels through the system understood. If the problem is approached haphazardly, any action may bring about results opposite from those intended.

Inflation can be defined as a general rise in the price level of goods and services. Prices are rising and falling all the time. As long as the *average* price level remains the same, inflation is 10 not a problem. When the average price level for all goods and services increases, we have inflation.

Primitive Production

Early humans had to struggle just to stay alive. Because groups were isolated, they had to be self-sufficient. A group produced its entire reserve of game, grain, shelter, and cloth or skins. Later, some groups began to specialize and trade with neighboring tribes. Specialization made 15 possible greater production so that the entire community could enjoy rising standards of living. Material gains were accomplished at the expense of self-sufficiency, but that was a small price to pay.

*LEARNING STRATEGY: Be able to define inflation, identify the possible causes, and explain the effects of inflation on different groups.

Specialization and trade required the use of money to overcome the difficulties of barter.
Primitive tribes used as money whatever tokens they found at hand—special beads and stones
and rare shells. As long as the supply of money remained in balance with the supply of goods,
there was no problem of rising prices. There was just enough money to exchange for goods at
their customary prices.

Economic Development

As knowledge expanded, however, output grew. More money was needed to symbolize the
greater values. A paradox arose: Money had to be of a scarce material to prevent misuse, but it
also had to be expansible if it was to be exchanged for a growing supply of goods. Gold
fulfilled both requirements for many centuries. But eventually, fewer new sources of gold (as
well as the difficulty of hauling it around in one's pockets) made it necessary to find a
substitute. Paper money ''tied'' to gold was the result.*

Balancing the supply of money and goods grew more difficult as economic life became more
complex. This might be seen as a problem of *form* versus *substance*. On the one hand, the
supply of goods (substance) might grow faster than the supply of money (form). Or, what is
more common, the supply of money might grow faster than the real substance of goods.

When the supply of money increases faster than the supply of goods, holders of money will
bid for the smaller quantity of goods. Prices will tend to rise; the economy will experience
inflation. When the supply of money increases more slowly than the supply of goods, sellers
will compete for the smaller quantity of money. Prices will tend to fall; the economy will
experience *deflation*.

Why All the Fuss About Inflation?

Why should inflation concern us? A one-dollar bill and a ten look pretty much the same. Why
should it matter whether a day's welding, a truckload of soybeans, a college course, or a suit
of clothes is counted as ten or one?

It matters if a day's welding *today* at forty dollars is to be exchanged in ten years for a suit
of clothes. By that time the value of the forty dollars may have evaporated and a suit might
cost as much as *five* days' welding. Inflation is especially hard on those people who depend on
stored money value: savers, the elderly, pensioners. (We'll all be there one day!)

It matters, too, if the price of a college course, for example, rises more slowly than the
price of a truckload of soybeans. Those groups who depend on income from the sale of college
courses may be unfairly penalized by uneven price changes. Inflation means a lower standard of
living for people whose occupations or incomes are relatively *fixed:* teachers, civil servants,
low-skilled or technically obsolete workers, and those who depend on government transfer
payments.

Inflation interferes with our ability to plan for the future. We have been taught to save part of
our income to provide security for our retirement years. Our savings may earn interest of up to,
say, 7 percent a year. But suppose the value of our money is declining at the rate of 10 percent
a year because of inflation. The thrifty saver will actually *lose* 3 percent in purchasing power.
The saver will be worse off than the scoundrel who squanders money on frivolous living!

What may be even more disturbing is the fact that the saver's interest earnings of 7 percent
are taxed as part of personal income. In effect, he or she is being taxed twice for being
virtuous—once through inflation and once by the Internal Revenue Service!

Those who make loans and borrow money (creditors and debtors) are also affected by
inflation. In fact, inflation may benefit the debtor, who pays back less in actual purchasing
power than originally borrowed. Lenders are understandably reluctant to lock themselves into
long-term loans when interest rates may not compensate for inflation.

Rampant inflation is often followed by recession or depression. During expansion, there is

*Our money is no longer tied to gold except in a very limited sense. When the U.S. Treasury buys newly
mined gold, it may issue currency in payment. However, most of our currency is issued by the Federal
Reserve banks which are not limited by the supply of gold.

65 feverish spending for capital investment and production of goods and services. The result may be overproduction and stockpiling inventories. Investment and production will eventually fall off, and unemployment and economic distress follow. /982

• *Comprehension Questions*

After reading the selection, answer the following questions with *a, b, c,* or *d.*

_____ 1. The best statement of the main idea of this selection is
   a. inflation is a complex and damaging imbalance in the supply of money and goods
   b. rapid economic development without government control created inflation
   c. in the economic cycle inflation predicts recession or depression
   d. inflation is a natural result of specialization and trade

_____ 2. The author's main purpose in this selection is to
   a. explain the causes and effects of inflation
   b. argue for policies to stop inflation
   c. discuss how to control inflation
   d. offer alternatives to the inflationary cycle

_____ 3. In early human history the need for money was created by
   a. self-sufficiency
   b. isolation
   c. agricultural production
   d. specialization

_____ 4. All of the following are desirable characteristics of material used for money except
   a. exhaustibility
   b. handiness
   c. scarcity
   d. expansibility

_____ 5. Applying the concept of *form* versus *substance,* inflation occurs when there are
   a. more mink coats and more money
   b. fewer mink coats and more money
   c. more mink coats and less money
   d. fewer mink coats and less money

_____ 6. Inflation definitely penalizes all of the following except
   a. savers
   b. social security recipients
   c. post-office workers
   d. debtors

_____ 7. According to the author, putting $1,000 in the bank at 7 percent a year, with an inflation rate of 10 percent a year, will result in a loss (because of inflation) for that year of
   a. less than $30   b. $30   c. $300 plus tax   d. $3.00

_____ 8. The author implies that during an inflationary period she would
   a. lend money
   b. produce fewer goods
   c. save money
   d. not want to tax interest earnings

_____ 9. The reader can conclude that all of the following represent an oversupply of goods except
   a. inflation
   b. deflation
   c. recession
   d. depression

_____ 10. The author points out that the irony of inflation is that it
   a. penalizes overindulgence
   b. raises the standard of living for everyone
   c. decreases product production
   d. hurts those who have conserved money prudently

Answer the following with *T* (true), *F* (false), or *CT* (can't tell).

_____ 11. Inflation is defined by the average price level rather than by an immediate price increase.

_____ 12. Specialization raised the standard of living in early times because more products were available.

_____ 13. More people rather than more products means that more money must be put into circulation.

_____ 14. In the United States the paper currency is directly tied to the supply of gold.

_____ 15. Economists predict a continued rise in the rate of inflation.

● *Vocabulary*

According to the way the boldface word was used in the selection, indicate *a, b, c,* or *d* for the word or phrase that gives the best definition.

____ 1. "is approached **haphazardly**"
   a. logically
   b. maliciously
   c. harshly
   d. randomly

____ 2. "had to be **self-sufficient**"
   a. selfish
   b. productive
   c. independently maintained
   d. self-disciplined

____ 3. "**Specialization** made possible"
   a. concentration of endeavor
   b. generalization of need
   c. mechanization
   d. technology

____ 4. "difficulties of **barter**"
   a. primitive deflation
   b. taxation
   c. trading by exchange of goods
   d. growing interest rates

_____ 5. "technically **obsolete** workers"
a. out-of-date
b. impoverished
c. sick
d. aimless

_____ 6. "taxed twice for being **virtuous**"
a. dishonest
b. unskillful
c. morally responsible
d. evasive

_____ 7. "(**creditors** and debtors)"
a. money lenders
b. authorities
c. originators
d. stockbrokers

_____ 8. "may benefit the **debtor**"
a. money manager
b. one who owes money
c. one who lends money
d. inflation controller

_____ 9. "**Rampant** inflation"
a. local
b. exaggerated
c. modified
d. widespread

_____ 10. "stockpiling of **inventories**"
a. paper money
b. supply of goods
c. investment capital
d. services

• *Possible Essay Exam Question*

Enumerate the financial difficulties that workers on fixed incomes experience during times of inflation. (Hint: Define inflation and its effect on buying power and wages. Then define fixed-income workers and list the resulting difficulties.)

• *Word Parts*

Study the meaning of the word parts and supply an additional example from your own vocabulary. In the second set of items, use the corresponding part to write the word that best fits the definition.

Word Part	Meaning	Example	Your Example
1. corp	body	corporation	_____
2. non	not	nonsense	_____
3. peri	around	periodontal	_____
4. mono	one	monopoly	_____
5. cycl	circle, wheel	cyclical	_____
6. en, em	into, in	employable	_____
7. as, ag	to, toward	assert	_____
8. ee	person who	nominee	_____
9. y	inclined to	faculty	_____
10. ine	like, related to	feline	_____

1. a dead body _____
2. making no monetary gain _____
3. circumference _____
4. exclusive control by one company _____
5. tornado _____
6. to register for entry _____
7. starting quarrels; bold, pushy _____
8. one who works for a company _____
9. tissues with excess flesh _____
10. relating to the dog family _____

Selection 2: Psychology

James V. McConnell, *Understanding Human Behavior*

Skill Development: Underscore the following selection as if you were preparing for an examination.

Monkey Love*

The scientist who has conducted the best long-term laboratory experiments on love is surely Harry Harlow, a psychologist at the University of Wisconsin. Professor Harlow did not set out to study love—it happened by accident. Like many other psychologists, he was at first primarily interested in how organisms learn. Rather than working with rats, Harlow chose to
5   work with monkeys.
Since he needed a place to house and raise the monkeys, he built the *Primate*(*) Laboratory at Wisconsin. Then he began to study the effects of brain lesions on monkey learning. But he soon found that young animals reacted somewhat differently to brain damage than did older monkeys, so he and his wife Margaret devised a breeding program and tried various ways of
10 raising monkeys in the laboratory. They rapidly discovered that monkey infants raised by their mothers often caught diseases from their parents, so the Harlows began taking the infants away from their mothers at birth and tried raising them by hand. The baby monkeys had been given cheesecloth diapers to serve as baby blankets. Almost from the start, it became obvious to the Harlows that their little animals developed such strong attachments to the blankets that, in the
15 Harlows' own terms, it was often hard to tell where the diaper ended and the baby began. Not only this, but if the Harlows removed the "security" blanket in order to clean it, the infant monkey often became greatly disturbed—just as if its own mother had deserted it.
The Surrogate Mother What the baby monkeys obviously needed was an artificial or *surrogate*(*) mother—something they could cling to as tightly as they typically clung to their

*LEARNING STRATEGY: Be able to explain the needs of the infant monkey and the effect that deprivation of those needs can have on the whole pattern of psychological development. Relate these findings to human behavior.

The surrogate cloth mother offers more security to the monkey than the wire mother.

20 own mother's chest. The Harlows sketched out many different designs, but none really appealed to them. Then, in 1957, while enjoying a champagne flight high over the city of Detroit, Harry Harlow glanced out of the airplane window and "saw" an image of an artificial monkey mother. It was a hollow wire cylinder, wrapped with a terry-cloth bath towel, with a silly wooden head at the top. The tiny monkey could cling to this "model mother" as closely as 25 to its real mother's body hair. This surrogate mother could be provided with a functional breast simply by placing a milk bottle so that the nipple stuck through the cloth at an appropriate place on the surrogate's anatomy. The cloth mother could be heated or cooled; it could be rocked mechanically or made to stand still; and, most important, it could be removed at will.

  While still sipping his champagne, Harlow mentally outlined much of the research that kept 30 him, his wife, and their associates occupied for many years to come. And without realizing it, Harlow had shifted from studying monkey learning to studying monkey love.

Infant-Mother Love

The chimpanzee or monkey infant is much more developed at birth than the human infant, and apes develop or mature much faster than we do. Almost from the moment it is born, the monkey infant can move around and hold tightly to its mother. During the first few days of its 35 life the infant will approach and cling to almost any large, warm, and soft object in its environment, particularly if that object also gives it milk. After a week or so, however, the monkey infant begins to avoid newcomers and focuses its attentions on "mother"—real or surrogate.

During the first two weeks of its life warmth is perhaps the most important psychological
thing that a monkey mother has to give to its baby. The Harlows discovered this fact by
offering infant monkeys a choice of two types of mother-substitutes—one wrapped in terry
cloth and one that was made of bare wire. If the two artificial mothers were both the same
temperature, the little monkeys always preferred the cloth mother. However, if the wire model
was heated, while the cloth model was cool, for the first two weeks after birth the baby
primates picked the warm wire mother-substitutes as their favorites. Thereafter they switched
and spent most of their time on the more comfortable cloth mother.

Why is cloth preferable to bare wire? Something that the Harlows call *contact comfort* (*)
seems to be the answer, and a most powerful influence it is. Infant monkeys (and chimps too)
spend much of their time rubbing against their mothers' skins, putting themselves in as close
contact with the parent as they can. Whenever the young animal is frightened, disturbed, or
annoyed, it typically rushes to its mother and rubs itself against her body. Wire doesn't ''rub''
as well as does soft cloth. Prolonged ''contact comfort'' with a surrogate cloth mother appears
to instill confidence in baby monkeys and is much more rewarding to them than is either
warmth or milk. Infant monkeys also prefer a ''rocking'' surrogate to one that is stationary.

According to the Harlows, the basic quality of an infant's love for its mother is *trust*. If the
infant is put into an unfamiliar playroom without its mother, the infant ignores the toys no
matter how interesting they might be. It screeches in terror and curls up into a furry little ball.
If its cloth mother is now introduced into the playroom, the infant rushes to the surrogate and
clings to it for dear life. After a few minutes of contact comfort, it apparently begins to feel
more secure. It then climbs down from the mother-substitute and begins tentatively to explore
the toys, but often rushes back for a deep embrace as if to reassure itself that its mother is still
there and that all is well. Bit by bit its fears of the novel environment are ''desensitized'' (*see*
Chapter 16) and it spends more and more time playing with the toys and less and less time
clinging to its ''mother.''

Good Mothers and Bad The Harlows found that, once a baby monkey has come to accept its
mother (real or surrogate), the mother can do almost no wrong. In one of their studies, the
Harlows tried to create ''monster mothers'' whose behavior would be so abnormal that the
infants would desert the mothers. Their purpose was to determine whether maternal rejection
might cause abnormal behavior patterns in the infant monkeys similar to those responses found
in human babies whose mothers ignore or punish their children severely. The problem was—
how can you get a terry-cloth mother to reject or punish its baby? Their solutions were
ingenious—but most of them failed in their main purpose. Four types of ''monster mothers''
were tried, but none of them was apparently ''evil'' enough to impart fear or loathing to the
infant monkeys. One such ''monster'' occasionally blasted its babies with compressed air; a
second shook so violently that the baby often fell off; a third contained a *catapult* (*) that
frequently flung the infant away from it. The most evil-appearing of all had a set of metal
spikes buried beneath the terry cloth; from time to time the spikes would poke through the cloth
making it impossible for the infant to cling to the surrogate.

The baby monkeys brought up on the ''monster mothers'' did show a brief period of
emotional disturbance when the ''wicked'' *temperament* (*) of the surrogates first showed up.
The infants would cry for a time when displaced from their mothers, but as soon as the
surrogates returned to normal, the infant would return to the surrogate and continue clinging,
as if all were forgiven. As the Harlows tell the story, the only prolonged distress created by the
experiment seemed to be that felt by the experimenters!

There was, however, one type of surrogate that uniformly ''turned off'' the infant monkeys.
S. J. Suomi, working with the Harlows, built a terry-cloth mother with ice water in its veins.
Newborn monkeys would attach themselves to this ''cold momma'' for a brief period of time,
but then retreated to a corner of the cage and rejected her forever.

90   From their many brilliant studies, the Harlows conclude that the love of an infant for its
      mother is *primarily a response to certain stimuli the mother offers*. Warmth is the most
      important stimulus for the first two weeks of the monkey's life, then contact comfort becomes
      paramount (*). Contact comfort is determined by the softness and "rub-ability" of the surface
      of the mother's body—terry cloth is better than are satin and silk, but all such materials are
      more effective in creating love and trust than bare metal is. Food and mild "shaking" or
95   "rocking" are important too, but less so than warmth and contact comfort. These needs—
      and the rather primitive responses the infant makes in order to obtain their satisfaction—are
      programmed into the monkey's genetic blueprint. The growing infant's requirement for social
      and intellectual stimulation becomes critical only later in a monkey's life. And yet, as we will
      see in this (and the next) chapter, if the baby primate is deprived of contact with other young
100   of its own species, its whole pattern of development can be profoundly disturbed.

Mother-Infant Love

      The Harlows were eventually able to find ways of getting female isolates pregnant, usually by
      confining them in a small cage for long periods of time with a patient and highly experienced
      normal male. At times, however, the Harlows were forced to help matters along by strapping
      the female to a piece of apparatus. When these isolated females gave birth to their first
105   monkey baby, they turned out to be the "monster mothers" the Harlows had tried to create
      with mechanical surrogates. Having had no contact with other animals as they grew
      up, they simply did not know what to do with the furry little strangers that suddenly
      appeared on the scene. These motherless mothers at first totally ignored their children,
      although if the infant persisted, the mothers occasionally gave in and provided the baby
110   with some of the contact and comfort it demanded.
          Surprisingly enough, once these mothers learned how to handle a baby, they did reasonably
      well. Then, when they were again impregnated and gave birth to a second infant, they took
      care of this next baby fairly adequately.
          Maternal affection was totally lacking in a few of the motherless monkeys, however. To
115   them, the newborn monkey was little more than an object to be abused the way a human child
      might abuse a doll or a toy train. These motherless mothers stepped on their babies, crushed
      the infant's face into the floor of the cage, and once or twice chewed off their baby's feet and
      fingers before they could be stopped. The most terrible mother of all popped her infant's head
      into her mouth and crunched it like a potato chip.
120   We tend to think of most mothers—no matter what their species—as having some kind of
      almost-divine "maternal instinct" that makes them love their children and take care of them no
      matter what the cost or circumstance. While it is true that most females have built into their
      genetic blueprint the *tendency* to be interested in (and to care for) their offspring, this inborn
      tendency is always expressed in a given environment. The "maternal instinct" is strongly
125   influenced by the mother's past experiences. Humans seem to have weaker instincts of all kinds
      than do other animals—since our behavior patterns are more affected by learning than by our
      genes, we have greater flexibility in what we do and become. But we pay a sometimes severe
      price for this freedom from genetic control.
          Normal monkey and chimpanzee mothers seldom appear to inflict real physical harm on their
130   children; human mothers and fathers often do. Serapio R. Zalba, writing in a journal called
      Trans-action, estimated in 1971 that in the United States alone, perhaps 250,000 children
      suffer physical abuse by their parents each year. Of these "battered babies," almost 40,000
      may be very badly injured. The number of young boys and girls killed by their parents annually
      is not known, but Zalba suggests that the figure may run into the thousands. Parents have
135   locked their children in tiny cages, raised them in dark closets, burned them, boiled them,

slashed them with knives, shot them, and broken almost every bone in their bodies. How can we reconcile these facts with the much-discussed maternal and paternal "instincts?"

140

The research by the Harlows on the "motherless mothers" perhaps gives us a clue. Mother monkeys who were themselves socially deprived or isolated when young seemed singularly lacking in affection for their infants. Zalba states that most of the abusive human parents that were studied turned out to have been abused and neglected *themselves* as children. Like the isolated monkeys who seemed unable to control their aggressive impulses when put in contact with normal animals, the abusive parents seem to be greatly deficient in what psychologists call "impulse control" (*see* Chapter 20). Most of these parents also were described as being socially

145

isolated, as having troubles adjusting to marriage, often deeply in debt, and as being unable to build up warm and loving relationships with other people—including their own children. Since they did not learn how to love from their own parents, these mothers and fathers simply did not acquire the social skills necessary for bringing up their own infants in a healthy fashion.   /2207

• *Comprehension Questions*

After reading the selection, answer the following questions with *a, b, c,* or *d.*

_____ 1. The best statement of the main idea of this selection is
  a. an infant develops a love relationship with its mother and later initiates this same relationship with its own child
  b. infant monkeys are very much like infant children
  c. trust is the quality in an infant's love for its mother
  d. a mother can easily fall into a pattern of child abuse

_____ 2. When Harry Harlow originally started his experiments with monkeys, his purpose was to study
  a. love
  b. breeding
  c. learning
  d. disease

_____ 3. The reason that the author mentions Harry Harlow's revelations on the airplane is to show
  a. that he had extrasensory perception
  b. that he liked to travel
  c. that he was always thinking of his work
  d. in what an unexpected way brilliant work often starts

_____ 4. In his experiments Harlow used all of the following in designing his surrogate mothers except
  a. a terry-cloth bath towel
  b. real body hair
  c. a rocking movement
  d. temperature controls

_____ 5. Harlow manipulated his experiments to show the early significance of warmth by
  a. heating wire

_____ b. cooling terry cloth
c. equalizing temperature
d. creating "monster mothers"

_____ 6. Harlow feels that for contact comfort the cloth mother was preferable to the wire mother for all of the following reasons except
a. the cloth mother instilled confidence
b. the wire mother doesn't "rub" as well
c. the wire mother was stationary
d. with the cloth mother, the infant feels a greater sense of security when upset

_____ 7. Harlow's studies show that when abused by its mother, infant monkeys will
a. leave the mother
b. seek a new mother
c. return to the mother
d. fight with the mother

_____ 8. For an infant to love its mother, Harlow's studies show that in the first two weeks the most important element is
a. milk
b. warmth
c. contact comfort
d. love expressed by the mother

_____ 9. In Harlow's studies with motherless monkeys he showed that the techniques of mothering are
a. instinctive
b. learned
c. inborn
d. natural

_____ 10. The Harlows feel that child abuse is caused by all of the following problems except
a. parents who were abused as children
b. socially isolated parents
c. parents who cannot control their impulses
d. parents who are instinctively evil

Answer the following with *T* (true), *F* (false), or *CT* (can't tell).

_____ 11. The authors feel that the studies of love in infant monkeys have a great deal of similarity to love in human children.

_____ 12. The author implies that isolated monkeys have difficulty engaging in normal peer relationships.

_____ 13. When taught how to be good mothers, all of the motherless mothers became fairly good parents.

_____ 14. Zalba's studies confirmed many of the findings of the Harlow studies.

_____ 15. Infant monkeys deprived of warmth become intellectually impaired.

• *Vocabulary*

According to the way the boldface word was used in the selection, indicate *a, b, c,* or *d* for the word or phrase that gives the best definition.

____1. "the **surrogate** mother"
   a. mean
   b. thoughtless
   c. loving
   d. substitute

____2. "a **functional** breast"
   a. mechanical
   b. operational
   c. wholesome
   d. imitation

____3. "on the surrogate's **anatomy**"
   a. body
   b. head
   c. offspring
   d. personality

____4. "begins **tentatively** to explore"
   a. rapidly
   b. hesitantly
   c. aggressively
   d. readily

____5. "fears of the **novel** environment"
   a. hostile
   b. literary
   c. dangerous
   d. new

____6. "fears . . . are **desensitized**"
   a. made less sensitive
   b. made more sensitive
   c. electrified
   d. communicated

____7. "solutions were **ingenious**"
   a. incorrect
   b. noble
   c. clever
   d. honest

____8. "**deprived** of contact"
   a. encouraged
   b. denied
   c. assured
   d. ordered into

____9. "if the infant **persisted**"
   a. stopped
   b. continued
   c. fought
   d. relaxed

____10. "to be greatly **deficient**"
   a. lacking
   b. supplied
   c. overwhelmed
   d. secretive

• *Possible Essay Exam Question*

Use Harlow's study to explain child abuse as a chain reaction. (Hint: Describe infant needs as demonstrated by Harlow's monkeys and the cause-and-effect nature of deprivation on future generations.)

• *Word Parts*

Study the meaning of the word parts and supply an additional example from your own vocabulary. In the second set of items, use the corresponding part to write the word that best fits the definition.

Word Part	Meaning	Example	Your Example
1. inter	between	interaction	_____
2. intra	within	intracellular	_____

3. fer	bring, bear, yield	fertile	_____
4. spir	breath	inspiration	_____
5. flex, flect	bend, turn aside	reflex	_____
6. rupt	break, burst	interrupt	_____
7. oper, opus	work	operable	_____
8. ive	quality of	aggressive	_____
9. ose	full	bellicose	_____
10. ance	state, condition of	elegance	_____

1. meddle in concerns of others _____

2. sports within the school _____

3. a boat for transporting cars over water _____

4. to breathe one's last breath _____

5. bendable _____

6. a volcanic explosion _____

7. to work with someone else _____

8. tending to agree _____

9. wordy _____

10. acceptance of differences _____

Selection 3: Geology

A. Lee McAlester, from *The Earth*

Skill Development: Underscore the following selection as if you were preparing for an examination.

Ice in the Ocean*

The formation of ice in sea water is a final important structural property of the ocean. We have seen that ice crystals forming in the ocean are made up of almost pure water; their formation increases the salinity of the remaining water so that further cooling is necessary for more freezing to take place. If this process continues, ice particles increase in abundance and freeze

5 into a solid framework enclosing small cells of sea water which have too high a salinity to freeze at that temperature. The result is a frozen mixture consisting mostly of relatively pure ice crystals enclosing small quantities of salt and brine.

*LEARNING STRATEGY: Visualize each step of the processes described and look for similarities and differences in ice masses.

Complete freezing of ocean water, in the manner just described, sometimes takes place in shallow bays and lagoons in polar regions, but in areas of deeper water only a thin surface
10   layer of **sea ice,** usually less than 3 m (10 ft) thick, forms in even the coldest polar seas. Such sea ice perpetually covers most of the Arctic Ocean and surrounds the ice-covered continent of Antarctica. It forms from the freezing of surface sea water and the accumulation of fresh water, as snow, on the surface. Sea ice seldom grows thicker than 3 m because as the waters beneath the ice are cooled, they increase in density and sink to be replaced by warmer waters from
15   below. Accumulation of snow and ice on the surface is also limited by the water temperature for, as snow accumulates on the surface, the ice below is depressed by the weight and an equivalent amount of ice is melted below by the warmer waters. Thus the thickness tends to remain constant even in areas of high snowfall.

In contrast to the thin sheets of sea ice that form on the oceans, ice on land, accumulating as
20   snow on a solid surface with no water below to cause melting, can reach tremendous thicknesses. Most of Greenland and the continent of Antarctica are now covered by huge ice sheets that are more than a kilometer thick. In addition to these extensive ice sheets, most mountains of polar regions have valleys filled by smaller **glaciers,** which are thick rivers of ice that accumulate on land as snow. Where either ice sheets or glaciers touch the ocean, huge
25   **icebergs** hundreds of meters thick may break away and float until they reach warmer water and melt. Icebergs (which along with sea ice form the two principal kinds of ice found in the ocean) therefore originate not from freezing of ocean water, but from the accumulation of fresh water, as snow, on the land surface. Most of the icebergs of the northern hemisphere occur in the North Atlantic and have their source in Greenland and arctic Canada. In the southern
30   hemisphere, the huge Antarctic ice cap in some places flows beyond the boundaries of the continent as **shelf ice** floating on the surrounding seas. The largest icebergs of the ocean originate when huge masses of this ice break off and float northward. During the Antarctic winter, this thick, floating, land ice is bounded on the seaward side by a much wider belt of thin sea ice similar to that which continually covers the Arctic Ocean.   /529

• *Comprehension Questions*

After reading the selection, answer the following questions with *a, b, c,* or *d.*

_____   1. The best statement of the central focus of this selection is
a. an ocean of ice fills the Arctic Ocean and surrounds Antarctica most of the year
b. the depth of sea ice is more constant than that of land ice

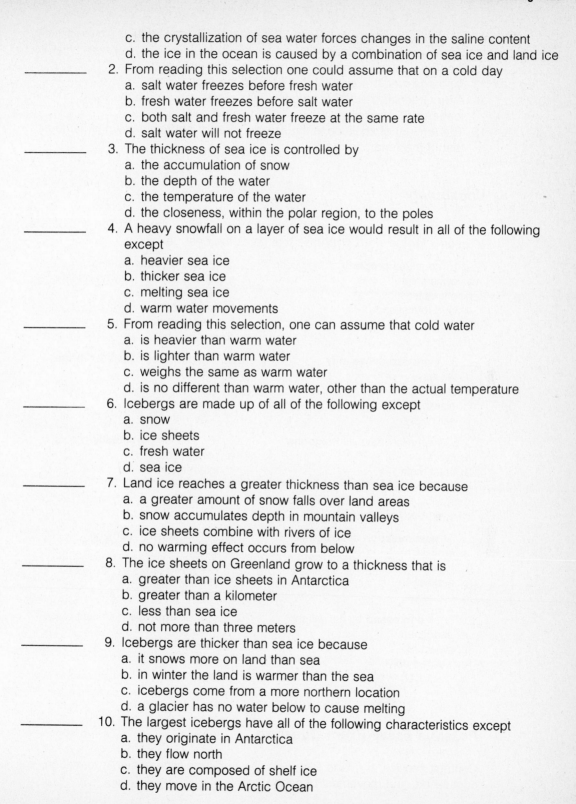

c. the crystallization of sea water forces changes in the saline content

d. the ice in the ocean is caused by a combination of sea ice and land ice

_____ 2. From reading this selection one could assume that on a cold day

a. salt water freezes before fresh water

b. fresh water freezes before salt water

c. both salt and fresh water freeze at the same rate

d. salt water will not freeze

_____ 3. The thickness of sea ice is controlled by

a. the accumulation of snow

b. the depth of the water

c. the temperature of the water

d. the closeness, within the polar region, to the poles

_____ 4. A heavy snowfall on a layer of sea ice would result in all of the following except

a. heavier sea ice

b. thicker sea ice

c. melting sea ice

d. warm water movements

_____ 5. From reading this selection, one can assume that cold water

a. is heavier than warm water

b. is lighter than warm water

c. weighs the same as warm water

d. is no different than warm water, other than the actual temperature

_____ 6. Icebergs are made up of all of the following except

a. snow

b. ice sheets

c. fresh water

d. sea ice

_____ 7. Land ice reaches a greater thickness than sea ice because

a. a greater amount of snow falls over land areas

b. snow accumulates depth in mountain valleys

c. ice sheets combine with rivers of ice

d. no warming effect occurs from below

_____ 8. The ice sheets on Greenland grow to a thickness that is

a. greater than ice sheets in Antarctica

b. greater than a kilometer

c. less than sea ice

d. not more than three meters

_____ 9. Icebergs are thicker than sea ice because

a. it snows more on land than sea

b. in winter the land is warmer than the sea

c. icebergs come from a more northern location

d. a glacier has no water below to cause melting

_____ 10. The largest icebergs have all of the following characteristics except

a. they originate in Antarctica

b. they flow north

c. they are composed of shelf ice

d. they move in the Arctic Ocean

Answer the following with *T* (True), *F* (false), or *CT* (can't tell).

_____ 11. Snow weighs more than ice.
_____ 12. Icebergs could be melted and used for drinking water.
_____ 13. Icebergs melt before they drift beyond the Arctic Circle.
_____ 14. After Greenland and Canada, the third greatest source of northern icebergs is Alaska.
_____ 15. The amount of shelf ice in the Arctic Ocean is approximately the same as that of the Antarctic region.

• Vocabulary

According to the way the boldface word was used in the selection, indicate *a, b, c,* or *d* for the word or phrase that gives the best definition.

____ 1. "structural **property** of the ocean"
a. ownership
b. characteristics
c. land formation
d. requirement

____ 2. "ice **crystals** forming"
a. solidified forms in symmetrical patterns
b. liquid drops
c. glass particles
d. rounded balls

____ 3. "increases the **salinity**"
a. wisdom
b. toughness
c. elasticity
d. saltiness

____ 4. "quantities of salt and **brine**"
a. dirt
b. scum
c. snowflakes
d. salty water

____ 5. "in shallow bays and **lagoons**"
a. rivers
b. coral reefs
c. tributaries
d. shallow lakes or ponds linked to a large body of water

____ 6. "sea ice **perpetually** covers"
a. permanently
b. intermittently
c. seasonally
d. largely

____ 7. "**accumulation** of fresh water"
a. arrangement
b. collection
c. acquisition
d. allocation

____ 8. "increase in **density**"
a. color
b. area
c. number per unit
d. temperature

____ 9. "is **depressed** by the weight"
a. saddened
b. dejected
c. pushed down
d. destroyed

____ 10. "an **equivalent** amount of ice"
a. greater
b. lesser
c. even
d. optimal

• Possible Essay Exam Question

Contrast sea ice and land ice. (Hint: Describe the differences in formation, accumulation, and movement of each.)

• *Word Parts*

Study the meaning of the word parts and supply an additional example from your own vocabulary. In the second set of items, use the corresponding part to write the word that best fits the definition.

Word Part	Meaning	Example	Your Example
1. micro	small	microscope	_____
2. macro	large	macronucleus	_____
3. dent	teeth	dentist	_____
4. ocul	eye	ocular	_____
5. pod, ped	foot	podiatrist	_____
6. derma	skin	dermatologist	_____
7. ortho	straight	orthodox	_____
8. itis	inflammation of	appendicitis	_____
9. scope	watch, see	periscope	_____
10. ectomy	cut out	vasectomy	_____

1. a small organism _____

2. chemistry requiring no microscope _____

3. artificial teeth _____

4. another name for an ophthalmologist _____

5. a stand with three legs _____

6. the outer layer of skin _____

7. doctor who straightens teeth _____

8. inflammation of a nerve _____

9. instrument to record earthquakes _____

10. removal of the appendix _____

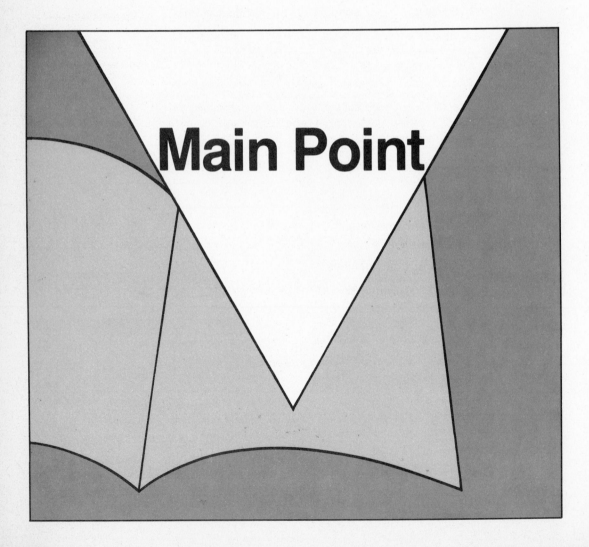

If all reading comprehension skills were reduced to one basic question, that question might possibly be, "What is the author's main point?" In answering, you must go beyond recognizing the general topic to understanding the author's message about a specific aspect of the topic.

For example, the general topic of an assignment might be advertising, but that is not a sufficient explanation or understanding of the main point. Is the assignment about new trends in advertising, consumer response, or unethical practices? In other words, what particular aspect of advertising is addressed?

Once the topic is narrowed, you can ask, "What point is the author trying to get across about this particular aspect of advertising?" Is it that new trends in advertising lack imagination, that new trends reach more consumers, or that new trends cost more money? Maybe the author's point is simply, "Here is a list of five new trends in advertising that you should know." Whatever the answer, your ultimate understanding of the material depends on determining *the point the author is trying to get across* and not just on summing up the subject matter under one general topic area.

Read the following paragraph by Mark Twain and then state the main point:

This creature's career could produce but one result, and it speedily followed. Boy after boy managed to get on the river. The minister's son became an engineer. The doctor's sons became "mud clerks;" the wholesale liquor dealer's son became a bar-keeper on a boat; four sons of the chief merchant, and two sons of the county judge, became pilots. Pilot was the grandest position of all. The pilot, even in those days of trivial wages, had a princely salary—from a hundred and fifty to two hundred and fifty dollars a month, and no board to pay. Two months of his wages would pay a preacher's salary for a year. Now some of us were left disconsolate. We could not get on the river—at least our parents would not let us.

Mark Twain, *Life on the Mississippi*

Is the main point of the paragraph that pilots have the best job on the river?

No—this is one of the interesting facts supporting and developing the author's main point.

Is it that Mississippi River life is exciting?

Yes and No—This is the general topic, but it is too broad to accurately describe the author's message in this particular paragraph. Such a broad statement would probably cover most of the paragraphs in this book.

Is it "The minister's son became an engineer"?

No—This is too specific and is merely one of the supporting details that adds interest to the paragraph.

Is it that young boys want interesting jobs?

No—This general statement applies but it is not specific enough to accurately describe this particular paragraph.

Is it that "the wholesale liquor dealer's son became a bar-keeper on a boat"?

No—This is only one of the supporting details.

Is it that pilots earn higher salaries than preachers?

No—This is just one of the minor details to add interest.

Is it that young boys in the area have a strong desire to leave home and get a job on the prestigious Mississippi River?

Yes—This is an accurate statement of the author's main point and the details support this message.

Imagine how the paragraph would have been if one of the details had actually been the main point. Rewrite the paragraph using as much of the same supporting material as possible, but change the author's main point to one of the following:

1. The minister's son became an engineer.
2. The wholesale liquor dealer's son became a barkeeper on a boat.
3. A river pilot is the best job on the river.
4. Parents object to sons leaving home for the jobs on the river.

Write your new paragraph in the space below.

_____

_____

_____

_____

_____

_____

_____

_____

_____

_____

_____

_____

_____

The reader can ask a series of three questions to arrive at the author's main point. These questions can be applied to a single paragraph or to an entire book.

1. Who or what is this about? (General Topic) _____

_____

2. What aspect of this who or what is the author addressing? (Narrowed

Aspect of the Topic) _____

3. What is the author trying to get across about this aspect of the who or what? (Main Point) _____

_____

• *Exercise 1*

Read the following paragraphs and use the three-question series to determine the author's main point.

Research is not a once-and-for-all-times job. Even sophisticated companies often waste the value of their research. One of the most common errors is not providing a basis for comparisons. A company may research its market, find a need for a new advertising campaign, conduct the campaign, and then neglect to research the results. Another may simply feel the need for a new campaign, conduct it, and research the results. Neither is getting the full benefit of the research. When you fail to research either the results or your position *prior* to the campaign, you cannot know the effects of the campaign. For good evaluation you must have *both* before *and* after data.

Edward Fox and Edward Wheatley, *Modern Marketing*

1. Who or what is this about? _____

2. What aspect of this who or what is the author addressing? _____

_____

3. What is the author trying to get across about this aspect of the who or what?

_____

_____

Under hypnosis, people may recall things that they are unable to remember spontaneously. Some police departments employ hypnotists to probe for information that crime victims do not realize they have. In 1976, twenty-six young children were kidnaped from a school bus near Chowchilla, California. The driver of the bus caught a quick glimpse of the license plate of the van in which he and the children were driven away. However, he remembered only the first two digits. Under hypnosis, he recalled the other numbers and the van was traced to its owners.

David Dempsey and Philip Zimbardo, *Psychology and You*

1. Who or what is this about?_____

2. What aspect of this who or what is the author addressing?_____

_____

3. What is the author trying to get across about this aspect of the who or what?

_____

_____

Crystal balls grow cloudy when it comes to predicting consumer behavior in the market. Who, in the 1960s, could have predicted the success of the CB radio or the disappointing performance of supersonic air travel during the 1970s? Consumers are influenced by such a wide range of circumstances that it is impossible to know for certain what products will sell, what businesses will be profitable, and what training will earn you the highest income.

Marilu Hurt McCarty, *Dollars and Sense*

1. Who or what is this about? _____

2. What aspect of this who or what is the author addressing? _____

_____

3. What is the author trying to get across about this aspect of the who or what?

_____

_____

If at any one time of my life more than another, I was made to drink the bitterest dregs of slavery, that time was during the first six months of my stay with Mr. Covey. We were worked in all weathers. It was never too hot or too cold; it could never rain, blow, hail, or snow, too hard for us to work in the field. Work, work, work, was scarcely more the order of the day than of the night. The longest days were too short for him, and the shortest nights too long for him. I was somewhat unmanageable when I first went there, but a few months of this discipline tamed me. Mr. Covey succeeded in breaking me. I was broken in body, soul, and spirit. My natural elasticity was crushed, my intellect languished, the disposition to read departed, the cheerful spark that lingered about my eye died; the dark night of slavery closed in upon me; and behold a man transformed into a brute!

Frederick Douglas, *Narrative of the Life of Frederick Douglas, an American Slave*

1. Who or what is this about? _____

2. What aspect of this who or what is the author addressing? _____

_____

3. What is the author trying to get across about this aspect of the who or what?

_____

_____

In the early nineteenth century Americans consumed an extraordinary amount of liquor. The average annual intake of spirituous and fermented alcohol per person of drinking age in the 1820s, for example, was seven to ten gallons—at least five times today's average. The most common distilled liquor in New England and seaport cities was rum; in the rest of the country it was usually whiskey. Beer and wine were drunk everywhere but the most popular fermented drink in those days was hard cider (about 20 proof). No social occasion, whether a cornhusking bee or the installation of a clergyman, was complete without heavy drinking. Whiskey was a form of money on the frontier, and even church subscriptions were payable in liquid coin. Wretched transportation facilities before the 1820s meant that grain could be marketed over distances only in distilled form. Liquor was cheap, untaxed in most areas, and constituted a considerable portion of people's daily calorie intake. Many men greeted each day with a gill (four fluid ounces) of grog; John Adams regularly drank a pint of hard cider before breakfast. European visitors were astonished by the "universal practice of sipping a little at a time . . . [every] half an hour to a couple of hours."

Carl N. Degler et al., *The Democratic Experience*

1. Who or what is this about? _____

_____

2. What aspect of this who or what is the author addressing? _____

_____

3. What is the author trying to get across about this aspect of the who or what?

_____

_____

Topic Sentences

A *paragraph* is a group of ideas expanded into sentences which specifically relate to the same topic. The *topic sentence* is a summary statement of the main idea of the paragraph. Sometimes the topic sentence is stated within the paragraph and sometimes it is not.

In the unit on previewing, the position of the topic sentence is discussed. The topic sentence can be stated in the beginning of the paragraph, as it frequently is, or at the end or in the middle or it may not be stated at all. What the reader needs to understand is that a great search for the topic sentence is not necessary in order to understand the author's main point. For example, pretend that the following are the key words from two different paragraphs:

Paragraph A		*Paragraph B*	
flies	insects	spring	fall
mosquitoes	fleas	summer	winter
gnats			

What is A about? _____   *What is B about?* _____

Note that in A the general topic is stated, whereas in B it is not; it is understood. These few key words from each paragraph give a general idea of the topic discussed, but you still do not have enough information about the paragraph to determine the author's main point.

If the key words are expanded into phrases, does that bring you any closer to the author's main point?

Paragraph A	*Paragraph B*
flies crawling over your food	pastel spring blossoms
bloodthirsty biting mosquitoes	green shade on hot summer days
to escape the busy gnats	fall's color festival
the purpose of flying insects	color for winter
to fight with the fleas	*What aspect of the topic in B is the author*
What aspect of the topic in A is the author	*addressing?*
addressing?	

The topics have been narrowed down somewhat, but the author's message is still unclear. For example, in A the author could use these details to make several points. Is it that flying insects have no purpose, or that they serve a major purpose in the food chain, or that their only purpose is to disturb life? Read the complete version of each paragraph and determine the author's main point.

Paragraph A
Have you ever been on a picnic with flies crawling over your food? On a summer night have you been driven from a moonlit patio by bloodthirsty biting mosquitoes? Have you had to forego the beauty of the ocean waves to escape the busy gnats that the land breeze brought to the beach? The purpose of flying insects seems to be to pester and annoy and to drive poor souls from the joys of nature. Even the dog has to fight with the fleas to enjoy a romp in the wilderness.

What is the author's main point? _____

_____

Paragraph B
A pastel spring blossoms in the south with dogwood, azaleas, and daffodils. The broad leaves of oaks cast a green shade on hot summer days and the grass grows lush between the toes. Fall's color festival opens with yellows, oranges, and reds and marks the end of another year's parade of color. The winter is gray because the color that is missing is the unfulfilled wish of a new-fallen snow.

What is the author's main point?_____

_____

This exercise demonstrates two points:

1. A topic sentence may be stated somewhere within the paragraph or it may be unstated. While a stated topic can help you, it is not necessary in determining the author's main point.
2. Finding the author's main point is a sequential process and cannot be determined until the entire paragraph is read.

• *Exercise 2*

Create your own key words for paragraphs using both stated and unstated topics. Be sure that each of your paragraphs is composed of ideas relating to a single specific topic.

Paragraph A (topic stated)

_____

_____

_____

_____

_____

Paragraph B (topic unstated)

_____

_____

_____

_____

_____

Paragraph C

_____

_____

_____

_____

Paragraph D

_____

_____

_____

_____

Details

Textbooks are packed full of details, and you must decide which are the most important to remember. The truth is that you cannot remember everything, and fortunately all details are not of equal importance. To decide which are the most important, go back to the central focus and ask the following questions.

1. Which details logically develop the main point?

2. Which details help you understand the main point?

3. Which details validate the main point?

Focus on the significant details that answer these questions and pay little attention to the rest. Your ability to select significant supporting details depends on your ability to determine the author's main point.

• *Exercise 3*

Answer the questions after reading each of the following paragaphs.

Adolescence is a period in which individuals are expected to express achievement motivation in some concrete fashion. Whether this entails academic success, athletic prowess, or social competence will vary from person to person. The general features of achievement motivation, such as autonomy, planning for the future, mastery of socially relevant skills, a devotion to effort and hard work, ambition, and a desire for upward mobility, all comprise a set of expectations that intrude heavily upon adolescents. Studies have demonstrated that social pressures toward the demonstration of achievement motivation are applied, often abruptly, early in adolescence and increase substantially throughout this period. Aversive behavior, such as the postponement of work activities, tardiness, erratic habits, and other forms of avoidance of responsibility, which would have been condoned in childhood are often severely punished in adolescence. He is expected to be an achiever, and to achieve consistently in many fields.

Burton Wright II, John P. Weiss and Charles M. Unkovic, *Perspective: An Introduction to Sociology*

1. This paragraph is mainly about
   a. the expectation of concrete achievements during adolescence
   b. the variety of avenues open to adolescents for achievement
   c. the aversive behavior caused by achievement pressure
   d. the parental pressure for adolescent achievement
2. Of the following details, the least significant in support of the main idea of the paragraph is
   a. areas of achievement will vary from person to person
   b. childhood aversive behavior is no longer acceptable
   c. social pressures for achievement increase after early adolescence
   d. academic success is stressed more than social competency

3. State the author's main point in this paragraph. _____
_____

4. Is the topic sentence stated within the paragraph? _____

If so, which sentence is it? _____

The furor over heart transplants died down as suddenly as it began. Once hailed as a medical triumph, transplants have fallen from grace over a period of a few years because most of the transplanted hearts are quickly rejected by the recipients. The job of actually removing the heart from the donor and suturing it into place was technically feasible from the inception of the idea, but the production of antibodies, which attack foreign cardiac tissue, was never successfully suppressed.

Shelby D. Gerking, *Biological Systems*

1. This paragraph is mainly about
   a. why heart transplants were unsuccessful
   b. how successful heart transplants were
   c. the change in public opinion over heart transplants
   d. the complex nature of heart transplants
2. Of the following details, the least significant in support of the main idea of the paragraph is
   a. recipients rejected most transplanted hearts
   b. the transplanted heart was a medical triumph
   c. antibodies attack new heart tissue
   d. unsuppressed antibodies cause rejection of a transplant

3. State the author's main point in this paragraph. _____

_____

4. Is the topic sentence stated within the paragraph? _____

If so, which sentence is it? _____

The water in a breaking wave climbs far up the beach and then, losing its momentum, flows back down the beach under the influence of gravity. In so doing, it passes beneath several subsequent waves, aiding greatly in upsetting them. This seaward-moving current operating beneath the landward-moving waves is called the undertow. When waves are large, the undertow is correspondingly powerful and is able to transport seaward great quantities of material.

Henry M. Kendall et al., *Introduction to Geography*

1. This paragraph is mainly about
   a. the influence of gravity
   b. waves
   c. currents in the ocean
   d. undertows
2. Of the following details, the least significant in support of the main idea of the paragraph is
   a. the undertow passes under waves
   b. if the waves are large, the undertow is therefore powerful
   c. the changes of the tides are governed by the moon
   d. the undertow carries material into the sea

3. State the author's main point in this paragraph. _____

_____

4. Is the topic sentence stated within the paragraph? _____

If so, which sentence is it? _____

The man's name was said to be Murlock. He was apparently seventy years old, actually about fifty. Something besides years had had a hand in his aging. His hair and long, full beard were white, his gray, lustreless eyes sunken, his face singularly seamed with wrinkles which appeared to belong to two intersecting systems. In figure he was tall and spare with a stoop of the shoulders—a burden bearer. I never saw him: these particulars I learned from my grandfather, from whom also I got the man's story when I was a lad. He had known him when living near by in that early day.

Ambrose Bierce, *The Boarded Window*

1. This paragraph is mainly about
   a. local people that grandfather had known
   b. Murlock's appearance, indicating age beyond his age
   c. the burdens that stooped Murlock's shoulders
   d. a description of Murlock's character

2. Of the following details, the least significant in support of the main idea is
   a. he appeared seventy but was only fifty
   b. his hair was white
   c. he had a beard
   d. his face was wrinkled

3. State the author's main point in this paragraph. _____
   _____

4. Is the topic sentence stated within this paragraph? _____

   If so, which sentence is it? _____
   _____

In addition to offsetting the tendency to overheat, insensible perspiration may be helpful, insofar as the palms and soles are concerned, for providing friction in order to facilitate the handling of objects and performing of work. The palms and soles do not secrete an oily sebum, as does the skin elsewhere on the body, and in the absence of moisture on their surface, it would be more difficult to get a good grip on certain things. In this connection, the reader may reflect on a baseball batter's habit of spitting on his hands when called to bat.

Roy Hartenstein, *Human Anatomy and Physiology*

1. This paragraph is mainly about
   a. offsetting the tendency to overheat
   b. the benefit of insensible perspiration on palms and soles
   c. the absence of oily sebum in palms and soles
   d. natural creation of friction

2. Of the following details, the least significant in support of the main idea of the paragraph is
   a. palms and soles do not secrete oily sebum
   b. a baseball batter spits on his hands before batting
   c. palms and soles perspire
   d. insensible perspiration cools the overheated body

3. State the author's main point in this paragraph. _____
   _____

4. Is the topic sentence stated within the paragraph? _____

   If so, which sentence is it? _____
   _____

Selection 1: Anthropology

Conrad Phillip Kottak, from *Anthropology: The Exploration of Human Diversity*

The Eskimos*

Among foragers, there is nothing that could accurately be called law in the sense of a legal code, including machinery of adjudication and enforcement, that applies to all members of the population. In some foraging societies, there may be a great deal of disorder. The Eskimos can serve as a good example. There are approximately 20,000 Eskimos, and the population extends
5 over approximately 6,000 miles in the extreme north, the Arctic region from eastern Siberia to eastern Greenland. The only significant social groups among Eskimos are the nuclear family and the local band. Bands are tied together through personal relationships established by each member individually. Some of the bands have headmen. There are also shamans, diviners, in Eskimo bands. These positions confer little power on those who occupy them.

10 Why do disputes arise among the Eskimos? Most involve males, and most originate over women. Wife stealing and adultery are common causes for disputes. Although it is acceptable for one man to have intercourse with another man's wife, access is by invitation only. If a man discovers that his wife has been having sexual relations without his sanction, he considers himself wronged, and he is expected to retaliate against the male offender. The manner of
15 retaliation will be examined after discussion of a related reason for disputes—wife stealing.

*LEARNING STRATEGY: Seek to explain how the Eskimo society has adapted and functions in a system that has no set legal code and no machinery for law enforcement.

The Eskimos, you will remember, practice female infanticide. There are several reasons for this. The male's role in Eskimo subsistence activity is primary; people prefer to have sons who can care for them when they become old. Furthermore, men have to travel on land and sea, hunting and fishing in a bitter environment. Their tasks are much more dangerous than those of

20   women. Female infanticide regulates the size of the Eskimo population: since the male role in the division of labor takes more lives, there would be an excess of females over males in the adult population if a proportion of female infants were not killed. Even with female infanticide, however, slightly more females survive than males. This demographic imbalance accommodates polygyny. Some men take two or three wives. Usually, it is a successful hunter-fisherman who

25   marries plural wives. The ability to support more than one wife confers a certain amount of prestige. Yet, it also encourages envy. If it becomes obvious that a man is marrying plural wives merely to increase his status, he is likely to have one of his wives stolen by a rival. This, like adultery, can lead to conflict.

A wronged man has several alternatives. Community opinion will not let him ignore

30   the offense; one way of avenging his tarnished honor is to kill the man who has stolen his wife. However, if he does this, he can be reasonably sure that one of the close kinsmen of the dead man will try to kill him in retaliation. Consider an example. Sam has two wives, Cynthia and Tricia. Irving, a younger man from another local group, manages to steal Tricia and take her home. Sam's social status and honor have now been tarnished.

35   He must avenge himself in some way. One way of doing it is to kill Irving. However, Sam knows that Irving has a brother, and if he kills Irving, Irving's brother will be bound by kinship to kill Sam. Sam also has a brother who will then be obliged to kill Irving's brother. One dispute could escalate into several deaths.

Once such a *blood feud* develops, there is no state authority to intervene and stop it.

40   However, an aggrieved individual always has the alternative of challenging the offending party to a song contest. This is a means of regaining lost honor. The two parties in the dispute make up insulting songs about one another. The audience listens and judges the insults. At the end of the song match, one of the two is declared the winner. If the man whose wife has been stolen wins the song contest, there is no guarantee that his wife will return to him. The woman

45   appears to have a good bit to say about where she will remain. Sometimes, she will decide to stay with her abductor.

There are several acts of killing which are deemed crimes in the contemporary United States and in other state-organized societies but which are not considered criminal among the Eskimos. Individuals who feel that, because of age or infirmity, they are no longer economically useful

50   may kill themselves or ask others to kill them. An old person or invalid who wishes to die will ask a close relative, a son perhaps, to end his life. It is necessary to ask a close relative to be sure that the kinsmen of the deceased will not take revenge on his killer.

Occasionally among the Eskimos we encounter something suggestive of law, the enforcement of a decision for the public good. An individual who has committed a single homicide is apt to

55   be attacked and perhaps killed by a close kinsman of his victim. Suppose, however, that before the avenger can kill him, he kills the avenger instead. He has now committed two murders. The Eskimos fear individuals who murder more than once. In such cases, there may be a meeting of adult male members of the offender's local group. It is apparently the headman of the group who initiates this meeting. If there is unanimous agreement that the individual must die, then

60   one of his close relatives is usually chosen to carry out the execution. Again, this is to avoid the possibility of revenge by kinsmen. There is some possibility, too, that the headman may do the killing.

To summarize, most disputes which arise among the Eskimos are related to the disposition of women. Murders must be avenged in some way, often leading to the blood feud. However,

65   peace may be restored through a song contest. The group may decide to execute a repeated murderer, perceived as a public threat. Disputes also arise if individuals believe that others are

practicing sorcery on them, and Hoebel (1954) reports that certain individuals have been killed because they are chronic liars.

70 Perhaps you have noted a major and significant difference between Eskimo conflicts and our own. Theft is not a problem for the Eskimos. Access to resources needed to sustain life is open to everyone. By virtue of his membership in a band, every individual has the right to hunt and fish and to manufacture all the tools he needs for subsistence activities. Individuals may even hunt and fish within the territories of other local groups. Conspicuously absent is the notion of private ownership of strategic resources. To describe the property notions of people who live in
75 nonstratified societies, the anthropologist Elman Service (1966) coined the term *personalty*. Personalty describes items other than strategic resources which are indelibly associated with a specific individual, things like the arrows he makes, the pouch he uses to carry his tobacco, his clothes. Service chose this term to point to the personal relationship between material items and the individual who owns them. So tied to specific individuals in public opinion are personalty
80 items that for another to steal them would be inconceivable. It may be that the grave goods found so often in pre-Neolithic archeological sites represent items of personalty, things which could not be passed on to heirs, so definite and inseparable was their association with the deceased.

Thus, in band-organized society, there is no differential or impeded access to strategic
85 resources; private property is personalty, and if one individual wants something which is owned by another, he simply asks for it and it is given. According to Hoebel, one of the basic postulates of Eskimo life is that "all natural resources are free or common goods." One of the corollaries of this is that "private property is subject to use claims by others than its owners [Hoebel, in Middleton, 1968, p. 96]." /1312

• *Skill Development*

Directions: Write the answers to the following questions.

1. The author's main point in this selection is _____

_____

2. In the first paragraph what aspect concerning foragers is the author addressing? _____

3. In the second paragraph what point is the author trying to get across about Eskimo disputes? _____

_____

4. In the third paragraph what is the author's point concerning the role of women in Eskimo society? _____

_____

5. In the fourth paragraph what is the author's main point about the Eskimo method of settling disputes? _____

_____

6. In the next to the last paragraph what is the author's main point about theft in the Eskimo society? _____

_____

• Comprehension Questions

After reading the selection, answer the following questions with *a, b, c,* or *d.*

_____ 1. The best statement of the main idea of this selection is
   a. since theft is not a problem for the foraging Eskimo society, a formal legal code is not necessary
   b. the foraging Eskimo society has developed its own system of settling disputes to match the needs of a band-organized society rather than adopt a formal legal code
   c. Eskimos settle injustices by killing or by song contests
   d. the greatest affront to an Eskimo is wife stealing, since he must retaliate to regain his honor

_____ 2. According to the article, the Eskimos of the Arctic region from eastern Siberia to eastern Greenland are ruled by
   a. the laws of the country in which they reside
   b. the headman of the band
   c. their desire for passion and revenge
   d. a traditional code of justice that is acceptable to the band

_____ 3. Most Eskimo disputes concern sexual relations without the permission of the
   a. wife
   b. husband
   c. father
   d. wife stealer

_____ 4. Eskimos practice female infanticide for all of the following reasons except
   a. the older people want someone to take care of them
   b. the male death rate is higher
   c. the male is primarily responsible for family security
   d. the successful male wants to have plural wives

_____ 5. The author implies that retaliation for wife stealing is
   a. forced by the community
   b. more vicious than retaliation for adultery
   c. not necessary if the husband is not upset
   d. dependent on the wishes of the wife

_____ 6. The purpose and practice of an Eskimo song contest is most similar to the elements of
   a. a courtroom trial
   b. a minstrel show
   c. a carnival
   d. an opera

_____ 7. The Eskimos condone killing in all of the following cases except
      a. a mother killing a baby girl
      b. a son killing an invalid father
      c. a murderer killing an avenger
      d. a kinsman killing a double murderer

_____ 8. The author suggests that Eskimos do not steal material goods because they
      a. have few personal needs
      b. lack the concept of contemporary private ownership
      c. have little access to manufactured products
      d. have strict laws against it

_____ 9. According to the definition, an item that would be most likely described as _personalty_ is a
      a. chair
      b. comb
      c. frying pan
      d. sled dog

_____ 10. The author probably believes the Eskimo practice of revenge by murder is
      a. just, but useless death
      b. against the laws of the community
      c. preferable to a song contest
      d. sinful and should be punished

Answer the following with _T_ (true), _F_ (false), or _CT_ (can't tell).

_____ 11. The author suggests that jealousy over prestige often motivates wife stealing.

_____ 12. The winner of the song contest automatically wins the wife.

_____ 13. Without female infanticide, many Eskimos would leave the northern region in search of food.

_____ 14. When requested, the Eskimos kill the old and the sick so they won't be a burden to society.

_____ 15. The author suggests that the Eskimo lifestyle dictates the code by which an Eskimo lives.

• _Vocabulary_

According to the way the boldface word was used in the selection, indicate _a, b, c,_ or _d_ for the word or phrase that gives the best definition.

____ 1. "machinery of **adjudication**"
    a. court decisions
    b. imprisonment
    c. apprehension
    d. arrest

____ 2. "some **foraging** societies"
    a. cold weather
    b. foreigners
    c. fighting
    d. searching for food

____ 3. "without his **sanction**"
a. attention
b. approval
c. noticing
d. suspicion

____ 4. "This **demographic** imbalance"
a. hereditary
b. democratic rule
c. scientifically frigid areas
d. science of vital statistics of populations

____ 5. "could **escalate** into several deaths"
a. demand
b. legislate
c. expand step by step
d. eliminate

____ 6. "are **deemed** crimes"
a. assigned
b. disfavored
c. forgiven
d. judged

____ 7. "practicing **sorcery**"
a. witchcraft
b. rebellion
c. bribery
d. untruths

____ 8. "**Conspicuously** absent"
a. frequently
b. centrally
c. noticeably
d. moderately

____ 9. "are **indelibly** associated with"
a. narrowly
b. permanently
c. marginally
d. sorrowfully

____ 10. "**impeded** access to"
a. promoted
b. regretted
c. obstructed
d. accelerated

• *Possible Essay Exam Question*

Analyze why an Eskimo might kill a man who has stolen his wife, yet would not steal the man's tobacco pouch. (Hint: Describe the disorder and then explain the "code" that has developed in the absence of law.)

• *Word Parts*

Study the meaning of the word parts and supply an additional example from your own vocabulary. In the second set of items, use the corresponding part to write the word that best fits the definition.

Word Part	Meaning	Example	Your Example
1. homo	man, same	homosexual	_____
2. anthrop	mankind	anthropoid	_____
3. ethno	race, tribe	ethnocentrism	_____
4. gene	race, kind, sex	indigenous	_____
5. spond, spons	pledge, answer	responsible	_____

6. mob, mot, mov	move	motivation	_____
7. forc, fort	strong	fortitude	_____
8. ure	state or condition of	pleasure	_____
9. ess	person who	actress	_____
10. trib	pay, bestow	contribution	_____

1. the killing of a human being   _____

2. study of mankind   _____

3. pertaining to groups of mankind   _____

4. study of heredity   _____

5. communicate through letters   _____

6. movable   _____

7. use pressure for compliance   _____

8. naive and unripened   _____

9. one who serves meals   _____

10. ascribe or assign to someone   _____

Selection 2: Biology

Shelby D. Gerking, from *Biological Systems*

Mountain Climbing and Scuba Diving*

Any flatlander who visits the mountains at 2150 meters (7000 feet) for the first time huffs and puffs during relatively mild exercise. His extra exertion is due to the fact that the barometric pressure as well as the partial pressure of oxygen lowers with increasing altitude. The smaller partial pressure at high altitudes reduces the transfer of oxygen from the inspired air to the
5   blood in the lungs. The flatlander breathes harder, his heart beats faster, and his cardiac output rises in order to compensate for the reduced amount of oxygen.

If a mountain climber wishes to be at peak performance at 2150 meters, he needs a week or 10 days to gradually acclimatize to the thinner air. At higher altitudes, acclimatization takes even longer; about a month is needed to adjust to 4600 meters (15,000 feet). Both the

*LEARNING STRATEGY: Since the title suggests a comparison, look for how the two activities and their effects on the body are alike and how they are different.

10 respiratory and cardiovascular systems respond to the need for the same amount of oxygen, but delivered at a lower partial pressure. We have already mentioned greater lung ventilation and greater ouput of blood from the heart as adaptations to stress, but even more profound changes in the circulatory system take place. If the mountain climber had some extra time, the quantity of hemoglobin in his blood would increase for two or three months and the number of red

15 blood cells would increase for about 38 weeks. Even with these acquired adaptations to high altitudes, the mountain climber is hard pressed to reach the summit at, say, 4600 meters without resting several minutes between his few feeble steps.

The Quechua Indians of the Peruvian Andes and the Sherpa tribes of the Himalayas spend their whole lives above 4500 meters. The highest inhabited settlement in the world is a mining

20 camp in the Andes at 5400 meters (17,500 feet). The Indians climb each day to work the mine at 5850 meters (19,000 feet) and come home each night. This is probably the highest that acclimatized man has lived and worked on a permanent basis. Both the Quechuas and Sherpas exhibit the acclimatization responses that a mountain climber would have if he lived with them for a year. They have seven million red blood cells per milliliter, a 40 per cent increase over

25 the usual number of five million. Along with the high red blood cell count is a corresponding increase in hemoglobin.

Some of the other adaptations are acquired only by living constantly at high altitudes. The Peruvian Indians have an exceptionally large chest for a great lung ventilation. Because they have an unusually large heart, the heart delivers a large volume of blood at each contraction

30 and they have a slower heart beat than one might expect. The lung capillaries are dilated to extract every bit of oxygen they can from the alveoli, and this means that the pulmonary circulation is carrying a much higher fraction of the blood volume than it does ordinarily. But the Quechuas and Sherpas pay a price for their acclimatization with a lower efficiency in the use of oxygen for work. The basal metabolic rate is slightly higher than normal; when this is

35 considered in terms of body mass, the rate of oxygen consumption per unit of metabolizing tissue is much higher than in a man living at sea level. If these Indian or Tibetan people were transported to sea level, they probably would be no better or worse off than we are. Although the question is still open, it appears that they would lose their adaptations to high altitudes and adjust to low-altitude living.

40 The scuba diver faces the reverse situation of the mountain climber—that of high pressure rather than low. When he dives beneath the surface of the water, he must bear the weight of the water immediately above him in addition to the normal atmospheric pressure, and this weight adds up fast. At a depth of 10 meters, the combined atmospheric and water pressure is double that at the surface. This means that his scuba tank must deliver air to the lungs under

45 pressure in order to overcome the amount compressing his chest. It also means that the diver cannot ascend without exhaling at the same time. If he fails to do this, the extraordinarily high air pressure in the lungs expands and finally ruptures the tissue. Even at two meters below the surface, the diver runs the risk of overdistending the lungs and rupturing the alveoli if he does not exhale on the way to the surface.

50 Another problem facing the deep diver is "the bends." When air is supplied under pressure, the greater partial pressure of nitrogen forces an extra amount of this inert gas into solution in the blood and in the tissues. The nitrogen is released from solution when the diver ascends. If he ascends rapidly, the nitrogen bubbles out of the blood and tissues, causing circulatory blockage and tissue damage. The effect is much like releasing the carbon dioxide from a

55 bottle of soda pop when the cap is taken off. If the ascent is more gradual, the bends, or pain in the joints, may be experienced several hours later. There is no acclimatization to the bends. The only way to relieve these symptoms is to recompress the afflicted individual in a high-pressure chamber and then slowly decompress him so that the nitrogen enters the blood slowly enough to be blown off from the lungs.   /897

• *Skill Development*

Directions: Write the answers to the following questions.

1. The author's main point in this selection is _____

_____

2. In the first paragraph what is the author's main point about a flatlander in the

mountains? _____

_____

3. In the third paragraph what is the author's main point about the Quechua Indians

and the Sherpa tribes? _____

_____

4. List four significant details that support the statement "Some of the other adaptations

are acquired only by living constantly at high altitudes."

_____

_____

_____

_____

5. In the fifth paragraph what is the author's main point about pressure on the scuba diver? _____

_____

6. In the last paragraph what is the author's main point about the bends? _____

_____

● **Comprehension Questions**

After reading the selection, answer the following questions with *a, b, c,* or *d.*

_____ 1. The best statement of the main idea of this selection is
   a. extremes of pressure either high or low, require adjustments in the body's respiratory and cardiovascular systems
   b. even though similar in nature, mountain climbing requires a greater adjustment of the red blood cells than scuba diving
   c. the danger of overexertion and the strain on the body is increased at both high- and low-pressure extremes
   d. the mountain climber's body is able to compensate for low pressure, whereas the scuba diver must rely on an artificial means of support

_____ 2. A flatlander gets out of breath exercising at high mountain altitudes because of
   a. fewer red blood cells
   b. less oxygen in the blood
   c. greater barometric pressure
   d. reduced blood transfer

_____ 3. A mountain climber's adjustment to thinner air means a change in
   a. the amount of oxygen needed
   b. the number of red blood cells
   c. the amount of blood in the body
   d. the size of the chest

_____ 4. The Peruvian Indians have a larger than normal heart to enable them to have
   a. larger lungs   c. more oxygen
   b. a slower heart beat   d. less need for oxygen

_____ 5. As compared to a flatlander, the Peruvian Indian
   a. uses less oxygen
   b. lives a shorter life due to a slower heart beat
   c. functions at a lower metabolic rate
   d. gets less benefit from a unit of oxygen

_____ 6. In the author's opinion, if Quechuas or Sherpas were relocated at sea level for several years they would
   a. experience no physical change
   b. maintain a high basal metabolic rate
   c. lose red blood cells
   d. be able to do more work than flatlanders

7. Because of the weight of the water and the normal atmospheric pressure, the scuba diver needs air under pressure to avoid
   a. nitrogen build up
   b. collapsed lungs
   c. ruptured alveoli
   d. overdistended lungs

8. Breathing from a scuba tank at a depth of 10 meters, the lungs of a scuba diver contain
   a. less air than at sea level
   b. more air than at sea level
   c. the same amount of air as at sea level
   d. a higher percent of oxygen than at sea level

9. "The bends" is caused by
   a. carbon dioxide in the blood
   b. the prolonged pressure of deep diving
   c. nitrogen in the blood
   d. improper descent in deep diving

10. In order to treat an individual for the "the bends," the body must
    a. adjust to the increase in nitrogen
    b. recompress in deep water
    c. inhale more oxygen to equalize the nitrogen
    d. artificially relive the condition of a correct dive

Answer the following with *T* (true), *F* (false), or *CT* (can't tell).

11. Nitrogen is a problem under high-pressure conditions, but not under low-pressure conditions.

12. Over a three-month period the body will make physical adjustments to both high- and low-pressure conditions.

13. Rapid descent from high altitudes can cause the lungs to rupture.

14. The author suggests that a key factor in scuba-diving safety is exhaling on ascent.

15. The higher metabolic rate of Quechuas and Sherpas is detrimental to their health.

• *Vocabulary*

According to the way the boldface word was used in the selection, indicate *a, b, c,* or *d* for the word or phrase that gives the best definition.

___ 1. "His extra **exertion**"
   a. problem
   b. difficulty
   c. effort
   d. manipulation

___ 2. "his **cardiac** output"
   a. heart
   b. lung
   c. pressure
   d. cell

___ 3. "to **compensate** for the reduced amount"
   a. signal
   b. make up
   c. demonstrate
   d. complete

___ 4. "**acclimatize** to the thinner air"
   a. centralize
   b. mobilize
   c. adjust
   d. suitable dress

_____ 5. "**respiratory** and cardiovascular system"
a. sleeping
b. veins and arteries
c. physical
d. breathing

_____ 6. "at each **contraction**"
a. attack
b. drawing up
c. intersection
d. breath

_____ 7. "capillaries are **dilated**"
a. expanded
b. damaged
c. destroyed
d. punctured

_____ 8. "**pulmonary** circulation"
a. pushing
b. affecting the lungs
c. automatic
d. primary

_____ 9. "**ruptures** the tissue"
a. bursts
b. encloses
c. fills
d. reaches

_____ 10. "of this **inert** gas"
a. unhealthy
b. radioactive
c. poisonous
d. inactive

• Possible Essay Exam Question

Compare the bodily needs and the adaptations to differing pressure in mountain climbing and in scuba diving. (Hint: Define the two divergent circumstances and explain the effect each has on the body and the manner in which these needs are met.)

• Word Parts

Study the meaning of the word parts and supply an additional example from your own vocabulary. In the second set of items, use the corresponding part to write the word that best fits the definition.

Word Parts	Meaning	Example	Your Example
1. aqua	water	aqualung	_____
2. aero	air	aeronautics	_____
3. pneuma, pneumo	wind	pneumatic	_____
4. card, cord	heart	cardiac	_____
5. osteo	bone	osteometry	_____
6. hemo	blood	hemoglobin	_____
7. ambi, amphi	both	ambidextrous	_____
8. arium, orium	place for	auditorium	_____
9. naut	voyager	astronaut	_____
10. oid	like, resembling	asteroid	_____

1. bluish-green color   _____

2. a type of map for aircraft   _____

3. disease of the lungs   _____

4. physician specializing in the heart   _____

5. person who treats bones by   _____
   manipulation

6. heavy bleeding   _____

7. lives both on land and in water   _____

8. glass tank where aquatic animals are   _____
   kept

9. voyager in the sea   _____

10. like or resembling man   _____

Selection 3: History

Leonard Pitt, from *We Americans*

Women and the Family *

Three radical women

Amelia Bloomer (1818-1894) published the first newpaper issued expressly for women. She
called it *The Lily*. Her fame, however, rests chiefly in dress reform. For six or eight years she
wore an outfit composed of a knee-length skirt over full pants gathered at the ankle, which
were soon known everywhere as ''bloomers.'' Wherever she went, this style created great
5   excitement and brought her enormous audiences—including hecklers. She was trying to make
the serious point that women's fashions, often designed by men to suit their own tastes, were
too restrictive, often to the detriment of the health of those who wore them. Still, some of her
contemporaries thought she did the feminist movement as much harm as good.
     Very few feminists hoped to destroy marriage as such. Most of them had husbands and lived
10 conventional, if hectic, lives. And many of the husbands supported their cause. Yet the
feminists did challenge certain marital customs. When Lucy Stone married Henry Blackwell,
she insisted on being called ''Mrs. Stone,'' a defiant gesture that brought her a lifetime of
ridicule. Both she and her husband signed a marriage contract, vowing ''to recognize the wife
as an independent, rational being.'' They agreed to break any law which brought the husband
15 ''an injurious and unnatural superiority.'' But few of the radical feminists indulged in ''free
love'' or joined communal marriage experiments. The movement was intended mainly to help
women gain control over their own property and earnings and gain better legal guardianship
over their children. Voting also interested them, but women's suffrage did not become a central
issue until later in the century.

*LEARNING STRATEGY: Look at the historical trend toward altering the image of women and note the
contributions to this change made by individuals and groups.

Sojourner Truth.

20   Many black women were part of the movement, including the legendary Sojourner Truth
(1797-1883). Born a slave in New York and forced to marry a man approved by her owner,
Sojourner Truth was freed when the state abolished slavery. After participating in religious
revivals, she became an active abolitionist and feminist. In 1851 she saved the day at a
women's rights convention in Ohio, silencing hecklers and replying to a man who had belittled
25   the weakness of women:

> The man over there says women need to be helped into carriages and lifted over ditches,
> and to have the best place everywhere. Nobody ever helps me into carriages or over
> puddles, or gives me the best place—and ain't I a woman? . . . Look at my arm! I have
> ploughed and planted and gathered into barns, and no man could head me—and ain't I
30   > a woman? I could work as much and eat as much as a man—when I could get it—and
> bear the lash as well! And ain't I a woman? I have borne thirteen children, and seen
> most of 'em sold into slavery, and when I cried out with my mother's grief, none but
> Jesus heard me—and ain't I a woman?

Changing the image and the reality

The accomplishments of a few women who dared pursue professional careers had somewhat
35   altered the image of the submissive and brainless child-woman. Maria Mitchell of Nantucket,
whose father was an astronomer, discovered a comet at the age of twenty-eight. She became the
first woman professor of astronomy in the U.S. (at Vassar in 1865). Mitchell was also the first
woman elected to the American Academy of Arts and Sciences and a founder of the
Association for the Advancement of Women. Elizabeth Blackwell applied to twenty-nine
40   medical schools before she was accepted. She attended all classes, even anatomy class, despite
the sneers of some male students. As a physician, she went on to make important contributions
in sanitation and hygiene.

        By about 1860 women had effected notable improvements in their status. Organized feminists
had eliminated some of the worst legal disadvantages in fifteen states. The Civil War altered the
45   role—and the image—of women even more drastically than the feminist movement did. As
men went off to fight, women flocked into government clerical jobs. And they were accepted in
teaching jobs as never before. Tens of thousands of women ran farms and businesses while the
men were gone. Anna Howard Shaw, whose mother ran a pioneer farm, recalled:

50 It was an incessant struggle to keep our land, to pay our taxes, and to live. Calico was selling at fifty cents a yard. Coffee was one dollar a pound. There were no men left to grind our corn, to get in our crops, or to care for our livestock; and all around us we saw our struggle reflected in the lives of our neighbors.

Women took part in crucial relief efforts. The Sanitary Commission, the Union's volunteer nursing program and a forerunner of the Red Cross, owed much of its success to women. They
55 raised millions of dollars for medicine, bandages, food, hospitals, relief camps, and convalescent homes.

North and South, black and white, many women served as nurses, some as spies and even as soldiers. Dorothea Dix, already famous as a reformer of prisons and insane asylums, became head of the Union army nurse corps. Clara Barton and ''Mother'' Bickerdyke saved
60 thousands of lives by working close behind the front lines at Antietam, Chancellorsville, and Fredericksburg. Harriet Tubman led a party up the Combahee River to rescue 756 slaves. Late in life she was recognized for her heroic act by being granted a government pension of twenty dollars per month.

Southern white women suffered more from the disruptions of the Civil War than did their
65 northern sisters. The proportion of men who went to war or were killed in battle was greater in the South. This made many women self-sufficient during the war. Still, there was hardly a whisper of feminism in the South.

The Civil War also brought women into the political limelight. Anna Dickson sky-rocketed to fame as a Republican speaker, climaxing her career with an address to the House of
70 Representatives on abolition. Stanton and Anthony formed the National Woman's Loyal League to press for a constitutional amendment banning slavery. With Anthony's genius for organization, the League in one year collected 400,000 signatures in favor of the Thirteenth Amendment.

Once abolition was finally assured in 1865, most feminists felt certain that suffrage would
75 follow quickly. They believed that women had earned the vote by their patriotic wartime efforts. Besides, it appeared certain that black men would soon be allowed to vote. And once black men had the ballot in hand, how could anyone justify keeping it from white women—or black women? Any feminist who had predicted in 1865 that women would have to wait another fifty-five years for suffrage would have been called politically naive.   /1108

• *Skill Development*

Directions: Write the answers to the following questions.

1. The author's main point in this selection is _____

_____

2. In the first paragraph what is the author's main point about Amelia Bloomer?

_____

_____

3. In the second paragraph what is the author's main point about Lucy Stone?

_____

_____

4. In the third paragraph what is the author's main point about Sojourner Truth?

_____

_____

5. In the fourth paragraph what is the author's main point about women in professional careers? _____

_____

6. In the last paragraph what is the author's main point about women's suffrage? _____

_____

- ## Comprehension Questions

   After reading the selection, answer the following questions with *a, b, c,* or *d.*

   _____ 1. The best statement of the main idea of this selection is
   a. the feminists as well as the Civil War helped change the female image and advance the woman's movement
   b. during the Civil War, females proved they could handle responsible jobs
   c. the work of the early feminist extremists led to suffrage for women
   d. women's suffrage was a long and difficult struggle

   _____ 2. In originating "bloomers," Amelia Bloomer's greatest concern was
   a. fashion   c. expense
   b. principle   d. good taste

   _____ 3. The major purpose of Sojourner Truth's quoted speech was to
   a. prove that women are stronger than men
   b. reprimand men for social courtesy
   c. dramatize the strengths of women
   d. praise childbearing as a womanly virtue

   _____ 4. Lucy Stone's major motive in retaining the name "Mrs. Stone" after marriage was to
   a. condone "free love" without marriage
   b. de-emphasize the responsibilities of marriage
   c. purchase property in her own name
   d. be recognized as an independent person equal to her husband

   _____ 5. The article states that women worked during the Civil War in all of the following except
   a. farms and businesses   c. government clerical jobs
   b. the military   d. the Red Cross

   _____ 6. The author implies that the eventual assumption of responsible roles by large numbers of women was primarily due to
   a. the feminist movement
   b. the determination and accomplishments of female professionals

      c. a desire to give women a chance

      d. economic necessity

_____ 7. The author believes that the Civil War showed southern women to be

      a. as capable but less vocal than northern women

      b. more capable than their northern sisters

      c. capable workers and eager feminists

      d. less able to assume responsible roles than northern women

_____ 8. The author's main purpose in mentioning the accomplishments of Maria Mitchell is to point out that

      a. she discovered a comet

      b. her professional achievements improved the image of women

      c. she was the first woman professor of astronomy in the U.S.

      d. she was a founder of the Association for the Advancement of Women

_____ 9. The article states or implies that all of the following women worked to abolish slavery except

      a. Anna Howard Shaw

      b. Harriet Tubman

      c. Anna Dickson

      d. Stanton and Anthony

_____ 10. In the author's opinion, the long wait by women after the Civil War for suffrage

      a. was predictable in 1865

      b. would not have been expected in 1865

      c. was due to the vote of black men

      d. was justified

Answer the following *T* (true), *F* (false), or *CT* (can't tell).

_____ 11. Women were granted the right to vote in 1920.

_____ 12. Sojourner Truth had been a southern slave.

_____ 13. The author implies that feminist leaders were more concerned with their own right to vote than with the abolition of slavery.

_____ 14. From the very beginning, the right to vote was the focal point of the woman's movement.

_____ 15. Many black slaves were led to freedom along an underground railway by Sojourner Truth.

• *Vocabulary*

According to the way the boldface word was used in the selection, indicate *a*, *b*, *c*, or *d* for the word or phrase that gives the best definition.

____ 1. "were too **restrictive**"

    a. showy

    b. expensive

    c. complicated

    d. limiting (confining)

____ 2. "to the **detriment** of"

    a. harm

    b. anger

    c. apology

    d. objection

_____ 3. " a **defiant** gesture"
  a. unlucky
  b. resistive
  c. admirable
  d. ignorant

_____ 4. "**communal** marriage experiments"
  a. permanent
  b. living together in groups
  c. illegal
  d. uncommon

_____ 5. "silencing **hecklers**"
  a. soldiers
  b. rioters
  c. disciples
  d. verbal harassers

_____ 6. "**pursue** professional careers"
  a. strive for
  b. abandon
  c. acknowledge
  d. indicate

_____ 7. "sanitation and **hygiene**"
  a. garbage disposal
  b. biology
  c. health care
  d. mental disorders

_____ 8. "an **incessant** struggle"
  a. earlier
  b. final
  c. novel
  d. unceasing

_____ 9. "**convalescent** homes"
  a. sanitary
  b. government
  c. reclaimed
  d. recuperating

_____ 10. "called politically **naive**"
  a. unsophisticated
  b. well informed
  c. dishonest
  d. unfortunate

• Possible Essay Exam Question

List five women who made early contributions toward altering the image of women and explain the way each changed stereotypical thinking. (Hint: Select five of the women mentioned whose actions represent an altering of accepted ideas and discuss each.)

• Word Parts

Study the meaning of the word parts and supply an additional example from your own vocabulary. In the second set of items, use the corresponding part to write the word that best fits the definition.

Word Part	Meaning	Example	Your Example
1. anti	against	antislavery	_____
2. temp	time	temporal	_____
3. per	through	periscope	_____
4. cent, hecto	hundred	centipede	_____

5. grad, gress, gred	go, take steps	progress	_____
6. equa	equal	equation	_____
7. un	not, opposite of	uncover	_____
8. chrome	color	chromosome	_____
9. less	without	helpless	_____
10. ship	state or quality of	citizenship	_____

1. used to prevent depression   _____

2. living during the same period of time   _____

3. through all seasons of the year   _____

4. a period of a hundred years   _____

5. taking of a degree   _____

6. divides the earth into north and south   _____

7. not fully completed   _____

8. a brand of color film   _____

9. without thinking   _____

10. agreeable sporting attitude   _____

VII Outlining

Outlining

Outlining

Outlining

Outlining

Freshman writing classes stress outlining as a necessary planning stage before writing. To communicate effectively, the writer must organize and plan so that the reader receives ideas in a grouped rather than a random fashion. Similarly, in order to remember ideas, the reader must also organize and plan; the informal outline can help in this task.

Organization

The outline organizes and highlights major points and subordinates items of lesser importance. In a glance the indentations, the numbers, and the letters quickly show how one idea relates to another and how all aspects relate to the whole. The layout of the outline is simply a graphic presentation of main ideas and significant supporting details. To outline correctly you must have a thorough understanding of the underlying structure of the material. The outline forms the skeleton of ideas from which the writer or speaker originally planned and worked.

The following example is the picture-perfect version of the basic outline form. In practice your "working outline" would probably not be as detailed or as rigid as this.

Title

I. First main idea
  A. Supporting idea
    1. Detail
    2. Detail
    3. Detail
      a. Minor detail
      b. Minor detail
  B. Supporting idea
    1. Detail
    2. Detail
  C. Supporting idea

II. Second main idea
  A. Supporting idea
  B. Supporting idea

Notetaking

Other than as a writing tool, you can use the outline in two important ways:

(1) To take notes from written material
(2) To take notes on class lectures

Outlining is a good notetaking strategy for library books and research material. Some students find that outlining textbook material helps them study, while others prefer underscoring and feel that textbook outlining is too time consuming. In actual practice underscoring requires the same thinking and priority-setting skills as outlining and is probably faster; however, when the book does not belong to you, underscoring is not possible. In this case, outlining offers an efficient method of recording material for later study.

Taking notes on class lectures places a tremendous burden on you as a student. Since these notes represent a large percentage of the material you will later study in order to pass the course, they are extremely important. Listening to the class lecture, you must almost instantly receive, synthesize, and select material and, at the same time, record something on paper for future reference. The difficulty of the task demands order and decision making. By far the easiest way to take notes is to use a working model of the outline form with the addition of stars, circles, and underlines to further emphasize the levels of importance.

Teachers say that after a class lecture they can walk around the room and look at the notes students have taken and tell how well each has understood the lesson. The errors most frequently observed fall into the following categories:

1. Poor organization
2. Failure to show importance
3. Writing too much
4. Writing too little

To avoid these pitfalls the most important thing to remember in outlining is *"What is my purpose?"* You don't need to include everything and you don't need a picture-perfect version for study notes. Include only what you feel you will need to remember later and use the numbering system and the indentations to show how one thing relates to another. Several other important guidelines to remember are as follows:

1. Get a general overview before you start.
   (How many main topics do there seem to be?)
2. Use phrases rather than sentences.
   (Can you state it in a few short words?)
3. Put it in your own words.
   (If you cannot paraphrase it, do you really understand it?)
4. Be selective
   (Are you highlighting or completely rewriting?)

Following is an example of how the outline can be used to highlight material from a text. Read the passage and then review the outline. Does the outline point out the key ideas at a glance? Does it include enough information, but not too much? Would this be useful to you in studying for a quiz on the circulatory system?

Circulatory Systems
When we examine the systems by which blood reaches all the cells of an animal, we find two general types, known as open and closed circulatory systems.

Open circulatory systems
The essential feature of the **open circulatory system** is that the blood moves through a body cavity—such as the abdominal cavity—and bathes the cells directly. The open circulatory system is particularly characteristic of insects and other arthropods, although it is also found in some other organisms.

In most insects the blood does not take a major part in oxygen transport. Oxygen enters the animal's body through a separate network of branching tubes that open to the atmosphere on the outside of the animal. (This type of respiratory system will be discussed in more detail in the next chapter.) Blood in an open circulatory system moves somewhat more slowly than in the average closed system. The slower system is adequate for insects because it does not have to supply the cells with oxygen.

Closed circulatory systems

In a **closed circulatory system,** the blood flows through a well-defined system of vessels with many branches. In the majority of closed systems the blood is responsible for oxygen transport. To supply all the body cells with sufficient oxygen, the blood must move quickly through the blood vessels. A closed circulatory system must therefore have an efficient pumping mechanism, or heart, to set the blood in motion and keep it moving briskly through the body.

All vertebrates possess closed circulatory systems. Simple closed systems are also found in some invertebrates, including the annelid worms. A good example of such a simple closed circulatory system can be seen in the earthworm.

Victor A. Greulach and Vincent J. Chiapetta, eds., *Biology*

Circulatory Systems

I. Open circulatory system
   A. Blood moves through body and bathes cells directly
   B. Found mostly in insects and other arthropods
   C. Oxygen supplied from outside air through tubes
   D. Slower blood movement since not supplying cells with oxygen
II. Closed circulatory system
   A. Blood flows through system of vessels
   B. Oxygen carried by blood so it must move quickly
   C. Heart serves as pumping mechanism
   D. Found in all vertebrates
   E. Found also in annelid worms (earthworms)

● *Exercise 1*

In the following passage, the author gives a numerical clue to the organizational pattern. Outline the key ideas as if you were studying for a quiz.

Psychologists separate the memory system into three parts: *sensory, short-term,* and *long-term.* Sensory memory performs a screening function. Incoming information reaches it first and is preserved just long enough to be used in perceiving, comparing, judging, and so on. It lasts for only a very brief time while the brain decides whether or not it needs this information for present or future use. If it seems useful, it is passed on to the short-term memory. If not, it is discarded. Sensory memory employs a "file or forget" approach to its job.

Short-term memory performs a second screening operation on the retained information. You can think of it as a sort of desk-top memory. Data arriving in the "in" box is looked over, sorted out, and acted on. Everything is there in front of you. Like most desk tops, however, short-term memory often gets cluttered up with many different items, some of which are more important than others. Often, too, a new item in the "in" box interferes with something you are working on. You put the old item aside and can't find it later. Generally speaking, you can deal with no more than seven or eight items at any one time. (There are strategies, however, for expanding the capacity of short-term memory and prolonging its duration.) To make room for more information, you clean off your "desk" every few minutes, throwing the "junk" mail into the wastebasket and sorting your ideas into meaningful groups. What remains will be filed in the "out" box for transmission to long-term memory.

Long-term memory is more permanent, and has a theoretically unlimited capacity. It used to be thought of as a kind of "dead storage," made up of information to be retrieved at some future time. Psychologists now think that long-term memory is a dynamic process, continually interacting with short-term memory to provide *operational,* or working, memory. To make decisions, for example, you constantly refer to material that has been filed away. Long-term memories are reactivated, combined with short-term memories, and then filed away again, along with any new material that seems worth saving.

David Dempsey and Philip G. Zimbardo, *Psychology and You*

I. _____

   A. _____

   B. _____

   C. _____

II. _____

   A. _____

   B. _____

   C. _____

   D. _____

III. _____

   A. _____

   B. _____

   C. _____

- *Exercise 2*

In the following passage the major divisions are obvious. Outline the key ideas as if you were studying for a quiz.

A fad is a product/service which is quickly accepted and then just as quickly rejected by a large number of consumers. The product life-cycle for a fad item is a highly compressed version of the typical product life-cycle. If the fad catches on, sales soar quickly in the introductory and growth phases. As the fad loses its novelty appeal, sales curves that went up quickly reverse their direction and decline with equal speed.

Experienced marketers of novelty fad items understand the compressed product life-cycle and are ready to supply a high volume of units to the market place quickly. They know that product acceptability will be short-lived. Some companies introduce a large number of such products to the market, knowing that many of the products will fail or have only limited or temporary success. (Most such products are inexpensive to produce.) On occasion, however, a product catches on, becomes a fad, and reaps high sales and profits for a short period of time. Hula-hoops, message-bearing T-shirts, and frisbees are examples of successful fads.

The fashion product life-cycle is less compressed than the fad cycle. But, like fads, fashion items are subject to quick and sometimes unpredictable swings in popularity and profitability. Innovation and emulation play important roles in the fashion life-cycle. Innovative individuals or firms develop a fashion product in the hope and expectation that it will be taken up by opinion leaders and trend setters who are highly visible in the fashion and general news media. If it is accepted and touted by such persons, the general public will likely emulate the fashion leaders and also demand the product. Mass production and marketing of the fashion will then ensue. (Recall the "diffusion of innovation" process discussed in Chapter 4: Understanding Consumer Behavior.) The process, however, is by no means automatic. Despite a good deal of media hoopla for midi- and maxi-length dresses in the 1970s, American women flatly rejected the innovative fashion.

Edward J. Fox and Edward W. Wheatley, Modern Marketing

_____

_____

_____

_____

_____

_____

_____

_____

• *Exercise 3*

In the following passage the divisions for outlining are less distinct. Read the passage and ask yourself what are the key ideas to remember and do these ideas fall into categories. Then list the ideas in outline form.

The constitutional guarantee of the writ of *habeas corpus* is designed to protect the most basic of all rights in a free society. This is the right not to be jailed unfairly. A writ is a court order and the writ of *habeas corpus* (once called the "great writ") is an order usually directed to prison officials. It requires them either to release someone held in custody or to show cause why the inmate should be charged with a crime. Thus it prevents indefinite imprisonment without trial merely "on suspicion," or as a weapon against political opponents.

The Constitution contains no provision relating this writ to the states. But Article I, Section 9 provides that the national government not suspend it "unless when in Cases of Rebellion or Invasion the public Safety may require it." Since the Civil War, the writ has been suspended only in Hawaii when martial law (military rule) was declared during World War II.

Charles Sohner, *American Government and Politics Today*

I. Description _____

_____

_____

_____

II. Constitutional Provisions _____

_____

_____

_____

• *Exercise 4*

Again the passage does not contain divisions that suggest clear distinctions. Read and outline the key ideas as if you were studying for a quiz.

Due to their widespread acceptance and the rapid advances in computer technology, bank credit cards are expected to replace cash in transactions of all types. As was discussed in Chapter 5, the development and linking together of electronic funds transfer systems (EFTS) and point of sale (POS) terminals will virtually eliminate the use of currency, coin, and checks in our society. In the not too distant future, each person will have a card that can be used to make all transactions. Paychecks will be deposited directly into people's bank accounts and the banks will be authorized to make certain fixed payments from these deposits. All other transactions will be made using the credit card. They will be electronically transmitted to the appropriate bank account and result in a series of bookkeeping entries. For example, if you buy a $50 radio at Store X, your credit card will be inserted in a terminal at the store, and the account number and information regarding the purchase will be transmitted to your bank. Upon receipt of this information, the bank will deduct $50 from your account and deposit it in Store X's account. If the store's account is not at the same bank as the customer's, the bank will electronically transfer the $50 to the appropriate bank.

Loans, loan payments, and payment of bills will all be transacted using the bank card. Regular statements will continue to be issued, but the system will make it virtually impossible to overdraw an account. Merchants will be certain to receive immediate and full payment for their goods and services. Although the need for pocket money to pay for inexpensive convenience items may continue for some time into the future, eventually bank cards will be used exclusively in all transactions.

Lawrence J. Gitman, *Personal Finance*

_____

_____

_____

_____

_____

_____

_____

_____

- ### *Exercise 5*

  Outline the key ideas in the following passage as if you were studying for a quiz.

  Punishment is the presentation of an aversive stimulus after a response. For example, children reach for an open flame and we slap their hands away. A dog snatches a steak off the table and we catch it by the scruff of the neck and scold it. Punishment is often an effective way of stopping a specific behavior, like shouting in class. It is less effective in stopping a general type of behavior, like "being uncooperative." Being uncooperative can mean anything from reading an English book in math class, to interrupting the teacher, to throwing spitballs.

  To stop a behavior, punishment should be swift and sure—given right away and given every time. It should also be severe enough to be worth avoiding but not *too* severe or prolonged, or it may have the reverse effect of causing more disobedience. The problem is that punishment may do more harm than good. Research has shown that:

  1. In the learning of a new response, punishment for errors may slow down learning instead of speeding it up. The learner needs to identify the differences between right and wrong answers, but giving punishment for this purpose may just create anxiety.

  2. In getting rid of "bad" behavior, punishment may suppress not only bad behavior but "good" behavior too. The school child who is repeatedly humiliated for clowning in class may lose all desire to please the teacher or do well in school, ending up with the attitude, "Why should I try harder? I'm not even Number 2."

  3. The punished behavior may disappear, only to surface later when the punisher is not around. You have probably known a child who was a "little angel" at home but a bully outside. Parents who don't spare the rod are often surprised to learn that their child is a troublemaker at school. "Willie wouldn't do a thing like that," they protest, "he's too well behaved."

  4. When human beings, especially children, are punished there is a danger that they will come to think *they*—rather than their behavior—are bad, stupid, or clumsy. With such an attitude, they expect to fail, to be inept, or to be unlovable. Children who are humiliated often become more concerned with protecting themselves against anxiety than with taking positive action. Such children may become withdrawn or may strike out in retaliation, thereby inviting a new round of punishment. In either case, the punishment becomes self-defeating.

5. If punishment is routinely used as the way to "enforce good behavior," children learn no other training method. They see it as the appropriate way for those in power to behave. So when they grow up, they treat their own children the same way. Studies have shown that the parents of battered children were usually abused themselves as children.

6. Punishment has an unfortunate effect on the punisher. Giving vent to frustration feels good. Thus, the punishing response is reinforced, especially if the bad behavior is stopped—at least for the moment. Besides being more likely to use punishment next time, the punisher is convinced that punishment produced whatever improvement there was. It is a short step from there to the belief that punishment is necessary; that without it, bad behavior can be expected. This starts a vicious circle in which more punishment is used. The person being punished has few chances to learn for positive reasons or to show that good behavior can come from anything but fear of punishment. The person punished may lose all motivation to do anything but avoid punishment—or get even with the punisher.

If punishment is used, it should be clear that certain behavior will also be *rewarded*. A stick works better if there is also a carrot in sight. In fact, in most cases, a good carrot works by itself. Research has shown that if children get attention for good behavior, they are less likely to try to get it by bad behavior.

David Dempsey and Philip G. Zimbardo, *Psychology and You*

_____

_____

_____

_____

_____

_____

_____

_____

_____

- ## *Exercise 6*

Outline the key ideas in the following passage as if you were studying for a quiz.

Until Andrew Jackson was elected in 1828, American presidents came from either Virginia or Massachusetts, and all Washington's successors had worked their way up through the cabinet. Jackson ended this "aristocratical" pattern and "toppled the Virginia-Massachusetts dynasty." Around the hero of New Orleans there formed a coalition of western farmers, city laborers, small bankers, tradespeople, and others who saw him as God's gift to the common people. They hoped to put him in the White House in 1824, and in the election of that year he did get the largest number of popular votes. But as Jackson's supporters saw it, a "corrupt bargain" between candidates John Quincy Adams and Henry Clay gave Adams the most electoral votes and the presidency. Adams then made Clay secretary of state.

Jackson—Old Hickory—succeeded in 1828 and was reelected president four years later. Jackson made good on the slogan "to the victors belong the spoils" by giving patronage jobs (positions filled by appointment) to his backers. He became the symbol of democracy at a time when the number of voters was expanding rapidly and when mobility—both social and geographical—was the keynote of American life.

Jackson waged two fierce contests as president. In one he tried to limit the activities of the federal government; in the other he greatly strengthened federal power. First, he destroyed the Bank of the United States, which had enjoyed special powers and privileges, and he placed its funds in state and local banks (1833). This pleased his backers, who wanted trade and finance to be free of central government control, but it helped cause a harsh economic depression in 1837. Second, he resisted South Carolina's attempt to "nullify" a tariff law that state disliked (1832-1833). This pitted him against Senator John C. Calhoun, a spokesman for the planter aristocracy of the Old South and for the idea that the states could declare federal laws unconstitutional. Jackson's victory in this nullification contest was a victory for centralism and the Union over "states' rights."

During Jackson's term the removal of Indians to the West became official government policy. The president ordered the Civilized Tribes of the South-east moved to the "permanent Indian Frontier" beyond the Mississippi. Some went peacefully, making new treaties and getting some payment for giving up their homes. Others resisted, like the Cherokees, who took their case all the way to the Supreme Court, and the Seminoles, who fought on until 1843, inflicting many casualties on the U.S. Army. By 1839 the military had removed most of the southern tribes, but the cost was enormous—both in wasted human lives and in the growing moral burden created by such acts. For example, forced marches over the "Trail of Tears" killed about four thousand Cherokees and subjected the survivors to intense suffering from hunger and exposure.

The same sad story was played out in the North, where in the Black Hawk War of 1832 the Sac and Fox tribes of Illinois tried to return to their lands and were crushed by the state militia. This removed the last Indian barrier to white expansion in the Old Northwest. The Bureau of Indian Affairs, created in 1836 to administer Indian treaties, was more notable for becoming the most durable federal bureaucracy than for protecting the rights or meeting the needs of Indians.

Leonard Pitt, *We Americans*

Selection 1

Karen Carlson and Alan Meyers, from *Speaking with Confidence*

Dr. Milton Rakove addressing
Chicago public school teachers.

Skill Development: After reading the following selection, outline the key ideas as if you were studying for a quiz.

Small-Group Speaking*

Formulating an Angle for Your Speech

Plan an angle for your speech, then explain your plan to the members of your small group, and get their reactions to it. Do they think it will touch the needs and interests of the entire class? Can they offer suggestions on what might better touch those needs and interests? After you've decided on your angle, make some notes so you don't forget it.

5   *Strengthening your introduction.* If you feel your introduction lacks sufficient strength to attract and hold your audience, you can choose from any of these standard devices, all of which should lead into your angle. One popular way to open a speech is with a question—like, "Do you share my rage about getting ripped off for auto repairs?" To be effective, though, your question should sound neither contrived, condescending, nor insulting to your audience's

10   intelligence. It must sound authentic. Asking "Did you ever think about what marsupials eat?" is silly unless you are speaking to kangaroos. Asking "Did you know there is a worldwide food shortage?" is insulting because anyone who reads the papers or watches the news knows that. Better to skip the question than ask a phony one.

A second possibility is to begin your speech with an anecdote, like the ones you told earlier

15   in the term. Here's a short one a Vietnam veteran might share to illustrate his feelings about combat, while inviting his audience to experience those feelings, too:

*LEARNING STRATEGY: As you read, think of how these techniques have been used in speeches that you have heard in the past. Formulate a speech in your mind and apply these suggestions.

Reading about the war won't tell you what it was like. You can't know what it's like until you've walked through a rice paddy and seen your best buddy's legs blown off by a land mine. After that, killing the enemy isn't scary; killing isn't disgusting. It's easy— especially if you call him a "gook" and he looks different from you and speaks a funny language. Somehow he seems less human, kind of like a pest or a snake. You want to step on his head before he strikes at you.

Additionally, you can begin your speech with a dramatic statement: "In ten years, we're going to be abandoning our cars and freezing in our homes. That's how serious the energy crisis is." And, finally, you can select among these possible openers: a joke, a quotation, an important fact from your research, or several such facts presented in rapid succession. But as you select from these devices, remember that a joke must be funny, a quote or a fact must be interesting, and anything you say must be short. Don't lose your audience with the very device you've chosen to gain their attention.

Announcing your destination and describing your route. The next step in your introduction is, of course, to state your *thesis* in a sentence or two so your listeners will know where you'll be taking them. But to help them follow your journey, you may want to draw them a general road map. In other words, you may want to include a brief *presummary* which outlines your arguments or points in the order you'll discuss them. Such presummaries aren't always necessary if you clearly label each argument or point you discuss within the body of your speech. Nevertheless, a presummary provides your audience with one more aid to understanding, so we'd recommend including it, especially in longer speeches. Here's an example. Dr. Milton Rakove, a political scientist, spoke to a college audience about the reasons that Mayor Richard J. Daley's Chicago Democratic political organization, or the "Machine," has thrived for two decades. Since his argument was long and complex, he made his thesis (which we've italicized) and his presummary explicit:

> What I'm going to talk about tonight is *why I think this "machine" has lasted as long as it has in Chicago.* It's a fascinating machine. All the other big city machines in this country have gone to hell; they all disappeared. [Newspaper writer] Mike Royko said in a column about eight years ago that one of the reasons the other machines went down is because they got into bad habits—and they reformed. But this one has never reformed. . . .
>
> I think that's an oversimplification of why the machine has lasted so long. And I think it's lasted as long as it has and done as well as it has primarily for five reasons: one, its ability to adapt to a changing city; two, the concept of its demand for efficiency within the machine; three, the demand for loyalty that the machine makes of its members; four, the fact of the almost single-minded concentration that the machine has on political power; and, five, you can't talk about this machine, of course, except within the context of the role that Mayor Daley has played. So let me take those five things and talk about them briefly.[1]

Note that Dr. Rakove not only mentioned all the points he would examine; he *enumerated* them as well. Throughout the speech, as he moved from point to point, he repeated the key terms and his numbering of them: "Let me start with adaptability," he said. Then later, "Secondly, I want to discuss the concept of efficiency," and so on.

Some speakers choose a looser kind of presummary, without the enumeration. They simply mention in a few sentences what they'll discuss, leaving the more explicit signposting for the body of the speech. Whichever method you choose, you will make the journey through your speech easier for your audience.

[1]Dr. Milton L. Rakove, "Chicago: The City That Works?" speech delivered at Wilbur Wright College, Chicago, Illinois, February 26, 1976.

Planning for your signposts along the way

As we've already suggested, short statements which indicate *transitions*—that is, which show the relationship between one idea and the next—are a further aid to clarity within the body of
65   your speech. They serve as signposts—"Leaving Idea Number One and entering Idea Number Two"—to guide your audience. Occasionally, in a longer speech, as you move from one major section to the next, you may wish to review where you've been before entering new territory. An audience has so much on their minds, so many noises in their brains and lives, that they may have missed parts of what you've said, especially at the end of each of your
70   major ideas. You can do them a favor by restating or bringing together your ideas in a section summary or an *internal summary,* then moving on to the next section.

Such summaries can be planned; but you must know the direction your speech is going and perceive the major breaks, the points at which your audience would appreciate a refresher. For example, Philip Hilts used the following one in the speech we first quoted in Chapter 5. More
75   than half an hour after he'd begun, after having related ten or more anecdotes and introduced a number of ideas, he summarized his main points (which we've italicized) before advancing into new territory. The words "The problem is" begin the transition.

> There is now no doubt as far as I am concerned that *behavior modification* is here permanently. . . . *I think the science of it is very clear and straightforward. I think the*
80   *science of it is right.* The problem is: What about the horror stories? What about the abuses? How do you put the two together—science that works and technology that is horrible, and sometimes good?[2]

Hilts then entered the next section of his speech, discussing a way to resolve—through political action—the problem of the "horror stories" and "abuses."
85   However, in shorter speeches where such internal summaries may be unnecessary, you can still indicate the relationship between ideas with a single sentence. It can be a statement ("In addition to learning the guitar chords, you must also learn a few strums."), or a question followed by your answer ("What can be done about the energy crisis? Here are a few suggestions."). The important point is, whenever possible, give your listeners the guidance to
90   stay on course.

Planning your ending

Since the last words in your speech will also be the last words in your audience's minds, a strong ending is crucial. You should plan your conclusion to accomplish two goals: (1) to *remind* your audience of what you've just said, and (2) to *show them the importance* of what you've just said. You'll be summarizing your speech and wrapping it up with a powerful
95   statement, which can take the form of a quotation or anecdote embodying your main idea, or a return to the beginning of your speech. Your ending also can carry your main ideas forward, suggesting the positive results of their application, or warning of the consequences if they're not carried out. In any case, your ending should be bold, forceful, vivid.

Here's a conclusion of a student's speech to his classmates in which he had explained the
100   disadvantages of buying a new car and the advantages of buying a used car. Notice how he summarizes most of his arguments and then ends on a firm positive note:

> So—to sum it all up—most of us can't really afford a new car. You could if you went out and borrowed, but then you are stuck with monthly payments. Monthly payments can cost a lot of money. Car insurance itself can be another thousand dollars. This is
105   really quite a lot of money. And, to be paying for the car for three or four years, I think, is just ridiculous for anyone going to school. When we get older and are making more

[2]Philip Hilts, "Behavior Modification: Its Uses and Implications," speech delivered at Wilbur Wright College, Chicago, Illinois, March 5, 1975.

money, then we can afford a new car. But right now, while we're in school, let's buy a used car we can fix up inexpensively, a car which fits both our basic needs and our budget.[3]   /1601

_____

_____

_____

_____

_____

_____

_____

_____

_____

_____

_____

_____

_____

_____

_____

_____

_____

• **Comprehension Questions**

After reading the selection, answer the following questions with *a, b, c,* or *d.*

_____ 1. The best statement of the main idea of this selection is
   a. in planning a speech, first attract the attention of the listeners and then guide them, step by step with frequent summaries, to a forceful conclusion
   b. a well-planned speech requires research into the topic and frequent practice sessions before the delivery

[3]Mark C. Puchalski, ''The Used Car,'' speech delivered at Wilbur Wright College, Chicago, Illinois, spring, 1976.

c. because the attention span of listeners vary, a good speech should be repetitious to allow for lapses of attention

d. the best speeches begin and end with amusing anecdotes to stress the theme and leave the listeners in a good mood

_____ 2. As an opening device for a speech, the author suggests all of the following except a
   a. joke
   b. question
   c. transition
   d. quotation

_____ 3. The author feels that beginning a speech with the anecdote on Viet Nam would serve all of the following purposes except
   a. attract the listeners' interest
   b. announce the destination of the speech
   c. dramatically introduce the topic
   d. create a mood for the speech

_____ 4. Stating the thesis of a speech is a statement of the
   a. main idea
   b. details in the order in which they will be covered
   c. signposts
   d. transition

_____ 5. The author suggests that an enumerated presummary accompany the introductory thesis statement of the speech when
   a. the audience is uneducated
   b. the speech is poorly organized
   c. the speech needs to be short and concise
   d. the speech is long and complicated

_____ 6. The author suggests that a speech without transitions might seem
   a. short
   b. disjointed
   c. hurried
   d. uninteresting

_____ 7. A transitional statement is all of the following except
   a. an internal summary
   b. a linking statement
   c. a dramatic device
   d. a restatement

_____ 8. The author feels that the conclusion of a speech is very important because
   a. the audience should leave in a good mood
   b. it's the last thing on the audience's mind
   c. it's the speaker's last chance to explain
   d. the audience is more attentive at the end

_____ 9. The author would probably consider the most successful speech one that
   a. shocked the audience
   b. aroused the audience to constructive action
   c. held the attention of the audience
   d. made the audience like the speaker

10. Of all of the hints mentioned, the author would probably consider the most important element of a good speech to be
  a. organization
  b. summaries
  c. anecdotes
  d. the introduction

Answer the following with *T* (true), *F* (false), or *CT* (can't tell).

11. Dr. Milton Rakove feels that a reformed political environment is not run by a machine.
12. The introduction to a speech is more important than the conclusion.
13. The angle of a speech is its focus of attention.
14. The purpose of enumeration and summary statements within a speech is to help the listener stay on course.
15. An anecdote should be used only in the introductory portion of a speech.

• *Vocabulary*

According to the way the boldface word was used in the selection, indicate *a, b, c,* or *d* for the word or phrase that gives the best definition.

1. "into your **angle**"
  a. ending
  b. point of view
  c. outline
  d. corner

2. "should sound neither **contrived**"
  a. fabricated
  b. easy
  c. serious
  d. disrespectful

3. "**condescending,** nor insulting"
  a. dishonest
  b. humorous
  c. lowering of oneself
  d. complex

4. "sound **authentic**"
  a. genuine
  b. heartwarming
  c. intelligent
  d. newly formed

5. "with an **anecdote**"
  a. synopsis
  b. quotation
  c. drama
  d. brief story

6. "in rapid **succession**"
  a. motions
  b. manipulations
  c. series
  d. trials

7. "**enumerated** them as well"
  a. specify one by one
  b. grouped
  c. changed
  d. sequenced

8. "more **explicit** signposting"
  a. complicated
  b. distinctly expressed
  c. difficult
  d. frequent

9. "begin the **transition**"
  a. new section
  b. central focus
  c. order of events
  d. passing from one part to another

10. "ending is **crucial**"
  a. final
  b. critical
  c. forceful
  d. desirable

- ## *Possible Essay Exam Question*

  Choose a subject and outline a speech that incorporates the suggestions in this selection. (Hint: Outline your speech and specifically note what you will use as the attention getter, the presummary, transitions, and the ending.)

- ## *Word Parts*

  Study the meaning of the word parts and supply an additional example from your own vocabulary. In the second set of items, use the corresponding part to write the word that best fits the definition.

Word Part	Meaning	Example	Your Example
1. voc, vok	voice, call	vocal	_____
2. neg, negat	say no, deny	negate	_____
3. tend, tens, tent	stretch	intensify	_____
4. sta, stit, sist	stand	resist	_____
5. loc	place, set	location	_____
6. plic, plex, ply	fold	complex	_____
7. er, errat	wander	errant	_____
8. esque	like in manner of style	arabesque	_____
9. ment	state or condition of	excitement	_____
10. ize	make or cause to be	idolize	_____

1. to bring forth anger _____

2. go back on a promise _____

3. concentration _____

4. to help _____

5. vicinity _____

6. entangled; difficult _____

7. wandering, irregular _____

8. looking like a picture _____

9. food for the body _____

10. to make thinner _____

Selection 2: Marketing

Edward J. Fox and Edward W. Wheatley, from *Modern Marketing*

Skill Development: After reading the following selection, outline the key ideas as if you were studying for a quiz.

Franchises—
A Special Case*

"IT'S DELICIOUS— JUST THE THING FOR OUR NATIONWIDE FRANCHISE OPERATION."

Holiday Inns, International House of Pancakes, Dairy Queen, McDonald's, U-Totem Stores, the Aapco (car painting) Systems—all saw unmatched growth in the 1960s. For marketers, that growth signified the opening of a new direct channel—franchising.

These operations and many more, some regional, some national, have the same general
5   pattern. The parent company first establishes a successful retail business. As it expands, it sees a profit potential in offering others the right to open similar businesses under its name. The parent company's methods and means of identification with consumers (color schemes, layouts, point-of-purchase displays) are included in this right. The franchising company supplies know-how, and may build and lease stores to franchisees. For these advantages the franchisee pays
10   the franchisor a substantial fee. Day-to-day operations are, for the franchisor, similar to those of the manufacturer selling direct to independent retailers. However, some of the advantages and disadvantages are different.

By extending a "proven" marketing method, a parent can profit in several ways. First, the

*LEARNING STRATEGY: From a marketing point of view, how does franchising work? What are the benefits to the franchisor and to the franchisee?

franchisee's purchase price gives the parent an immediate return on the plan. Then, the sale of
supplies to the franchisee provides a continuing source of profits. As new businesses are added
and the company's reputation spreads, the value of the franchise increases and sales of
franchises become easier. The snowballing effect can be dramatic. McDonald's, for example,
once announced that commitments for new franchises were so heavy it would not undertake
more accounts for about 18 months. Such growth, too, brings into play the economies of scale.
Regional or national advertising that might be financially impossible for a franchisor with 20
franchises could be profitable for one with 40.

The parent, then, finds immediate gains from the opportunity to expand markets on the basis
of reputation alone, without having to put up capital or take the risk of owning retail outlets.
Added to this advantage is a less obvious but material one. Skilled, conscientious retail
managers are rare. People who invest their capital in franchises, though, probably come closer
to the ideal than do paid managers. In effect, the franchisee is an independent store operator
working for the franchisor, but without an independent's freedom to drop suppliers at will. Of
course the factory's costs of selling supplies are less. But also certainly the franchisee buying
goods that have had broad consumer acceptance will not casually change suppliers, even when
the contract permits. If the hamburger or french fries are not what customers expected, they
may not return. Having paid for the goodwill, the franchisee won't thoughtlessly jeopardize it.

Our description of franchising may give you the idea that as a franchisor you need only relax
in your rocking chair. Few marketers can do that. Franchising, like any other channel, has
problems to be solved.

Selling franchises is not simple. Buyers need not only capital to invest but also a willingness
to invest in and supervise what is in many ways a new outlet. Few franchisors can easily round
up such people. Franchisees who do not follow the format are threats to both franchisors and
themselves. Badly managed operations with poor service hurt the image that is a major part of
what a company is selling. Even when an agreement specifically states the franchisee's
obligations, enforcement can be impracticable. In fact, the conformity problem could become
so difficult that the firm might be forced to revert to a company-owned operation. Reportedly,
Howard Johnson stopped franchising its restaurants primarily for this reason.

Franchisors (who are, after all, manufacturers) often have little experience in some aspects
of the business. Suitable sites for outlets must be found and buildings constructed. Vastly
different types of franchisees in various areas must be counseled and controlled. These and
many other jobs all compete for management time and capital.

The immediate consumer for the franchisor's goods is, of course, the franchisee. Many of
these people could start a business of their own. Why, then, would someone who wanted,
say, a restaurant, choose to pay for the use of someone else's name and agree to all the
operating restrictions? The answer is probably an expectation of greater profits. Franchisees'
dollars buy, first, established names that are promoted continually at less cost to them than the
amount needed to promote an independent business. Second, they buy an established line of
products and procedures that have a proven track record. In effect, they buy consumer
acceptance that would have taken years to establish alone (or perhaps never could have been
established).

Franchisees do take risks. New and untried franchises may well fail. Minnie Pearl's and
Broadway Joe's franchisees have not done well. Franchisees who invest in established names—
and pay the higher asking price—could fail, although the risks are lessened. No one can predict
with certainty if or how consumer tastes might change or sites deteriorate to the point of
unprofitableness. "Investigate before you invest" is old, wise advice.

Although franchising grew up in the 1960s, relatively few companies (concentrated in a few
products and services) have taken the franchise route to consumers. Most of these companies
apparently started from a strong nucleus of company-owned operations. They have been well
financed and have vigorously promoted the franchises. And because of their continual heavy
advertising, franchisees have been able to attract consumers.

The range of products and services a franchise offers is limited. Although these products and services vary among franchises from 15¢ hamburgers to over $100 transmission services, the companies do have some things in common. Since operations can be standardized, people need few skills to manage and service them. Franchisees need no great buying or supervising skills (workers at hamburger or pizza counters need be neither high-powered salespeople nor master chefs).

70

The offerings are of a kind to which consumers can be attracted by advertising. Few car owners, for example, can judge in advance whether a paint job will be worth the price. Advertising for an established name, though, lends confidence to a choice. Too, a large market exists for most franchise offerings. Marketers of highly specialized or expensive products would have little use for this channel (diamond producers don't sell franchises). Prompt volume sales must be expected.

75

How much of the growth in franchising is a basic trend, how much is fad, only time will show. As better locations become scarce and competition among franchised operations sharpens, the method will be tested. Evidence already shows much disillusionment. Clearly, however, the new franchising is firmly established. Almost gone are the old "franchised dealers" who pay nothing for the privilege. They operate under their own names, may or may not have exclusive areas, and may sell both competing and noncompeting products.

80

The new franchising, though, has a lot going for it. Population and incomes are expanding. Retailing is becoming more and more automated. Longevity is increasing and retirees and others are seeking new channels for both energy and capital. The new franchising, then, could be for more marketers the answer to "which channel shall I choose?"   /1169

85

_____

_____

_____

_____

_____

_____

_____

_____

_____

_____

_____

_____

_____

_____

_____

_____

• *Comprehension Questions*

After reading the selection, answer the following questions with *a, b, c,* or *d*.

_____ 1. The best statement of the main idea of this selection is
   a. the rise of franchising in the 60's does not mean continued growth in the 70's
   b. franchising is a type of direct channel route in marketing for buyers to evaluate and consider
   c. successful franchising depends on good management
   d. franchising benefits the consumer because of product standardization

_____ 2. The author's main purpose in this selection is
   a. to favorably influence the reader toward franchise investing
   b. to warn the public of the dangers of franchise investing
   c. to give an example of a decrease in marketing competition in the 60's
   d. to explain the advantages and disadvantages of franchising

_____ 3. The franchising operation might best be defined as a successful parent company
   a. selling name-brand goods to a private investor
   b. renting proven ideas and techniques for investment capital
   c. selling an independent investor the right, as well as the guidance, to open a business under its name
   d. assuming management and advertising responsibility for individual investors

_____ 4. The advantages of franchising to the parent company are all the following except
   a. the ownership of additional retail outlets
   b. an immediate investment return
   c. the development of a future market for sale of supplies
   d. the opportunity for more extensive advertising

_____ 5. The advantages of franchising to the franchisee are all of the following except
   a. use of proven procedures
   b. insurance of greater profits
   c. greater advertising than an independent could afford
   d. starting out with customer acceptance of the product

_____ 6. According to the author, a significant danger of franchising to the franchisor is
   a. overspending advertising dollars on regional markets
   b. establishing a line of products that the franchisee does not want to sell
   c. the bad image a franchisee can give to the total business
   d. the franchisee deciding to open an independent business operation without the parent company

_____ 7. According to the author a business that would lend itself well to franchising usually has all of the following characteristics except
   a. limited products and services   c. cheap locations
   b. standardized operations   d. no need for highly skilled employees

_____ 8. According to the author, the trend of franchising may continue to grow because
   a. fads continue for many years
   b. good locations are becoming scarce
   c. competition is keen
   d. retailing is becoming more automated

_____ 9. The snowballing effect in franchising referred to by the author is best stated as
   a. success breeds success
   b. the first is the easiest
   c. overextending causes failure
   d. greater quality increases volume

_____ 10. An important motivating and management key on which franchising capitalizes is
   a. cheap labor
   b. parent company leasing
   c. individual ownership
   d. local marketing controls

Answer the following with *T* (true), *F* (false), or *CT* (can't tell).

_____ 11. In the author's opinion, a franchisor should sell to anyone who has the capital to invest.

_____ 12. The author implies that franchisees of the Howard Johnson restaurants did not always meet the standards of the parent company.

_____ 13. According to the author, as the franchisor becomes more established, the price of a franchise usually becomes higher.

_____ 14. McDonald's is the number one franchising business in the world.

_____ 15. Minnie Pearl's and Broadway Joe's franchisees failed because of inferior products.

• *Vocabulary*

According to the way the boldface word was used in the selection, indicate *a*, *b*, *c*, or *d* for the word or phrase that gives the best definition.

____ 1. "sees a profit **potential**"
   a. area
   b. undeveloped power
   c. reality
   d. notion

____ 2. "The **parent** company's methods"
   a. original
   b. responsible
   c. independent
   d. family

____ 3. "The **snowballing** effect"
   a. chilling
   b. accumulating
   c. circling
   d. playful

____ 4. "**conscientious** retail managers"
   a. willing to learn
   b. specifically trained
   c. intelligent
   d. honest and hardworking

_____ 5. "won't thoughtlessly **jeopardize** it"
a. endanger
b. forget
c. fail
d. slander

_____ 6. "follow the **format**"
a. manner
b. plan
c. legality
d. leadership

_____ 7. "the franchisee's **obligations**"
a. payments
b. practices
c. commitments
d. privileges

_____ 8. "from a strong **nucleus**"
a. energy area
b. center of growth
c. research base
d. module

_____ 9. "shows much **disillusionment**"
a. animosity
b. fantasy
c. disenchantment
d. bitterness

_____ 10. "**Longevity** is increasing"
a. available money
b. length of loans
c. interest rate
d. long life

• *Possible Essay Exam Question*

Describe how franchising helped McDonald's grow into a bigger and better company than might otherwise have been possible. (Hint: Relate the strengths and weaknesses of franchising to McDonald's Corporation.)

• *Word Parts*

Study the meaning of the word parts and supply an additional example from your own vocabulary. In the second set of items, use the corresponding part to write the word that best fits the definition.

Word Part	Meaning	Example	Your Example
1. a, an	without, not	atypical	_____
2. bene	well, good	benefactor	_____
3. mal	ill, wrong	malady	_____
4. extra	beyond, outside, without	extraordinary	_____
5. intro	into	introduce	_____
6. ver, veri	true, genuine	veracity	_____
7. pel, puls	drive, push, throw	propel	_____
8. ity	state or quality of	adversity	_____
9. ant	quality of	repentant	_____
10. ian	person who	disciplinarian	_____

1. without a name _____

2. a nonmalignant tumor _____

3. discontented, ill-tempered _____

4. senses beyond the normal _____

5. inward examination of self _____

6. opinion of the jury _____

7. to push out of school _____

8. quality of helpfulness toward the needy _____

9. being demanding _____

10. one skilled in grammar _____

Selection 3

Gardner Lindzey, Calvin Hall, and Richard F. Thompson, from *Psychology*

Skill Development: After reading the following selection, outline the key ideas as if you were studying for a quiz.

Creative Thinking and Critical Thinking[*]

Creative thinking is thinking that results in the discovery of a new or improved solution to a problem. *Critical thinking* is the examination and testing of suggested solutions to see whether they will work. Creative thinking leads to the birth of new ideas, while critical thinking tests ideas for flaws and defects. Both are necessary for effective problem-solving, yet they are
5 incompatible—creative thinking interferes with critical thinking, and vice versa. To think creatively we must let our thoughts run free. The more spontaneous the process, the more ideas will be born and the greater the probability that an effective solution will be found. A steady stream of ideas furnishes the raw material. Then critical judgment selects and refines the best ideas, picking the most effective solution out of the available possibilities. Though we must
10 engage in the two types of thinking separately, we need both for efficient problem-solving.

Inhibitions of Creative Thinking
Conformity—the desire to be like everyone else—is the foremost barrier to creative thinking. A person is afraid to express new ideas because he thinks he will make a fool of himself and be ridiculed. This feeling may date back to his childhood, when his spontaneous and imaginative ideas may have been laughed at by parents or older people. During adolescence, conformity is

[*]LEARNING STRATEGY: Be able to describe the factors involved in both creative and critical thinking and explain how the two interact.

Thomas Edison with his early phonograph, 1888.

15   reinforced because young people are afraid to be different from their peers. Then, too, history
      teaches us that innovators often are laughed at and even persecuted.

      Censorship—especially self-imposed censorship—is a second significant barrier to creativity.
      External censorship of ideas, the thought-control of modern dictatorships, is dramatic and
      newsworthy; but internal censorship is more effective and dependable. External censorship
20   merely prevents public distribution of proscribed thoughts; the thoughts may still be expressed
      privately. But people who are frightened by their thoughts tend to react passively, rather than
      think of creative solutions to their problems. Sometimes they even repress those thoughts, so
      that they are not aware they exist. Freud called this internalized censor the *superego*.

      A third barrier to creative thinking is the rigid *education* still commonly imposed upon
25   children. Regimentation, memorization, and drill may help instill the accepted knowledge of
      the day, but these classroom methods cannot teach students how to solve new problems or how
      to improve upon conventional solutions. On the other hand, the progressive movement in
      education often has been criticized on the ground that its emphasis on creative thinking also
      encourages intellectual nonconformity and radicalism. Such critics fear that new ideas may
30   threaten the established order. Others simply believe that creative thinking must be balanced by
      critical thinking if it is to be useful.

      A fourth barrier to creative thinking is the great *desire to find an answer quickly*. Such a
      strong motivation often narrows one's consciousness and encourages the acceptance of early,
      inadequate solutions. People tend to do their best creative thinking when they are released from
35   the demands and responsibilities of everyday living. Inventors, scientists, artists, writers, and
      executives often do their most creative thinking when they are not distracted by routine work.
      The value of a vacation is not that it enables a person to work better on his return but rather
      that it permits new ideas to be born during the vacation.

The daydreamer often is criticized for wasting his time. Yet without daydreams, society's progress would be considerably slower, since daydreaming often leads to the discovery of original ideas. This is not to suggest that all daydreaming or leisurely contemplation results in valid and workable ideas—far from it. But somewhere, among the thousands of ideas conceived, one useful idea will appear. Finding this one idea without having to produce a thousand poor ones would achieve a vast saving in creative thinking. But such a saving seems unlikely, especially since creative thinking is generally enjoyable whether its results are useful or not.

Critical Thinking

Creative thinking must be followed by critical thinking if we want to sort out and refine those ideas that are potentially useful. Critical thinking is essentially an idea-testing operation. Will it work? What is wrong with it? How can it be improved? These are questions to be answered by a critical examination of newly hatched ideas. You may be highly creative, but if you cannot determine which ideas are practical and reasonable, your creativity will not lead to many fruitful consequences. In order to make such distinctions, you must maintain some distance and detachment, so that you can appraise your own ideas objectively.

Critical thinking requires some criteria by which to judge the practicality of the ideas. For example, if a community wants to do something about crime, it must decide what limitations are to be imposed upon the measures that are suggested. One limitation is the amount of money available; many proposals for curbing crime cost more than the community is willing or able to pay. Critical thinking must always take such realities into account.

What barriers stand in the path of critical thinking? One is the *fear of being aggressive and destructive*. We learn as children not to be critical, not to differ with what someone says, especially an older person. To criticize is to be discourteous.

A closely related barrier is the *fear of retaliation*. If I criticize your ideas, you may turn about and criticize mine. This often involves yet another barrier, the *overevaluation* of one's own ideas. We like what we have created, and often we are reluctant to let others take apart our creation. By and large, those who are least secure hang on most tenaciously to their original ideas.

Finally, we should note again that if too much emphasis is placed upon being creative, the critical faculty may remain undeveloped. In their zeal to stimulate creativity in their pupils, teachers often are reluctant to think critically. This is unfortunate, since for most people life requires a balance between creative and critical thinking.

Critical Attitudes. There is an important distinction between critical thinking and a *critical attitude*. Critical thinking tries to arrive at a valid and practical solution to a problem. However much it may reject and discard, its final goal is constructive. A critical attitude, on the other hand, is destructive in intent. A person with a critical attitude tends to criticize solely for the sake of criticizing. Such an attitude is emotional rather than cognitive.

The Creative Person

In recent years, psychologists have studied creativity intensively. The first challenge they faced was how to define and recognize creativity. One common solution to this problem is to ask knowledgeable people to name the most creative individuals in their own field. Architects are asked to identify the most creative members of their profession or authors are asked to name the most creative writers. These highly creative people then are studied by means of interviews, questionnaires, tests, and other devices to see how they differ from less creative members of the same profession. These studies show that exceptionally creative people are characteristically:

1. flexible   3. perceptive

2. intuitive   4. original

5. ingenious

6. dedicated

7. hardworking

8. persistent

9. independent

10. unconventional

11. courageous

12. uninhibited

13. moody

14. self-centered

15. self-assertive

16. dominant

17. eccentric

Creative people often have vivid and sometimes even flamboyant personalities. They prefer complexity to simplicity. And those who are males accept the feminine side of their nature

85   without being effeminate (Barron, 1959).

Isolating such characteristics of highly creative people may be useful. If these traits are related to creativity, child training and educational procedures may be tailored to produce more creative people. Still, we are only assuming that these traits have anything to do with being creative. They may merely be associated with creativity, rather than being determinants of it.

90   Or, they may be necessary but not sufficient conditions for being creative. Flexibility, originality, and hard work, for example, may be requirements for creativity but they certainly are not sufficient to insure it. The creative genius displayed by Shakespeare, Leonardo da Vinci, Einstein, and Beethoven remains a mystery that has so far eluded scientific analysis./1340

_____

_____

_____

_____

_____

_____

_____

_____

_____

_____

_____

_____

_____

_____

_____

• *Comprehension Questions*

After reading the selection, answer the following questions with *a, b, c,* or *d.*

————— 1. The best statement of the main idea of this selection is
   a. both creative and critical thinking are necessary for efficient problem solving
   b. creative and critical thinking are not compatible
   c. creative thinking is more important than critical thinking
   d. creative thinking is more easily inhibited than critical thinking

————— 2. According to the author, creative thinking includes all of the following except
   a. improved solutions to old problems
   b. the birth of new ideas
   c. a spontaneous flow of free thoughts
   d. an evaluation of effective alternatives

————— 3. The author implies that critical thinking could be characterized as all of the following except
   a. selective   c. spontaneous
   b. judgmental   d. organized

————— 4. Of the following barriers to creative thinking, the single individual would probably have the most control over
   a. conformity   c. education
   b. external censorship d. the desire for a quick answer

————— 5. Of the following statements, the author would agree that
   a. in general, today's educational system encourages creativity
   b. creative people must dare to be different
   c. dictatorships cannot stop creative ideas
   d. creativity should not interfere with daily duties

————— 6. The author believes that daydreaming
   a. is a waste of time
   b. slows society's progress
   c. fosters creative thinking
   d. saves time in problem solving

————— 7. The author would agree with all of the following statements except
   a. creative thinking comes before critical thinking
   b. critical thinking requires guidelines for evaluating ideas
   c. critical thinking must be realistic
   d. creative thinking should be done by one person and critical thinking by another

————— 8. All of the following are barriers to critical thinking except
   a. the threat of returned criticism
   b. the chance of offending someone
   c. an aggressive desire for improvement
   d. the possible destruction of cherished ideas

————— 9. The author feels that a critical attitude is
   a. desirable   c. unintentional
   b. undesirable   d. destructive

_____ 10. The author believes that highly creative people
   a. cannot isolate the determinants of creativity
   b. tend to be effeminate
   c. make simple solutions complicated
   d. do not need to work hard

Answer the following with *T* (true), *F* (false), or *CT* (can't tell).

_____ 11. The author believes that rest is the most important result of a vacation.
_____ 12. The author suggests that the progressive movement in education should be followed.
_____ 13. The author implies that a teacher's constructive criticism helps students develop critical thinking.
_____ 14. The author feels that conformity is at its worst during adolescence.
_____ 15. The author feels that creative thinking is fun.

• *Vocabulary*

According to the way the boldface word was used in the selection, indicate *a*, *b*, *c*, or *d* for the word or phrase that gives the best definition.

____ 1. "yet they are **incompatible**"
   a. untouched
   b. not understood
   c. similar in nature
   d. unsuitable together

____ 2. "The more **spontaneous** the process"
   a. demanding
   b. momentarily impulsive
   c. reliable
   d. advantageous

____ 3. "**Inhibitions** of Creative Thinking"
   a. variations
   b. objections
   c. motivators
   d. restraints

____ 4. "**innovators** often are laughed at"
   a. clowns
   b. introducers of the new
   c. people who fail
   d. adventurers

____ 5. "nonconformity and **radicalism**"
   a. conservatism
   b. extremism
   c. isolationism
   d. romanticism

____ 6. "leisurely **contemplation**"
   a. relaxation
   b. conversation
   c. meditation
   d. manipulation

____ 7. "maintain some distance and **detachment**"
   a. outside advice
   b. separation
   c. sophistication
   d. emotional involvement

____ 8. "hang on most **tenaciously**"
   a. strongly
   b. loosely
   c. quickly
   d. quietly

____ 9. "in their **zeal** to stimulate"
   a. attempt
   b. goal
   c. rush
   d. eagerness

____ 10. "**flamboyant** personalities"
   a. annoying
   b. likeable
   c. showy
   d. intelligent

• *Possible Essay Exam Question*

List items that a classroom teacher should consider in attempting to create a desirable balance of creative and critical thinking in students. (Hint: Define both terms and form a list from the needs for interaction, the inhibitions, and the barriers mentioned in the selection.)

• *Word Parts*

Study the meaning of the word parts and supply an additional example from your own vocabulary. In the second set of items, use the corresponding part to write the word that best fits the definition.

Word Part	Meaning	Example	Your Example
1. psych	mind	psychotherapy	_____
2. multi	many	multimillionaire	_____
3. morph	body	ectomorphic	_____
4. proto	first	prototype	_____
5. trans	across	translucent	_____
6. sub	under	subconscious	_____
7. ambi	both	ambivalent	_____
8. er	person who	laborer	_____
9. ancy, ency	state or condition of	militancy	_____
10. ite	quality of	suburbanite	_____

1. a physician who studies the mind   _____

2. speaking many languages   _____

3. a study of structure of form   _____

4. minute one-cell animals   _____

5. to send or forward   _____

6. to plunge under water   _____

7. using both hands equally well   _____

8. one who fights   _____

9. flowing ease with language   _____

10. to speed up or hasten   _____

Chapter Eight

Inference

Inference

Inference

Inference

Inference

Notice the power of suggested meaning in responding to the following questions:

1. Which is the sexiest?
   a. lingerie
   b. underwear
   c. undergarments
2. Which would you find in a small town?
   a. movies
   b. flickers
   c. picture shows
3. Who probably earns the most money?
   a. a businessman in a dark suit, white shirt, and tie
   b. a businessman in slacks and a sport shirt
   c. a businessman in a pale blue uniform

Can you prove your answers? It's not the same as proving when the Declaration of Independence was signed, yet you still have a feeling for how each question should be answered. Even though a right or wrong answer is more difficult to explain in this type of question, certain answers can still be supported as correct—they are *a, c,* and *a.* The answers are based on feelings, attitudes, and knowledge commonly shared by society. Perhaps you can't prove lingerie is sexier than underwear, but everyone has a feeling that it must be.

In categorizing reading skills, the first and most basic level of reading is the literal level—what are the facts? In reacting to a literal question, you can actually point to the words on the page that answer the question. Reading, however, progresses beyond this initial stage. A second and more sophisticated level of reading deals with motives, feelings, and judgments—this is the inferential level. At this level you no longer can point to the answer, but instead must form opinions from suggestions within the selection. In a manner of speaking, the reader must "read between the lines" for the implied meaning.

Rather than directly stating, authors often subtly suggest and thus manipulate the reader. Suggestion can be a more effective method of getting the message across than a direct statement. Suggestion requires greater writing skill, and it is also usually more artistic, creative, and entertaining. The responsible reader searches beyond the printed word for insights into what was left unsaid.

An example of the power of implied meaning and its effective everyday use is found in the advertising business. In the example of cigarette advertisements, the public has been enticed through suggestion, not facts, into spending millions of dollars on a product that is presumably unhealthful. According to the choice of a particular brand, smoking offers the refreshment of a mountain stream, the liberation of a successful woman, the masculinity of a rugged cowboy, or the sophisticated elegance of the rich and famous. The emotionalism of the full-page advertisement is so overwhelming that the consumer hardly notices the warning peeking from the daisies at the bottom of the page—"Warning: The Surgeon General Has Determined That Cigarette Smoking Is Dangerous to Your Health."

Never is smoking directly praised or pleasure promised; these things are implied. A lawsuit for false advertising is out of the question because nothing tangible has been put into print. The cigarette and advertising companies profit financially from manipulating the consumer through suggestion.

Authors and advertisers have not invented a new comprehension skill; they are merely capitalizing on an already highly developed skill of daily life. When asked by a co-worker, "How do you like your boss?", the employee might answer, "I think he wears nice ties," rather than "I don't like my boss." A lack of approval has been suggested, while the employee has avoided a direct statement of dislike. In life, just as in literature, traits of character unfold by examining what people say, what they do, and what others say about them. The intuition of everyday life applied to the printed word is the inferential level of reading.

Connotation

Seemingly an innocent tool, the writer's choice of words is the lowest denominator of implied meaning. For example, if a person is skinny, he is unattractive, but if he is slender or slim he must be attractive. All three words might refer to the same underweight person, but *skinny* communicates a negative feeling while *slender* or *slim* communicates a positive one. This feeling or emotionalism surrounding a word is called *connotation. Denotation* is the specific meaning of a word, but the connotative meaning goes beyond this to reflect certain attitudes and prejudices of society. Even though it may not seem premeditated, writers select words, just as advertisers select symbols and models, to manipulate the reader's opinions.

● *Exercise 1*

In each of the following word pairs, write the letter of the word that connotes a more positive emotional feeling:

_____   1. (a) guest   (b) boarder

_____   2. (a) surplus   (b) waste

_____   3. (a) conceited   (b) proud

_____   4. (a) hawk   (b) nightingale

_____   5. (a) heavyset   (b) obese

_____   6. (a) Richard   (b) Elmer

_____   7. (a) house   (b) mansion

_____   8. (a) song   (b) serenade

_____   9. (a) calculating   (b) clever

_____ 10. (a) neglected   (b) deteriorated

———————— 11. (a) colleague   (b) accomplice

———————— 12. (a) ambition   (b) greed

———————— 13. (a) kitten   (b) cat

———————— 14. (a) courageous   (b) audacious

———————— 15. (a) contrived   (b) designed

———————— 16. (a) flower   (b) orchid

———————— 17. (a) distinctive   (b) peculiar

———————— 18. (a) baby   (b) kid

———————— 19. (a) persuasion   (b) propaganda

———————— 20. (a) gold   (b) tin

———————— 21. (a) slump   (b) decline

———————— 22. (a) lie   (b) misrepresentation

———————— 23. (a) janitor   (b) custodian

———————— 24. (a) offering   (b) collection

———————— 25. (a) soldiers   (b) mercenaries

Reading would be rather dull if the author stated every idea, never giving you a chance to figure things out for yourself. For example, in a mystery novel you carefully weigh each word, each action, each conversation, each description, and each fact in an effort to identify the villain and solve the crime before it is revealed at the end. Although textbook material may not have the Sherlock Holmes' spirit of high adventure, authors use the same techniques to imply meaning. The following examples, both from factual material and from fiction, show how authors use suggestion, and from the clues given, you can deduce the facts.

• *Exercise 2: Inference from Description*

Looking back on the Revolutionary War, one cannot say enough about Washington's leadership. While his military skills proved less than brilliant and he and his generals lost many battles, George Washington was the single most important figure of the colonial war effort. His original appointment was partly political, for the rebellion that had started in Massachusetts needed a commander from the South to give geographic balance to the cause. The choice fell to Washington, a wealthy and respectable Virginia planter with military experience dating back to the French and Indian War. He had been denied a commission in the English army and had never forgiven the English for the insult. During the war he shared the physical suffering of his men, rarely wavered on important questions, and always used his officers to good advantage. His correspondence with Congress to ask for sorely needed supplies was tireless and forceful. He recruited several new armies in a row, as short-term enlistments gave out.

Leonard Pitt, *We Americans*

Answer the following with *T* (true), *F* (false), or *CT* (can't tell).

_____   1. The author regards George Washington as the most brilliant military genius in American history.

_____   2. A prime factor in Washington's becoming President was a need for geographic balance.

_____   3. Washington gained early military experience as a member of the British army.

_____   4. The Revolutionary War started as a rebellion in the northeast.

_____   5. The author feels that Washington's leadership was courageous and persistent even though not infallible.

● *Exercise 3: Inference from Action*

When he came to the surface he was conscious of little but the noisy water. Afterward he saw his companions in the sea. The oiler was ahead in the race. He was swimming strongly and rapidly. Off to the correspondent's left, the cook's great white and corked back bulged out of the water, and in the rear the captain was hanging with his one good hand to the keel of the overturned dinghy.

   There is a certain immovable quality to a shore, and the correspondent wondered at it amid the confusion of the sea.

Stephen Crane, *The Open Boat*

Answer the following with *a, b, c,* or *d.*

_____   1. The reason that the people are in the water is because of
            a. a swimming race
            b. an airplane crash
            c. a capsized boat
            d. a group decision
_____   2. In relation to his companions, the correspondent is
            a. closest to the shore
            b. the second or third closest to the shore
            c. farthest from the shore
            d. in a position that is impossible to determine
_____   3. The member of the group that had probably suffered a previous injury is the
            a. oiler
            b. correspondent
            c. cook
            d. captain
_____   4. The uninjured member of the group that the author seems to regard as the least physically fit is the
            a. oiler
            b. correspondent

c. cook
d. captain
_____ 5. The story is being told through the eyes of the
a. oiler
b. correspondent
c. cook
d. captain

• *Exercise 4: Inference from Figurative Language*

> He clasps the crag with crooked hands;
> Close to the sun in lonely lands,
> Ringed with the azure world, he stands.
>
> The wrinkled sea beneath him crawls;
> He watches from his mountain walls
> And like a thunderbolt he falls.
>
> Alfred Lord Tennyson, "The Eagle"

Answer the following with *a, b, c,* or *d.*

_____ 1. For an overall effect in this poem the author wants the reader to see the eagle as
a. majestic
b. violent
c. ancient
d. frightened
_____ 2. Using *wrinkled* and *crawls* to describe the sea suggests
a. the movement of the ocean waves
b. the eagle's dominance over the sea
c. the eternal age of the sea
d. the changing ocean tides
_____ 3. The "crooked hands" suggest a relationship between the eagle and
a. a deformed person
b. a dishonest villain
c. an aging monarch
d. other birds of prey
_____ 4. "Close to the sun" is suggestive primarily of the eagle's
a. superb flying ability
b. superiority over earthly things
c. warm-hearted manner
d. bald head
_____ 5. *Thunderbolt* suggests all of the following except
a. speed
b. destruction
c. power
d. failure

• *Exercise 5: Inference from Conversation*

"Well, Miss Whitcomb, I suppose I—may as well come to—the point. There was—a little—matter I wished to speak to you about. I don't suppose you were—at least I can't suppose you were—aware of it, but—this morning, during the singing by the choir, you played and—sung a little too—loud. That is, with—the windows open. It—disturbed us—a little. I hope you won't feel hurt—my dear Miss Candace, but I knew you would rather I would speak of it, for I knew—you would be more disturbed than anybody else at the idea of such a thing."

Candace did not raise her eyes; she looked as if his words might sway her through the window. "I ain't disturbed at it," said she. "I did it on purpose; I meant to."

Mary Wilkins Freeman, *A Village Singer*

Answer the following with *a, b, c,* or *d.*

_____ 1. The man speaking is probably
   a. a friend   c. the minister
   b. a choir member   d. a relative

_____ 2. The pattern of the man's speech indicates that he
   a. has a speech defect   c. knows he is right
   b. is nervous   d. is self-confident

_____ 3. When Candace was singing and playing too loudly, she was probably located
   a. in the basement of the church   c. in the back of the church
   b. in a house next to the church   d. in the choir

_____ 4. When he first started to talk, the man probably believed that Candace was
   a. aware of disturbing the choir
   b. unaware of disturbing the choir
   c. concerned about disturbing the choir
   d. a force of evil against the church

_____ 5. Candace's attitude toward disturbing the choir is probably due to her
   a. not being a church member
   b. own selfish desires
   c. having been mistreated by the church or choir
   d. evil and destructive nature

• *Exercise 6: Inference from Factual Material*

Except for some minor internal disturbances in the nineteenth century, Switzerland has been at peace inside stable boundaries since 1815. The basic factors underlying this long period of peace seem to have been (1) Switzerland's position as a buffer between larger powers, (2) the comparative defensibility of much of the country's terrain, (3) the relatively small value of Swiss economic production to an aggressive state, (4) the country's value as an intermediary between belligerents in wartime, and (5) Switzerland's own policy of strict and heavily armed neutrality. The difficulties which a great power might encounter in attempting to conquer Switzerland have often been popularly exaggerated since the Swiss Plateau, the heart of the country, lies open to Germany and France, and even the Alps have frequently been traversed by strong military forces in past times. On the other hand, resistance in the mountains might well be hard to thoroughly extinguish. In World War II Switzerland was able to hold a club over the head of Germany by mining the tunnels through which Swiss rail lines avoid the crests of the Alpine passes. Destruction of these tunnels would have been very costly to Germany, as well as to its military partner, Italy, since the Swiss railways were depended on to carry much traffic between them.

Wheeler, Kostbade and Thoman, *Regional Geography of the World*

Answer the following with *T* (true), *F* (false), or *CT* (can't tell).

1. In 1814 Switzerland was fighting a war with its neighbors.
2. The most important economic area of Switzerland is protected from its neighbors by the Alps.
3. In World War II Germany did not invade Switzerland primarily because of the five basic factors listed by the author.
4. The maintenance of a neutral Swiss position in World War II was due in part to a kind of international blackmail.
5. If it had not been for the railroad access to Italy through Switzerland, Germany would have been defeated sooner.

Selection 1: Poetry

Robert Frost, ''The Death of the Hired Man''

The Death of the Hired Man*

Mary sat musing on the lamp-flame at the table
Waiting for Warren. When she heard his step,
She ran on tip-toe down the darkened passage
To meet him in the doorway with the news
5   And put him on his guard. ''Silas is back.''
She pushed him outward with her through the door
And shut it after her. ''Be kind,'' she said.
She took the market things from Warren's arms
And set them on the porch, then drew him down
10   To sit beside her on the wooden steps.

''When was I ever anything but kind to him?
But I'll not have the fellow back,'' he said.
''I told him so last haying, didn't I?
'If he left then,' I said, 'that ended it.'
15   What good is he? Who else will harbour him
At his age for the little he can do?
What help he is there's no depending on.
Off he goes always when I need him most.

*LEARNING STRATEGY: Visualize the scene and try to piece together the character of the hired man as the parts unfold one by one.

'He thinks he ought to earn a little pay,
20   Enough at least to buy tobacco with,
So he won't have to beg and be beholden.'
'All right,' I say, 'I can't afford to pay
Any fixed wages, though I wish I could.'
'Someone else can.' 'Then someone else will have to.'
25   I shouldn't mind his bettering himself
If that was what it was. You can be certain,
When he begins like that, there's someone at him
Trying to coax him off with pocket-money,—
In haying time, when any help is scarce.
30   In winter he comes back to us. I'm done.''

"Sh! not so loud: he'll hear you," Mary said.

"I want him to: he'll have to soon or late."

"He's worn out. He's asleep beside the stove.
When I came up from Rowe's I found him here,
35   Huddled against the barn-door fast asleep,
A miserable sight, and frightening, too—
You needn't smile—I didn't recognize him—
I wasn't looking for him—and he's changed.
Wait till you see."

40   "Where did you say he'd been?"

"He didn't say. I dragged him to the house,
And gave him tea and tried to make him smoke.
I tried to make him talk about his travels
Nothing would do: he just kept nodding off."

45   "What did he say? Did he say anything?"

"But little."

                "Anything? Mary, confess
He said he'd come to ditch the meadow for me."

"Warren!"

50   "But did he? I just want to know."
"Of course he did. What would you have him say?
Surely you wouldn't grudge the poor old man
Some humble way to save his self-respect.
He added, if you really care to know,
55   He meant to clear the upper pasture; too.
That sounds like something you have heard before?
Warren, I wish you could have heard the way
He jumbled everything. I stopped to look
Two or three times—he made me feel so queer—

60   To see if he was talking in his sleep.
           He ran on Harold Wilson—you remember—
           The boy you had in haying four years since.
           He's finished school, and teaching in his college.
           Silas declares you'll have to get him back.
65   He says they two will make a team for work:
           Between them they will lay this farm as smooth!
           The way he mixed that in with other things.
           He thinks young Wilson a likely lad, though daft
           On education—you know how they fought
70   All through July under the blazing sun,
           Silas up on the cart to build the load,
           Harold along beside to pitch it on.''

           ''Yes, I took care to keep well out of earshot.''

           ''Well, those days trouble Silas like a dream.
75   You wouldn't think they would. How some things linger!
           Harold's young college boy's assurance piqued him.
           After so many years he still keeps finding
           Good arguments he sees he might have used.
           I sympathise. I know just how it feels
80   To think of the right thing to say too late.

85   Harold's associated in his mind with Latin.
        He asked me what I thought of Harold's saying
        He studied Latin like the violin
        Because he liked it—that an argument!
        He said he couldn't make the boy believe
90   He could find water with a hazel prong—
        Which showed how much good school had ever done him.
        He wanted to go over that. But most of all
        He thinks if he could have another chance
        To teach him how to build a load of hay—''

95   ''I know, that's Silas' one accomplishment.
        He bundles every forkful in its place,
        And tags and numbers it for future reference,
        So he can find and easily dislodge it
        In the unloading. Silas does that well.
100   He takes it out in bunches like big birds' nests.
        You never see him standing on the hay
        He's trying to lift, straining to lift himself.''

        ''He thinks if he could teach him that, he'd be
        Some good perhaps to someone in the world.
105   He hates to see a boy the fool of books.
        Poor Silas, so concerned for other folk,
        And nothing to look backward to with pride,
        And nothing to look forward to with hope,
        So now and never any different.''

110   Part of a moon was falling down the west,
        Dragging the whole sky with it to the hills.
        Its light poured softly in her lap. She saw it
        And spread her apron to it. She put out her hand
        Among the harp-like morning-glory strings,
115   Taut with the dew from garden bed to eaves,
        As if she played unheard some tenderness
        That wrought on him beside her in the night.
        ''Warren,'' she said, ''he has come home to die:
        You needn't be afraid he'll leave you this time.''

120   ''Home,'' he mocked gently.
                                ''Yes, what else but home?
        It all depends on what you mean by home.
        Of course he's nothing to us, any more
        Than was the hound that came a stranger to us
125   Out of the woods, worn out upon the trail.''

        ''Home is the place where, when you have to go there,
        They have to take you in.''
                                ''I should have called it
        Something you somehow haven't to deserve.''

130   Warren leaned out and took a step or two,

Picked up a little stick, and brought it back
And broke it in his hand and tossed it by.
"Silas has better claim on us you think
Than on his brother? Thirteen little miles
135   As the road winds would bring him to his door.
Silas has walked that far no doubt to-day.
Why didn't he go there? His brother's rich.
A somebody—director in the bank."

"He never told us that."

140   "We know it though."
"I think his brother ought to help, of course.
I'll see to that if there is need. He ought of right
To take him in, and might be willing to—
He may be better than appearances.
145   But have some pity on Silas. Do you think
If he had any pride in claiming kin
Or anything he looked for from his brother,
He'd keep so still about him all this time?"

"I wonder what's between them."

150   "I can tell you.
Silas is what he is—we wouldn't mind him—
But just the kind that kinsfolk can't abide.
He never did a thing so very bad.
He don't know why he isn't quite as good
155   As anybody. Worthless though he is,
He won't be made ashamed to please his brother."

"I can't think Si ever hurt anyone."

"No, but he hurt my heart the way he lay.
And rolled his old head on that sharp-edged chair-back.
160   He wouldn't let me put him on the lounge.
You must go in and see what you can do.
I made the bed up for him there to-night.
You'll be surprised at him—how much he's broken.
His working days are done; I'm sure of it."

165   "I'd not be in a hurry to say that."

"I haven't been. Go, look, see for yourself.
But, Warren, please remember how it is:
He's come to help you ditch the meadow.
He has a plan. You mustn't laugh at him.
170   He may not speak of it, and then he may.
I'll sit and see if that small sailing cloud
Will hit or miss the moon."

                 It hit the moon.
Then there were three there, making a dim row,

175   The moon, the little silver cloud, and she.

Warren returned—too soon, it seemed to her,
Slipped to her side, caught up her hand and waited.

"Warren?" she questioned.

"Dead," was all he answered.   /1402

• *Skill Development*

According to the implied meaning in the selection, answer the following with *T* (true), *F* (false), or *CT* (can't tell).

_____   1. Warren had just come back from the grocery store.
_____   2. Silas always asked Warren for higher wages than the other workers.
_____   3. Silas had gone to see his brother before coming to Mary and Warren's farm.
_____   4. Each year when Silas returned he always said the same thing to Warren about why he had come back.
_____   5. Silas wanted to teach Harold to load hay only to enhance his own ego, and not at all for Harold's benefit.
_____   6. This time Warren probably would have absolutely made Silas leave if he had not been dead.
_____   7. Silas' brother probably has more money than Mary and Warren.
_____   8. Mary seems to understand Silas better than Warren.
_____   9. Warren had been told, not by Silas but by his brother, that the two were kin.
_____   10. Mary was particularly fond of Silas because she did not have any children.

• *Comprehension Questions*

After reading the selection answer the following questions with *a, b, c,* or *d.*

_____   1. The best statement of the main idea of this selection is
              a. Warren and Mary did not want to be burdened with Silas for another winter
              b. when a man is not accepted by his family, his friends are burdened with his problems
              c. the unreliable hired man had accomplished little in his life and returned home to the place he felt most comfortable to die
              d. Silas ruined his life by using the same excuses for his lack of accomplishment

_____ 2. If this selection were presented in exactly the same format as a stage play, the number of characters seen on stage would be
a. two
b. three
c. four
d. five

_____ 3. Warren does not want to hire Silas again because of Silas' past history of
a. arguing with Warren
b. deserting Warren at harvest time
c. causing unpleasant friction with Harold
d. doing careless and unsatisfactory work

_____ 4. Silas said he had come back "to ditch the meadow" and "clear the upper pasture" because
a. he knew it needed to be done
b. he had always done it in the past
c. he knew they expected him to say it
d. he wanted to feel as if he had an important reason for being there

_____ 5. The author suggests that Harold probably thought of Silas as all of the following except
a. an uneducated man
b. a failure
c. an expert teacher of haying technique
d. an argumentative know-it-all

_____ 6. The author's major purpose in contrasting Harold Wilson and Silas is to show that
a. Silas was not respected for his one accomplishment and had little hope for the future
b. Harold was too well educated to be working in haying for the rest of his life
c. a young person needs more than book learning to become educated
d. Silas was not able to teach his expertise to anyone

_____ 7. In his life, as well as in his resting position by the stove, Silas is compared to
a. a gypsy
b. a family member
c. a hound dog
d. a lonely child

_____ 8. Mary and Warren define home as a place that must be
a. accepting
b. approving
c. deserved
d. welcoming

_____ 9. Silas did not go to his brother's house because
a. his brother would make him feel shame at his failure
b. he and his brother had an argument over money
c. his brother threw him out of the house
d. his brother is a banker and does not want Silas around

_____ 10. The feeling that Mary and Warren had for Silas was
     a. respect for his ability to work
     b. dislike for his worthlessness
     c. pretended belief that he was better than he was
     d. understanding and acceptance of what he was

Answer the following with *T* (true), *F* (false), or *CT* (can't tell).

_____ 11. Mary had been at home all day.
_____ 12. The setting for the story is the porch steps of a farmhouse.
_____ 13. The time-setting of the poem is sunset.
_____ 14. The author implies that Silas probably knew he was going to die.
_____ 15. Mary and Warren did not care that Silas had died.

● *Vocabulary*

According to the way the boldface word was used in the selection, indicate *a, b, c,* or *d* for the word or phrase that gives the best definition.

_____ 1. "Mary sat **musing**"
  a. dozing
  b. pondering
  c. weaving
  d. warming

_____ 2. "Trying to **coax** him off"
  a. persuade
  b. force
  c. steal
  d. rush

_____ 3. "Some **humble** way"
  a. sly
  b. secret
  c. desperate
  d. lowly

_____ 4. "**daft** on education"
  a. foolish
  b. capable
  c. intelligent
  d. spoiled

_____ 5. "young college boy's **assurance**"
  a. agility
  b. knowledge
  c. confidence
  d. mannerism

_____ 6. "**piqued** him"
  a. interested
  b. endangered
  c. flattered
  d. provoked

_____ 7. "**taut** with the dew"
  a. shining
  b. covered
  c. tightly stretched
  d. wet

_____ 8. "from garden bed to **eaves**"
  a. barns
  b. edges of the roof
  c. windows
  d. trees

_____ 9. "he **mocked** gently"
  a. attacked
  b. realized
  c. ridiculed
  d. questioned

_____ 10. "kinsfolk can't **abide**"
  a. put up with
  b. respect
  c. forget
  d. invite

- ### *Possible Essay Exam Question*

  Explain why the hired man felt that Mary and Warren's place was his home. (Hint: Discuss his character traits and how his experiences with Mary and Warren related to his sense of worth.)

- ### *Word Parts*

  Study the meaning of the word parts and supply an additional example from your own vocabulary. In the second set of items, use the corresponding part to write the word that best fits the definition.

Word Part	Meaning	Example	Your Example
1. lith	stone	lithograph	_____
2. dox	opinion, belief	paradox	_____
3. agon	contest, struggle	antagonist	_____
4. soph	wise	sophomore	_____
5. solus	alone	soliloquy	_____
6. loc, loqui	speak	circumlocution	_____
7. verbum	word	verbatum	_____
8. fix	fix	affix	_____
9. agi, ager	move, go, do	agenda	_____
10. meta	change	metaphor	_____

1. large single stone or structure _____

2. conventional; conforming to religious doctrine _____

3. to cause to suffer; to torture _____

4. urban; cultured _____

5. confinement alone _____

6. extremely talkative _____

7. unnecessarily wordy _____

8. to focus on intensely _____

9. skillful; active; quick _____

10. process of energy use by living cells _____

Selection 2: Literature

Mark Twain, from *Huckleberry Finn*

Col. Grangerford*

There was another clan of aristocracy around there—five or six families—mostly of the name of Shepherdson. They was as high-toned and well born and rich and grand as the tribe of Grangerfords. The Shepherdsons and Grangerfords used the same steamboat landing, which was about two mile above our house; so sometimes when I went up there with a lot of our folks I used to see a lot of the Shepherdsons there on their fine horses.

One day Buck and me was away out in the woods hunting, and heard a horse coming. We was crossing the road. Buck says:

"Quick! Jump for the woods!"

We done it, and then peeped down the woods through the leaves. Pretty soon a splendid young man came galloping down the road, setting his horse easy and looking like a soldier. He had his gun across his pommel. I had seen him before. It was young Harney Shepherdson. I heard Buck's gun go off at my ear, and Harney's hat tumbled off from his head. He grabbed his gun and rode straight to the place where we was hid. But we didn't wait. We started through the woods on a run. The woods warn't thick, so I looked over my shoulder to dodge the bullet, and twice I seen Harney cover Buck with his gun; and then he rode away the way he come—to get his hat, I reckon, but I couldn't see. We never stopped running till we got home. The old gentleman's eyes blazed a minute—'twas pleasure, mainly, I judged—then his face sort of smoothed down, and he says, kind of gentle:

"I don't like that shooting from behind a bush. Why didn't you step into the road, my boy?"

"The Shepherdsons don't, father. They always take advantage."

Miss Charlotte she held her head up like a queen while Buck was telling his tale, and her nostrils spread and her eyes snapped. The two young men looked dark, but never said nothing. Miss Sophia she turned pale, but the color come back when she found the man warn't hurt.

Soon as I could get Buck down by the corncribs under the trees by ourselves, I says:

"Did you want to kill him, Buck?"

"Well, I bet I did."

"What did he do to you?"

"Him? He never done nothing to me."

"Well, then, what did you want to kill him for?"

"Why, nothing—only it's on account of the feud."

"What's a feud?"

"Why, where was you raised? Don't you know what a feud is?"

"Never heard of it before—tell me about it."

"Well," says Buck, "a feud is this way: A man has a quarrel with another man, and kills him; then that other man's brother kills *him*; then the other brothers, on both sides, goes for one another; then the *cousins* chip in—and by and by everybody's killed off, and there ain't no more feud. But it's kind of slow, and takes a long time."

"Has this one been going on long, Buck?"

"Well, I should *reckon!* It started thirty years ago, or som'ers along there. There was trouble 'bout something, and then a lawsuit to settle it; and the suit went agin one of the men, and so he up and shot the man that won the suit—which he would naturally do, of course. Anybody would."

"What was the trouble about, Buck?—land?"

"I reckon maybe—I don't know."

"Well, who done the shooting? Was it a Grangerford or a Shepherdson?"

"Laws, how do *I* know? It was so long ago."

*LEARNING STRATEGY: Imagine the scenes in your mind and try to understand Huck's difficulty in accepting Buck's philosophy and way of life. Look for the irony in each situation.

"Don't anybody know?"

"Oh, yes, pa knows, I reckon, and some of the other old people; but they don't know now what the row was about in the first place."

50   "Has there been many killed, Buck?"

"Yes; right smart chance of funerals. But they don't always kill. Pa's got a few buckshot in him; but he don't mind it 'cuz he don't weigh much anyway. Bob's been carved up some with a bowie, and Tom's been hurt once or twice."

"Has anybody been killed this year, Buck?"

55   "Yes; we got one and they got one. 'Bout three months ago my cousin Bud, fourteen year old, was riding through the woods on t'other side of the river, and didn't have no weapon with him, which was blame' foolishness, and in a lonesome place he hears a horse a-coming behind him, and sees old Baldy Shepherdson a-linkin' after him with his gun in his hand and his white hair a-flying in the wind; and 'stead of jumping off and taking to the brush, Bud 'lowed he

60   could outrun him; so they had it, nip and tuck, for five mile or more, the old man a-gaining all the time; so at last Bud seen it warn't any use, so he stopped and faced around so as to have the bullet holes in front, you know, and the old man he rode up and shot him down. But he didn't git much chance to enjoy his luck, for inside of a week our folks laid *him* out."

"I reckon that old man was a coward, Buck."

65   "I reckon he *warn't* a coward. Not by a blame' sight. There ain't a coward amongst them Shepherdsons—not a one. And there ain't no cowards amongst the Grangerfords either. Why, that old man kep' up his end in a fight one day for half an hour against three Grangerfords, and come out winner. They was all a-horseback; he lit off of his horse and got behind a little woodpile, and kep' his horse before him to stop the bullets; but the Grangerfords

70   stayed on their horses and capered around the old man, and peppered away at him, and he peppered away at them. Him and his horse both went home pretty leaky and crippled, but the Grangerfords had to be *fetched* home and one of 'em was dead, and another died the next day. No, sir; if a body's out hunting for cowards he don't want to fool away any time amongst them Shepherdsons, becuz they don't breed any of that *kind*."

75   Next Sunday we all went to church, about three mile, everybody a-horseback. The men took their guns along, so did Buck, and kept them between their knees or stood them handy against the wall. The Shepherdsons done the same. It was pretty ornery preaching—all about brotherly love, and such-like tiresomeness; but everybody said it was a good sermon, and they all talked it over going home, and had such a powerful lot to say about faith and good works

80   and free grace and preforeordestination, and I don't know what all, that it did seem to me to be one of the roughest Sundays I had run across yet.   /1134

• *Skill Development*

According to the implied meaning in the selection, answer the following with *T* (true), *F* (false), or *CT* (can't tell).

_____   1. Huck probably is not a member of the Grangerford family.

_____   2. The Shepherdsons had more money than the Grangerfords.

_____   3. Miss Sophia's reaction indicates that she might have had a feeling of affection for Harney Shepherdson.

_____   4. Miss Charlotte probably would have been pleased if Harney Shepherdson had been killed.

_____   5. Buck's father seemed rather happy to hear that Buck had shot at Harney.

_____ 6. The author feels that Harney probably does not know what the feud is about.

_____ 7. The author probably feels that both the Shepherdsons and Grangerfords are cowards.

_____ 8. The author feels that the church service softened the hearts of the feuding families and gave them a hope of peace.

_____ 9. Buck seems to admire the courage of Baldy Shepherdson even though he killed an unarmed boy.

_____ 10. In a previous encounter Buck had killed a Grangerford.

- ## Comprehension Questions

  After reading the selection, answer the following questions with *a, b, c,* or *d.*

_____ 1. The best statement of the main idea of this selection is
   a. families can feud and kill but still respect each other
   b. the status of the family has a bearing on the legal severity of the alleged crime
   c. feuding is an accepted tradition of southern aristocracy
   d. feuding is nothing more than senseless killing, regardless of the social status of the families involved

_____ 2. All of the following are untrue about the shooting incident between Buck and Harney Shepherdson except
   a. to Huck's surprise Buck stepped into the road and shot at Harney
   b. Buck shot from behind a bush and then ran away
   c. Harney provoked Buck into an attack
   d. Huck took pleasure in the excitement of the surprise attack

_____ 3. Harney's reaction to the surprise attack was to
   a. shoot at Buck and Huck   c. pick up his hat and run away
   b. shoot only at Huck   d. chase the boys all the way home

_____ 4. The author implies that Pa Grangerford is primarily concerned with
   a. the well-being of his sons
   b. the honor of the family name
   c. teaching his family the Christian way of life
   d. finding a solution to the feud

_____ 5. In Buck's explanation of the feud, all of the following are true except
   a. it started before he was born
   b. the original conflict between the families was probably solved in a court of law
   c. no one now living remembers the exact reason for the lawsuit
   d. the disagreement was definitely over land claims

_____ 6. Bud was killed by Baldy Shepherdson because
   a. Bud had killed his cousin
   b. Bud jumped off his horse and ran into the brush
   c. Bud was not able to outrun the pursuing Baldy
   d. Baldy was intimidated by Bud's face-to-face confrontation

_____ 7. The author suggests that Huck interpreted the killing of Bud as
  a. a lucky break for Baldy Shepherdson
  b. a cowardly old man killing an unarmed boy
  c. a foolish mistake on the part of Bud
  d. his friend Buck interpreted it

_____ 8. The incident in which the three Grangerfords were chasing after Baldy resulted in
  a. Baldy's being killed
  b. the death of Baldy's horse
  c. the death of two Grangerfords
  d. the death of all three Grangerfords

_____ 9. The author's purpose in including a description of the Sunday church service is to show
  a. the hypocrisy of the situation
  b. that Huck didn't like to go to church
  c. that a good sermon can change a person's life
  d. that the feuding families were religious at heart

_____ 10. In the author's characterization of the two boys, Huck is portrayed as
  a. less mature in moral concerns than Buck
  b. innocent while Buck is portrayed as evil
  c. a person with little understanding of life who now has Buck as a teacher
  d. more understanding of human values than Buck

Answer the following questions with *T* (true), *F* (false), or *CT* (can't tell).

_____ 11. The steamboat landing was neutral territory in which no killing was allowed.

_____ 12. No guns were allowed inside the church.

_____ 13. When the shooting incident with Harney Shepherdson occurred, Buck and Huck had been hunting in the woods for rabbits.

_____ 14. The women in the feuding families were never killed.

_____ 15. Buck's mother was dead and Miss Charlotte was the female head of the family.

• *Vocabulary*

According to the way the boldface word or phrase was used in the selection, indicate *a, b, c,* or *d* for the word or phrase that gives the best definition.

_____ 1. "clan of **aristocracy**"
  a. believers
  b. warriors
  c. country people
  d. privileged upper class

_____ 2. "his gun across his **pommel**"
  a. stomach
  b. lap
  c. saddle front
  d. shoulder pads

_____ 3. "on account of the **feud**"
  a. lawsuit
  b. quarrel for revenge
  c. secret mission
  d. compromise

_____ 4. "what the **row** was"
  a. dispute
  b. line
  c. oar
  d. race

_____ 5. "carved up some with a **bowie**"
a. sword
b. hunting knife
c. kitchen carver
d. hachet

_____ 6. "**nip and tuck** for five mile"
a. uneven
b. familiar territory
c. exhausting
d. closely contested

_____ 7. "**capered** around the old man"
a. combined
b. spread out
c. frisked
d. organized

_____ 8. "pretty **ornery** preaching"
a. inspiring
b. low-down
c. high-minded
d. relevant

_____ 9. "and such-like **tiresomeness**"
a. boredom
b. cleverness
c. dishonesty
d. commonness

_____ 10. "free grace and
preforeordestination"
a. spiritual leadership
b. the holy spirit
c. forgiveness
d. mispronunciation of _predestination_

• *Possible Essay Exam Question*

Explain why Huck finds it difficult to accept Buck's philosophy of life. (Hint: Discuss the irony that Huck sees in specific incidents such as explaining a feud, defining a coward, and going to church. What does he question about these situations?)

• *Word Parts*

Study the meaning of the word parts and supply an additional example from your own vocabulary. In the second set of items, use the corresponding part to write the word that best fits the definition.

Word Part	Meaning	Example	Your Example
1. cred, credit	believe	incredulous	_____
2. amor	love	amiable	_____
3. biblio	book	bibliotheraphy	_____
4. pseudo	false	pseudoclassical	_____
5. syn, sys, syl	with, together	system	_____
6. lingua	language	linguist	_____
7. nyn, nomen, nomin	name	nomenclature	_____
8. sangui	blood	sangfroid	_____

9. tui, tuit, tut   guard, teach   tutorial   _____

10. techni   skill, art   pyrotechnics   _____

1. qualifications   _____

2. strongly loving; enamored   _____

3. list of writings referred to in a text   _____

4. false name; pen name   _____

5. emotional feeling for another's misfortune   _____

6. proficient in two languages   _____

7. word of opposite meaning   _____

8. blood red, ruddy; confident   _____

9. immediate insight without rational thought   _____

10. particular method   _____

Selection 3: History

Shepard B. Clough et al., from *A History of the Western World*

Mary of Scotland*

Some months before Philip II went home to Spain, his second wife, Mary of England, died (1558). Her twenty-five-year-old half sister Elizabeth, daughter of the indiscreet and unfortunate Ann Boleyn, succeeded her to the English throne. Three years later, Elizabeth's young second cousin, Mary Stuart, now dowager queen of France after the death of her husband, Francis II,
5   returned to Scotland, a land that she barely remembered. Already, at the age of nineteen, this young lady had begun to style herself Queen of England as well as of Scotland and to assert that she, not Elizabeth, was the legitimate heiress of Mary Tudor.

Mary Stuart was an altogether remarkable young woman, about whom it is almost impossible to remain objectively impartial. Even when one discounts the flattery that crept into descriptions
10   of her, one is inclined to accept the contemporary evidence that Mary was extraordinarily beautiful, though tall for a girl—perhaps over six feet. In addition to beauty, she had almost every other attractive attribute in high degree: courage, wit, resourcefulness, loyalty, and responsiveness, in short everything needful for worldly greatness save discretion in her relations with men and a willingness to compromise, if need be, on matters of religion. She was a
15   thoroughgoing Roman Catholic, a good lover, and a magnificent hater.

During much of Mary's sojourn in France, Scotland was ruled in her name and in French interests by her mother, Mary of Guise. Ostensibly, Scotland still adhered to its traditional

*LEARNING STRATEGY: Look for the opportunities that Mary had for greatness and analyze the events in her life and flaws in her character that led to her demise.

Beheading of Mary, Queen of Scots, 1587.

20

French alliance; in fact, the marriage of young Mary with the French *dauphin* had made the Franco-Scottish connection seem even closer and to point toward the time when the two kingdoms would be united under one ruler. But religious changes that had been taking place in Scotland during the regency made such a result more and more unlikely.

Mary's Romantic End as Queen of Scotland

There is little doubt that Mary thought of the Scottish throne as a stepping-stone to the crown of England. She remarkably improved her chances of achieving that goal when she married her cousin who was next in line, after her, to the English throne. Henry, Lord Darnley, was also

25

a great-grandchild of Henry VII. Mary seemed at first truly to love her new husband, and was thus enabled to perform a rare feat: to combine guileful statecraft with the satisfaction of personal desires. Darnley's main function, from a historical point of view, was to get Mary with the child who eventually became James VI of Scotland and James I of England. Darnley was not an admirable human being, as Mary came bitterly to realize. He repeatedly betrayed

30

his wife in a number of political schemes in which he fully revealed his grasping shallowness at

the same time that his attitude toward Mary was embittered by her unfaithfulness. As Darnley's despicable character became more and more apparent, Mary seemed to come under the influence, politically and emotionally, of her Italian secretary, David Rizzio, and, after him, of a hardy ruffian named Bothwell. One of Darnley's plots led to Rizzio's being murdered in
35   Mary's presence by a band of conspirators. Although she was anxious to be rid of this difficult husband, Mary quailed at "divorce"[1] because she feared that such a move would jeopardize the legitimacy of her son. Accordingly, Darnley was killed, either blown up with a charge of gunpowder or strangled. It would seem that there is no way for historians to determine whether Mary had a hand in this murder; but it is quite clear that, within a shockingly short period of
40   time, she married Bothwell, who was thought by almost everyone to have killed Darnley.[2]

This had all the appearances of a very nasty business; and the upshot was that Mary lost all significant support in Scotland. For a while she was romantically locked up in a castle on an island in a loch from which she just as romantically escaped; and eventually she fled to England (1569) where she threw herself on the mercy of her cousin Queen Elizabeth. Mary left behind
45   her an infant son in whose name a series of regents governed tempestuous Scotland as the new kirk tried to consolidate its position. When he came of age, James Stuart, a striking contrast to his mother, lent his learned mind to the task of trying to transform Scotland into a modern and centralized absolutism. Though a Protestant, he came into conflict with the Presbyterians over the question of how the kirk should be governed. James believed strongly that an episcopal
50   organization of the kirk was necessary to support the kind of monarchy that he had in mind. In this regard, his ideas were the ones entertained by most contemporary monarchs, whether they were Protestant or Roman Catholic. Later, after little success on the Scottish scene, James was to try to apply these notions on the larger state of English affairs.

The story of his mother in Scotland was also a tale of failure. She proved powerless to act as
55   an effective instrument of the Catholic Counter Reformation or to introduce the new style of government in Scotland because she was not *of* the society she came briefly to rule. In short, she was Mary, Queen over Scotland, and not Mary, Queen of Scots. One is permitted privately to play the game of speculating about what would have happened in Scotland if Mary Stuart had been able to control her love life, to galvanize the large number of Scottish Roman
60   Catholics, and to survive her cousin Elizabeth. But that is not the way it happened. Mary failed; she went to England; Elizabeth incarcerated her and eventually consented to her execution.   /1049

• *Skill Development*

According to the implied meaning in the selection, answer the following with *T* (true), *F* (false), or *CT* (can't tell).

_____   1. Mary was queen of Scotland, while she lived in France.
_____   2. The author suggests that Ann Boleyn was somewhat responsible for her own misfortunes.
_____   3. Because of exaggerated accounts, Mary's actual beauty is questionable.

[1]It is to be remembered that the Roman Catholic Church does not recognize divorce *per se*. According to the Roman Catholic Church the only grounds for dissolving a marriage is the fact that the marriage never existed as a valid sacrament.
[2]Bothwell was brought to trial. Inasmuch as he brought 4,000 armed men with him, it is not surprising that the prosecution could find no one to testify against him and that he was found guiltless.

_____ 4. The author feels that Mary's unwillingness to compromise on religious matters was a greater failure than her indiscretion with men.

_____ 5. Darnley was attempting to gain power for himself in his political plots against Mary.

_____ 6. Darnley's men killed Rizzio because he and Mary were having a love affair.

_____ 7. The author believes that Bothwell killed Darnley at Mary's request.

_____ 8. Darnley would have been hanged for Rizzio's murder if he had not been killed.

_____ 9. Darnley's body was mutilated and it was difficult to tell how he died.

_____ 10. There was an attempt in Scotland to punish Mary after the death of Darnley.

• **Comprehension Questions**

   After reading the selection, answer the following questions with *a, b, c,* or *d.*

_____ 1. The best statement of the main idea of this selection is
   a. Mary of Scotland's success as a queen was marred by her love life, her religion, and her foreign upbringing
   b. Mary of Scotland had her first husband killed to strengthen her rule over Scotland
   c. Mary spent much of her life in an unsuccessful quest for the English throne
   d. Mary's greatest success was her son James, who became king of England

_____ 2. The ruler of England directly before Elizabeth was
   a. Mary of Guise
   b. Ann Boleyn
   c. Mary Stuart
   d. Mary Tudor

_____ 3. The author suggests that Scotland and France did not unite under one ruler because of
   a. Mary's love affairs
   b. religious changes in Scotland
   c. Queen Elizabeth's power
   d. Mary's Roman Catholic belief

_____ 4. The author suggests the development of an early conflict between Mary Stuart and Elizabeth because
   a. they were jealous of each other's beauty
   b. they both wanted to be queen of England
   c. Elizabeth was childless and Mary's son later became king of England
   d. Mary was Catholic and Elizabeth was Protestant

_____ 5. The author suggests that the primary reason Mary married Lord Darnley was
   a. for love
   b. to have a child who would be next in line to rule England

     c. to make herself eventually queen of England

     d. to aggravate Elizabeth who was still unmarried

_____ 6. In the author's opinion, Lord Darnley's "despicable character" was

     a. a result of Mary's infidelity

     b. inherited from Henry VII

     c. an unfortunate fact that Mary gradually realized

     d. revealed first in the murder of Rizzio

_____ 7. The death of Darnley resulted in all of the following except

     a. the trial and conviction of Bothwell

     b. a loss of support for Mary

     c. the continued legitimacy of James Stuart

     d. the marriage of Mary and Bothwell

_____ 8. How many times was Mary of Scotland married?

     a. one   c. three

     b. two   d. four

_____ 9. According to the author, all of the following are true of James Stuart except

     a. his religion was different from his mother's

     b. his rule of Scotland was very successful

     c. he became king while still an infant

     d. he attempted to do more than his mother had to strengthen the monarchy in Scotland

_____ 10. From information in this selection the reader might infer that Elizabeth consented to Mary's execution because

     a. she thought Mary had killed Darnley

     b. Elizabeth did not want Mary to return to Scotland

     c. Mary wanted to be queen of England

     d. Elizabeth was not of the Roman Catholic faith

Answer the following questions with *T* (true), *F* (false), or *CT* (can't tell).

_____ 11. Bothwell engineered Mary's escape from the castle in which she was imprisoned.

_____ 12. The author implies that Mary did not readily forgive her enemies.

_____ 13. Mary of Scotland was older than Queen Elizabeth.

_____ 14. Queen Elizabeth did not want to be allied with the Germans.

_____ 15. Bothwell used a show of force to influence his trial for murder.

• *Vocabulary*

According to the way the boldface word was used in the selection, indicate *a*, *b*, *c*, or *d* for the word or phrase that gives the best definition.

____ 1. "**indiscreet** and unfortunate"

     a. disagreeable

     b. unkind

     c. uninteresting

     d. imprudent

____ 2. "**dowager** queen of France"

     a. foreign

     b. titled widow

     c. unpopular

     d. withdrawn

_____ 3. "Mary's **sojourn** in France"
a. brief stay
b. rule
c. long journey
d. exile

_____ 4. "**adhered** to its traditional French alliance"
a. prayed
b. stuck
c. falsely admitted
d. secretly rejected

_____ 5. "**guileful** statecraft"
a. honest
b. hopeful
c. courageous
d. cunning

_____ 6. "a hardy **ruffian**"
a. lawless person
b. follower
c. countryman
d. revolutionary

_____ 7. "Mary **quailed**"
a. cried
b. fought
c. lost courage
d. flew out

_____ 8. "an island in a **loch**"
a. cage
b. country
c. lake
d. city

_____ 9. a series of **regents** governed
a. appointed rulers
b. poor leaders
c. lords of parliament
d. elderly cousins

_____ 10. "**tempestuous** Scotland"
a. loyal
b. calm
c. official
d. turbulent

• *Possible Essay Exam Question*

Trace the major events that contributed to Mary's failure as queen of Scotland. (Hint: Select the most important events in Mary's failure to rule in Scotland and explain their significance in time order.)

• *Word Parts*

Study the meaning of the word parts and supply an additional example from your own vocabulary. In the second set of items, use the corresponding part to write the word that best fits the description.

Word Parts	Meaning	Example	Your Example
1. lin	line, thread	linear	_____
2. anni	year	annually	_____
3. the, theo	god	theology	_____
4. idio	peculiar, private	idiomatic	_____
5. se	apart, away	secular	_____
6. ced, cess, ceed	go, move along	recession	_____

7. dyn, dynamo	power	dynasty	_____
8. intellect, intellig	power to know and think	intelligentsia	_____
9. nunci, nounc	declare, warn	denunciation	_____
10. grat	pleasing	ingratitùde	_____

1. ancestry   _____

2. annual celebration of a special day   _____

3. one who does not believe in God   _____

4. personal peculiarity or quirk   _____

5. withdrawal of states from the union   _____

6. dead   _____

7. an explosive   _____

8. understandable; clear   _____

9. to make public knowledge   _____

10. felicitations; good wishes   _____

Chapter Nine

How many of the following statements are true?

1. Textbooks contain facts and not opinions.
2. The historical account of an incident is based on fact and thus does not vary from one author to another.
3. Except for the style of the author, freshman biology textbooks do not vary in their informational content.
4. Textbooks are supposed to be free from author's interpretation.

Unfortunately, too many students tend to answer, "all of the above." Paying big money for a thick book with lots of facts and an authoritative title does not necessitate, contrary to student belief, that the text be an unbiased chronicle of the nation's past. No purity rule applies to textbook writing. In the case of history, the author portrays the past from a personal and unique perspective. The name of the first President of the United States does not vary from one text to another, but the emphasis on the importance of Washington's administration might.

Authors of factual material, like authors of fiction, have opinions, theories, and prejudices that influence their presentation of the subject matter. When facts are slanted, though not necessarily distorted, toward the author's personal beliefs, the written material reflects the *biases* of that author. Bias is not an indication of evil intent; it is merely a signpost to the aware and responsible reader.

Would a London professor write the same account of American history during the revolutionary period as a native Philadelphia scholar? Probably not, because they look at the problem from different angles—one as a colonial uprising on a distant continent and the other as a struggle for personal freedom and survival. The two authors are writing from different points of view; identifying each particular viewpoint helps you evaluate the material. For example, how would you evaluate the validity of the descriptions of your blind date for Friday night by the following three persons: (1) the date's mother, (2) the person setting up the date, (3) someone who dated the person last weekend? To objectively evaluate, it is important to recognize the speaker's point of view.

The Author's Purpose

When putting the words on paper, the author always has a purpose in mind. As long as you are aware of that purpose, it doesn't matter whether it is to explain, persuade, or entertain. However, when the author's intent is to persuade but you see the material as an objective explanation, the author has gained a distinct advantage. Recognizing the author's purpose does not mean that you won't buy the product; it just means that you are a more cautious, well-informed consumer.

In both fiction and nonfiction, the author can create a consistent feeling that mirrors his own attitude toward a topic. This tone might be serious, sympathetic, cynical, argumentative, humorous, satirical, or ironical. Again, as the tone reflects the author's biases, it influences you.

To psyche out the author, ask the following questions:

1. What is the author's background?
2. Why is the author an authority on this particular subject?
3. What is the author's purpose or intent in writing this?
4. What is the author's point of view?
5. Is there another side to the issue that is not presented?

Emotional Words

The techniques of persuasion deal with selection and serve to manipulate the reader on an emotional level of decision making. In shaping opinion, certain words trigger emotional, rather than logical, reactions, and authors deliberately choose such words to elicit positive or negative responses. This same ploy is used by political campaigners to influence public opinion during elections. Notice the emotionalism surrounding the following words:

1. Positive—*the free world, efficient, patriotic, the American people, freedom loving*
2. Negative—*industrialist, opportunism, hippie, capitalism, socialistic tendencies*

Both fact and opinion are used persuasively to support positions. It is up to you to determine which is which and then to judge the issue accordingly. Adding the quoted opinion of a well-known authority to a few bits of evidence does not increase the data, yet this is an effective persuasive technique. Even though the opinion may be valid, it should not be viewed as fact.

A fact is a statement based on actual evidence or personal observation. It can be checked objectively with empirical data and proved to be either true or false. On the other hand, an opinion is a statement of personal feeling or a judgment. It reflects a belief or an interpretation rather than an accumulation of evidence, and it cannot be proved true or false. Both fact and opinion play a role in evaluation and in decision making, but you need to tell the difference between the two.

• *Exercise 1*

Read each of the following and indicate *a* for fact and *b* for opinion.

————— 1. For women locked into socioeconomic situations that cannot promise financial independence, liberation is relatively meaningless and sometimes suggests the denial of femininity as a goal.

Reece McGee et al., Sociology: An Introduction

————— 2. The territorial base from which Soviet ambitions proceed is the largest country in area on the globe.

Wheeler, Kostbade and Thoman, Regional Geography of the World

————— 3. Company sources attribute Coors' success to product quality, boasting that it "is the most expensively brewed beer in the world."

Louis Boone and David L. Kurtz, Contemporary Business

_____ 4. If you wish to "break the hunger habit" in order to gain better control over your own food intake, you might be wise to do so slowly—by putting yourself on a very irregular eating schedule.

James V. McConnell, *Understanding Human Behavior*

_____ 5. The first step in running for the nomination is to build a personal organization, because the party organization is supposed to stay neutral until the nomination is decided.

James M. Burns, J. W. Peltason and Thomas E. Cronin, *Government by the People*

_____ 6. It is true that American politics often rewards with power those who have proved that they can direct the large institutions of commerce and business, of banking, and of law, education, and philanthropy.

Kenneth Prewitt and Sidney Verba, *An Introduction to American Government*

_____ 7. Precipitation is not uniform, and neither is the distribution of population.

Robert J. Foster, *Physical Geology*

_____ 8. Through classical conditioning, infants and young children learn to respond to social or man-made stimuli (with smiles to the nursing bottle, with tears at the sight of bitter-tasting medicine) just as through operant conditioning they learn to inhibit certain responses and adopt others as habitual.

Leonard Broom and Philip Selznick, *Sociology*

_____ 9. The great affair of Henry's reign was his divorce and the separation of the English Church from Rome, which occupied the decade and a half after 1527.

Shepard B. Clough et al., *A History of the Western World*

_____ 10. Women, young girls, and even mere children were tortured by driving needles under their nails, roasting their feet in the fire, or crushing their legs under heavy weights until the marrow spurted from their bones, in order to force them to confess to filthy orgies with demons.

Edward M. Burns, *Western Civilizations*

The following exercises use examples from different subject-matter areas. Notice the authors' biases creeping into the factual presentations.

● *Exercise 2: Government*

Propaganda has been treated as an unmitigated evil, but that is a simplistic approach. Indeed, it is hard to say just where propaganda ends and education starts. Effective education may include some propaganda (in favor, say, of democratic values, the virtues of which must be taken in part on faith). And if propaganda is defined as a "method used for influencing the conduct of others on behalf of predetermined ends," then almost every person who writes or talks with a purpose becomes a propagandist. Lasswell has described propaganda as a technique for social control—"the manipulation of collective attitudes by the use of significant symbols (words, pictures, and tunes) rather than violence, bribery, or boycott." Obviously propaganda in these terms may be used for good causes as well as bad.

Burns, Peltason and Cronin, *Government by the People*

_____ 1. The author's major objective in this paragraph is to point out
   a. the good side of propaganda
   b. the bad side of propaganda
   c. both the good and bad sides of propaganda
   d. how education can combat propaganda

_____ 2. The author is assuming that the reader is already greatly aware of all of the following except
   a. the benefits of propaganda
   b. the dangers of propaganda
   c. the traditional definition of propaganda
   d. the techniques of propaganda

_____ 3. Which of the following sentences, except for a few emotive words, is a statement of fact?
   a. "Propaganda has been . . . ."
   b. "Effective education may . . . ."
   c. "And if propaganda . . . ."
   d. none of the above

_____ 4. The author's primary reason for using the quotation by Lasswell is to
   a. give an unbiased, authoritative definition of propaganda
   b. show the good and bad in propaganda
   c. add credibility to his own argument by quoting an authority
   d. give a modern definition to an overused word

_____ 5. Which of the following words, as used in this paragraph, is the least emotional?
   a. _evil_
   b. _democratic_
   c. _virtues_
   d. _education_

• _Exercise 3: Science_

The seas contain very few animals outwardly as unattractive as the oyster. Misshapen, drab, practically motionless, and devoid of expression, the oyster presents little to stir in the imagination or aesthetic sensibilities. Nevertheless, in its prosaic way, the oyster contributes more to the welfare of man than any other invertebrate of the sea, and its geologic history is long and informative. Kilometer after kilometer of oyster banks and reefs fringe the warmer borders of the continents, furnishing food and raw materials for man. The approximate annual world production of oyster meat approaches 54 million kilograms, and in several countries, especially the United States, France, the Netherlands, Japan, and Australia, oyster fishing is an important industry. Oyster shells are dredged by the thousands of tons from shallow banks and used for construction material and other purposes. A number of mollusks popularly called oysters are not really members of the genus Ostrea; among these are "pearl oysters," genus Melagrina. More than 1,000 species of oysters, including fossil and living species are known.

William Lee Stokes, _Essentials of Earth History_

_____ 1. The author's major objective in this paragraph is to emphasize the
   a. unattractive appearance of the oyster
   b. importance of the oyster to man
   c. many different species of oysters
   d. many ways in which oyster shells are used

_____ 2. Which of the following sentences is a statement of fact?
   a. "The seas contain . . . ."
   b. "Nevertheless, in its . . . ."
   c. "The approximate annual . . . ."
   d. none of the above

_____ 3. Which of the following words, as used in this paragraph, is the least emotional?
   a. *unattractive*   c. *invertebrate*
   b. *drab*   d. *welfare*

_____ 4. By stating that the "pearl oyster" is not really a member of the genus *Ostrea,* the author is trying to do all of the following except
   a. relate to what the reader already knows
   b. dispel a myth
   c. show that everything that looks like an oyster isn't one
   d. explain the process of pearl formation

_____ 5. The author seems to be most intrigued with the oyster's
   a. geologic history
   b. practically motionless position in the sea
   c. annual production of food for the world
   d. contrasting bad looks and extreme importance

• *Exercise 4: Sociology*

The American school has thus become the victim of its own success. Particularly during the decades of the great immigrations, the schools were called upon almost to create a nation. Despite the overapplication of the melting pot metaphor, they succeeded sufficiently well to cause amazement in many places abroad. But that very success, and our overcelebration of it, created further expectations that cannot be fulfilled. The public school—or the more vague conception of "education"—has become the American equivalent of a magic wand: virtually no personal or social problem exists that someone, somewhere—often educators, who ought to know better—has not assured us can be overcome through education. The current crises of our schools, from Head Start through multiversity, are testimony to the falsity of that belief. Social problems are the problems of the society as a whole. No single institution, from school to court, can hope to cope with them. Until that realization becomes widespread, the problems of the schools—and the society—will remain unresolved.

Reece McGee et al., *Sociology: An Introduction*

_____ 1. The author's major objective in this paragraph is to convince the reader that
   a. we can't expect schools to solve all problems
   b. schools create many of their own problems
   c. schools in the past shaped American society
   d. schools are not as good as they used to be

_____ 2. Which of the following sentences is, except for a few emotive words, a statement of fact?
   a. "The American school . . . ."
   b. "The public school . . . ."
   c. "The current crises . . . ."
   d. none of the above

_____ 3. The author attributes the present crises in American schools primarily to
   a. teachers
   b. students
   c. parents
   d. overexpectations

_____ 4. The author's reason for putting the word _education_ in quotation marks is
   a. because it is quoted from another source
   b. to stress a suggested meaning beyond the traditional definition
   c. to relate it personally to students
   d. to support his argument with an authoritative quote.

_____ 5. Which of the following words, as used in this paragraph, is the least emotional?
   a. _victim_   c. _vague_
   b. _amazement_   d. _multiversity_

• _Exercise 5: Literature_

love, _n._ A temporary insanity curable by marriage or by removal of the patient from the influences under which he incurred the disorder. This disease, like caries and many other ailments, is prevalent only among civilized races living under artificial conditions; barbarous nations breathing pure air and eating simple food enjoy immunity from its ravages. It is sometimes fatal, but more frequently to the physician than to the patient.

Ambrose Bierce, The Devil's Dictionary

_____ 1. The author's major objective in this selection is to
   a. praise love   c. condemn love
   b. ridicule love   d. dismiss love as a joke

_____ 2. The author feels that marriage is
   a. the beginning of love
   b. the end of love
   c. the continuation of love
   d. the vehicle of a greater growth of love

_____ 3. The author believes that love is
   a. a social necessity
   b. a part of the natural order
   c. a disease like tooth decay
   d. a lasting bond of affection

_____ 4. The author believes that the most dangerous position is
   a. to be in love
   b. to be loved by someone
   c. not to be loved
   d. to try to prevent love

_____ 5. Which of the following words, as used in this paragraph, is the least emotional?
   a. *insanity*
   b. *barbarous*
   c. *races*
   d. *ravages*

• *Exercise 6: History*

The surprising thing about the War of Independence when you compare it with other wars of liberation is not that the Americans won, but that they did not win more easily. All they had to do to gain independence was to hold what they had. The British, on the contrary, had to reconquer a vast territory in order to win. To get troops in action against the 'rebels' of 1775-83, the British government had to send them by bulky, slow-moving sailing vessels which never took less than four weeks (and often ten) to cross the Atlantic. Moreover, those who 'came three thousand miles and died, to keep the Past upon its throne,' had to be armed, clothed, and even partly fed from England, which meant more shipping, more delays, more losses at sea, and such expense as had never been known in English history.

Morison, Commager and Leuchtenburg, *A Concise History of the American Republic*

_____ 1. By referring to the war as the War of Independence, rather than the American Revolution, the author is connoting that he
   a. sympathizes with the British
   b. sympathizes with the Americans
   c. is an impartial observer
   d. is careful to use the correct terminology
_____ 2. The author's major objective in this paragraph is to
   a. show the dedication of the British to the war
   b. emphasize the difficulties confronting the British in the war
   c. minimize the American accomplishments in the war
   d. chastize the Americans for their inefficiency
_____ 3. The author is assuming that the reader
   a. has a preconceived bias in favor of the American war effort
   b. has a preconceived bias in favor of the British
   c. is unbiased in viewing the war
   d. is trying to decide which side deserved to win
_____ 4. Which of the following sentences, except for a few emotive words, is a statement of fact?
   a. "The surprising thing . . . ."
   b. "All they had . . . ."
   c. "To get troops . . . ."
   d. none of the above
_____ 5. Which of the following words, as used in this paragraph, is the least emotional?
   a. *surprising*   c. *vessels*
   b. *'rebels'*   d. *liberation*

Selection 1: Literature

Jonathan Swift, ''A Modest Proposal''

A Modest Proposal*

for Preventing the Children of Poor People in Ireland From Being a Burden to Their Parents or Country, and for Making Them Beneficial to the Public.

It is a melancholy object to those who walk through this great town or travel in the country, when they see the street, the roads, and cabin doors, crowded with beggars of the female sex, followed by three, four, or six children, all in rags, and importuning every passenger for an alms. These mothers, instead of being able to work for their honest livelihood, are forced to employ all their time in strolling to beg sustenance for their helpless infants, who, as they grow up, either turn thieves for want of work, or leave their dear native country, to fight for the Pretender in Spain, or sell themselves to the Barbadoes.

I think it is agreed by all parties that this prodigious number of children in the arms, or on the backs, or at the heels of their mothers, and frequently of their fathers, is in the present deplorable state of the kingdom a very great additional grievance; and therefore whoever could find out a fair, cheap, and easy method of making these children sound and useful members of the common-wealth, would deserve so well of the public as to have its statue up for a preserver of the nation.

But my intention is very far from being confined to provide only for the children of professed beggars; it is of much greater extent, and shall take in the whole number of infants at a certain age, who are born of parents in effect as little able to support them, as those who demand our charity in the streets.

As to my own part, having turned my thoughts, for many years, upon this important subject, and maturely weighed the several schemes of other projectors, I have always found them grossly mistaken in their computation. It is true, a child just dropt from its dam, may be supported by her milk for a solar year with little other nourishment, at most not above the value of two shillings, which the mother may certainly get, or the value in scraps, by her lawful occupation of begging; and it is exactly at one year old that I propose to provide for them in such a manner, as, instead of being a charge upon their parents, or the parish, or wanting food and raiment for the rest of their lives, they shall, on the contrary, contribute to the feeding and partly to the clothing of many thousands.

There is likewise another great advantage in my scheme, that it will prevent those voluntary abortions, and that horrid practice of women murdering their bastard children, alas! too frequent among us—sacrificing the poor innocent babes, I doubt, more to avoid the expense than the shame—which would move tears and pity in the most savage and inhuman breast.

The number of souls in this kingdom being usually reckoned one million and a half, of these I calculate there may be about two hundred thousand couples whose wives are breeders; from which number I subtract thirty thousand couples, who are able to maintain their own children, although I apprehend there cannot be so many, under the present distresses of the kingdom; but this being granted, there will remain an hundred and seventy thousand breeders. I again subtract fifty thousand, for those women who miscarry, or whose children die by accident or

*LEARNING STRATEGY: Look for the irony in this selection. What is the difference between what Swift is saying and what he really means?

William Hogarth print, Gin Lane, *broadly depicting eighteenth-century Britain.*

disease within the year. There only remain an hundred and twenty thousand children of poor
parents annually born: The question therefore is, How this number shall be reared, and
provided for: which, as I have already said, under the present situation of affairs, is utterly
40 impossible by all the methods hitherto proposed; for we can neither employ them in handicraft
or agriculture; we neither build houses (I mean in the country) nor cultivate land: They can very
seldom pick up a livelihood by stealing till they arrive at six years old, except where they are
of towardly parts, although, I confess, they learn the rudiments much earlier; during which
time they can however be properly looked upon only as probationers; as I have been informed
45 by a principal gentleman in the county of Cavan, who protested to me, that he never knew
above one or two instances under the age of six, even in a part of the kingdom so renowned
for the quickest proficiency in that art.

I am assured by our merchants, that a boy or a girl before twelve years old, is no saleable
commodity, and even when they come to this age, they will not yield above three pounds, or
50 three pounds and a half a crown at most, on the exchange; which cannot turn to account either
to the parents or kingdom, the charge of nutriment and rags having been at least four times that
value.

I shall now therefore humbly propose my own thoughts, which I hope will not be liable to
the least objection.
55 I have been assured by a very knowing American of my acquaintance in London, that a
young healthy child well nursed is at a year old a most delicious nourishing and wholesome
food, whether stewed, roasted, baked, or boiled; and I make no doubt that it will equally serve
in a fricassee, or a ragout.

I do therefore humbly offer it to public consideration, that of the hundred and twenty
60 thousand children, already computed, twenty thousand may be reserved for breed, whereof
only one-fourth part to be males; which is more than we allow to sheep, black cattle, or swine;
and my reason is that these children are seldom the fruits of marriage, a circumstance not much
regarded by our savages; therefore one male will be sufficient to serve four females. That the
remaining hundred thousand may, at a year old, be offered in the sale to the persons of quality
65 and fortune through the kingdom; always advising the mother to let them suck plentifully in the
last month, so as to render them plump and fat for a good table. A child will make two dishes
at an entertainment for friends; and when the family dines alone, the fore or hind quarter will
make a reasonable dish, and seasoned with a little pepper or salt will be very good boiled on
the fourth day, especially in winter.
70 I have reckoned upon a medium that a child just born will weight 12 pounds, and in a solar
year, if tolerably nursed, increaseth to 28 pounds. I grant this food will be somewhat dear,
and therefore very proper for landlords, who, as they have already devoured most of the
parents, seem to have the best title to the children.

Infants' flesh will be in season throughout the year, but more plentiful in March, and a little
75 before and after; for we are told by a grave author, and eminent French physician, that fish
being a prolific diet, there are more children born in Roman Catholic countries about nine
months after Lent than at any other season; therefore, reckoning a year after Lent, the markets
will be more glutted than usual, because the number of popish infants is at least three to one in
this kingdom; and therefore it will have one other collateral advantage, by lessening the number
80 of papists among us.

I have already computed the charge of nursing a beggar's child (in which list I reckon all
cottagers, laborers, and four-fifths of the farmers) to be about two shillings per annum, rags
included; and I believe no gentleman would repine to give ten shillings for the carcass of a
good fat child, which, as I have said, will make four dishes of excellent nutritive meat, when
85 he hath only some particular friend or his own family to dine with him. Thus the squire will
learn to be a good landlord, and grow popular among his tenants; the mother will have eight
shillings net profit, and be fit for work till she produces another child.

90   Those who are more thrifty (as I must confess the times require) may flay the carcass, the skin of which artificially dressed will make admirable gloves for ladies, and summer boots for fine gentlemen.

As to our city of Dublin, shambles may be appointed for this purpose in the most convenient parts of it, and butchers we may be assured will not be wanting; although I rather recommend buying the children alive and dressing them hot from the knife, as we do roasting pigs.

95   I can think of no one objection that will possibly be raised against this proposal, unless it should be urged that the number of people will be thereby much lessened in the kingdom. This I freely own, and 'twas indeed one principal design in offering it to the world. I desire the reader will observe that I calculate my remedy for this one individual kingdom of Ireland, and for no other that ever was, is, or, I think, ever can be upon earth. Therefore let no man talk to me of other expedients: of taxing our absentees at five shillings a pound: of using neither
100   clothes, nor household furniture, except what is of our own growth and manufacture: of utterly rejecting the materials and instruments that promote foreign luxury: of curing the expensiveness of pride, vanity, idleness, and gaming in our women: of introducing a vein of parsimony, prudence and temperance: of learning to love our country, where in we differ even from Laplanders, and the inhabitants of Topinamboo: of quitting our animosities, and factions, not
105   act any longer like the Jews, who were murdering one another at the very moment their city was taken: of being a little cautious not to sell our country and consciences for nothing: of teaching landlords to have at least one degree of mercy towards their tenants. Lastly, of putting a spirit of honesty, industry, and skill into our shop-keepers, who, if a resolution could now be taken to buy only our native goods, would immediately unite to cheat and exact upon us in the
110   price, the measure, and the goodness, nor could ever yet be brought to make one fair proposal of just dealing, though often and earnestly invited to it.

I profess, in the sincerity of my heart, that I have not the least personal interest in endeavoring to promote this necessary work, having no other motive than the public good of my country, by advancing our trade, providing for infants, relieving the poor, and giving
115   some pleasure to the rich. I have no children by which I can propose to get a single penny; the youngest being nine years old, and my wife past child-bearing.   /1869

• *Skill Development*

Answer the following with *T* (true), *F* (false), or *CT* (can't tell).

_____   1. The author's major purpose in this selection is to make the reader laugh.
_____   2. The author uses statistics to add credibility to his proposal.
_____   3. The author's organizational strategy is to sell the reader on the need and advantages of his plan before explaining it.
_____   4. The author feels that poor families take advantage of landlords.

Which of the following word(s), as used in this selection, is the least emotional?

_____   5. a. *cabin doors*
                  b. *honest livelihood*
                  c. *helpless infants*
                  d. *native country*

_____ 6. a. *parties*
b. *prodigious*
c. *great*
d. *deplorable*

_____ 7. a. *breeders*
b. *miscarry*
c. *stealing*
d. *agriculture*

For each of the following excerpts, indicate *a* for fact and *b* for opinion.

_____ 8. "It is true, a child just dropt from its dam, may be supported by her milk for a solar year with little other nourishment . . . ."

_____ 9. "The number of souls in this kingdom being usually reckoned one million and a half . . . ."

_____ 10. "I have no children by which I can propose to get a single penny . . . ."

• **Comprehension Questions**

After reading the selection, answer the following questions with *a, b, c,* or *d.*

_____ 1. The best statement of the main idea of this selection is
a. the poverty in Ireland is so desperate that only a drastic reduction in the population can save the country from complete desolation
b. the solution to the problem of poverty in Ireland is not the eating of children, as the author suggests, but the positive movement of the government and people toward honesty, industry, and national support
c. the eating of meat, as dramatized by the eating of children, is savage and cruel and serves only to further reduce the ability of a poor country to produce food for its inhabitants
d. even though eating the children is an exaggerated solution, the poor deserve to be punished for the problems of poverty that they have created in Ireland

_____ 2. The author states that he intends his proposal to apply to the children of
a. professional beggars only
b. the rich and poor alike
c. parents who cannot afford them
d. beggars and politicians

_____ 3. The major reason the author proposes the age of one year for the sale of a child is because the child would then
a. be most plump and tender
b. not yet be educated in the ways of thievery
c. be taken away before parental attachment develops
d. bring the greatest profit for the least expense

_____ 4. The author feels that abortion is mainly due to
   a. unfeeling mothers
   b. financial necessity
   c. shame
   d. the country's laws regarding unwed mothers

_____ 5. The author proposes, through careful calculation, that the number of children to be sold for food each year should be
   a. two hundred thousand
   b. one hundred and seventy thousand
   c. one hundred and twenty thousand
   d. one hundred thousand

_____ 6. In the author's proposal the sex ratio of the children who are to be sold for food at the age of one year
   a. should be half male and half female
   b. should be one fourth male and three fourths female
   c. should be largely female
   d. is not determined

_____ 7. The author implies that landlords
   a. have good taste and deserve the best
   b. take unfair advantage of the poor
   c. are popular among their tenants
   d. teach mercy to their tenants

_____ 8. Underlying the satire of this selection, the author seriously proposes all of the following solutions to the poverty problems of Ireland except
   a. a form of absentee taxation
   b. the purchase of native goods before foreign imports
   c. a national concern for thrift and a love of country
   d. an extermination of the poor similar to the murdering of Jews

_____ 9. The irony of the author's final statements is that
   a. his concern is purely for the good of the country
   b. he will not be affected by the cruelty of his proposal
   c. he cannot realize any profits from his own proposal
   d. he does not care about the poor or the country

_____ 10. The author uses satire in this selection for all of the following reasons except
   a. to dramatize the horror and desperation of the problem
   b. to entertain
   c. to lessen the impact of the problem
   d. to shock

Answer the following with _T_ (true), _F_ (false), or _CT_ (can't tell).

_____ 11. The author feels that the Irish should leave their country and fight for the Pretender of Spain.

_____ 12. The author implies that Americans are somewhat savage.

_____ 13. The author implies that there is an unemployment problem in Ireland.

_____ 14. The Roman Catholics composed a minority of the Irish population.

_____ 15. The author has lived in Ireland all of his life.

• **Vocabulary**

According to the way the boldface word was used in the selection, indicate *a,* *b, c,* or *d* for the word that gives the best definition.

____ 1. "**importuning** every passenger"
   a. begging
   b. welcoming
   c. introducing
   d. attacking

____ 2. "for an **alms**"
   a. sympathy
   b. job
   c. money
   d. flower

____ 3. "to beg **sustenance**"
   a. shelter
   b. food
   c. forgiveness
   d. mercy

____ 4. "**prodigious** number of children"
   a. increasing
   b. unmanageable
   c. enormous
   d. solitary

____ 5. "the present **deplorable** state"
   a. unfortunate
   b. convincing
   c. remorseful
   d. unstable

____ 6. "wanting food and **raiment**"
   a. money
   b. lodging
   c. pension
   d. clothing

____ 7. "more **glutted** than usual"
   a. depleted
   b. expensive
   c. flooded
   d. popular

____ 8. "one other **collateral** advantage"
   a. opposite
   b. parallel
   c. antagonistic
   d. redeeming

____ 9. "would **repine** to give"
   a. fail
   b. request
   c. neglect
   d. complain

____ 10. "introducing a vein of **parsimony**"
   a. stinginess
   b. trust
   c. loyalty
   d. pride

• **Possible Essay Exam Question**

Explain how Swift strengthens his argument through the use of irony. (Hint: Use specific examples to illustrate the dramatic impact that he is able to achieve through irony.)

● *Word Parts*

Study the meaning of the word parts and supply an additional example from your own vocabulary. In the second set of items, use the corresponding part to write the word that best fits the definition.

Word Part	Meaning	Example	Your Example
1. fin, finis	end, limit	indefinite	_____
2. cycl	circle	cycle	_____
3. med	middle	mediate	_____
4. greg	group	gregarious	_____
5. mill	thousand	mile	_____
6. omni	all	omniscient	_____
7. neo, nov	new	neoclassical	_____
8. poten, posse	power	potentiality	_____
9. vac	empty	vacancy	_____
10. magna, magni	great	magnanimously	_____

1. endless _____

2. series of pictures encircling room _____

3. descriptive of the Middle Ages _____

4. to flock together _____

5. a thousand-year period _____

6. both meat- and plant-eating _____

7. a beginner or neophyte _____

8. all powerful _____

9. a holiday _____

10. to enlarge or intensify _____

Selection 2: History

Leonard Pitt, from *We Americans*

LET THEM HAVE IT ALL, AND BE DONE WITH IT!

The robber barons divided the country among themselves, creating monopolies.

The Ruthless Power of Big Business*

Natural resources and technological ability alone would probably not have made America the leading industrial nation. Big business was a vital link. America's new wealth came primarily from manufacturing. Most impressive were the advances in railroads, steamships, farm tools, and the steel and chemical industries.

*LEARNING STRATEGY: Look critically at how the ruthless power of big business was both an advantage and a disadvantage to the nation and its creation of wealth.

5   The railroad was the first to leap ahead. In the spring of 1869 at Promontory Point, Utah, a golden spike was driven into the rail that completed the first transcontinental line. Chugging across flat plains and through high mountain passes, scattering the buffalo in their paths, railroads could now carry goods and passengers from coast to coast.

       The new east-west rail line did more than mark the finish of the first railroad to cross the

10   continent. It also opened the Age of Big Business. The railroads were the first of the giant corporations that were to assume such a commanding place in American life. Their owners— the empire builders whose vision spanned the continent—needed more capital and labor than ever before. Banks and financial syndicates sprang up to lend them money. Construction companies were organized to carry out their plans. New and bigger unions were formed to

15   organize railroad workers. The government set up the first regulatory agencies to control the lines. As their finances increased, the railroads organized their own subsidiaries to store grain, drill oil, cut timber, or mine coal and ore on their own land. They spent millions in lobbying— and graft—to get grants of money and land from federal and state governments. And they also sold and leased the land on a huge scale.

20   The era gave rise to a new type of business leader. Called "robber barons" or "tycoons," they were known for their ruthless competition and their indifference to the needs of either their workers or the public. "The public be damned!" Cornelius Vanderbilt once exclaimed. Vanderbilt and Collis P. Huntington in railroads, Andrew Carnegie in steel, John D. Rockefeller in oil, Phillip D. Armour in meat packing, Cyrus McCormick in farm machinery,

25   and Jay Cooke and J. P. Morgan in finance controlled enormous chunks of money and power. They considered themselves rugged individualists. A few rose from rags to riches, but most worked their way up from moderately comfortable surroundings.

       While the new tycoons were thought of as self-made men, it is misleading to ignore the help they got from Uncle Sam and from state governments. Some of the largest fortunes in

30   railroads, oil, timber, water power, coal, cattle, and land were made from the public domain. The federal government granted 131 million acres of public land to the railroads, and the states added another 40 million acres.

       Andrew Carnegie, who emigrated from Scotland with his poor parents in 1848, amassed a fortune in iron and steel. In 1872 he began using the new Bessemer process to make steel for

35   railroad tracks. Seven years later he had virtually cornered the market on steel production. His own barges and railroad cars carried mountains of iron ore and coal to his giant mills in Pennsylvania. The secret to his success, Carnegie said, was to control the resources:

       Two pounds of ironstone mined upon Lake Superior and transported nine hundred miles
       to Pittsburgh; one pound and one-half of lime, mined and transported to Pittsburgh; a

40   small amount of manganese ore mined in Virginia and brought to Pittsburgh—and these four pounds of materials manufactured into one pound of steel, for which the consumer pays one cent.

       Some tycoons built their fortunes by ruthlessly destroying the competition. A classic example was John D. Rockefeller. He organized Standard Oil in 1870 and in 1882 formed the Standard

45   Oil Trust—the first trust ever organized—which represented a combination of 77 different oil companies. A master of cutthroat competition, Rockefeller also organized the South Improvement Company, a transportation business that has been called by Stewart Holbrook "the boldest, most naked attempt at dry-land piracy" in all of history. It contracted for special rebates with leading eastern railroads that shipped its oil. From them it got in exchange secret

50   information about competitors, as well as secret rebate payments for shipping the oil of competitors. In effect it was getting some of the profit of competing firms. When necessary, the early Rockefeller companies used hired goons to dynamite the refineries of competitors and bribed various elected officials in New Jersey and Pennsylvania. Six U.S. senators were on the company payroll (one received a salary of $100,000) and were expected to favor Standard Oil

55   with special laws. The company contracted with more than a hundred Ohio newspapers to print

only stories that put Standard Oil in a favorable light. By these methods—and through new
technology and efficient management—Rockefeller amassed a personal fortune of $800 million
and created a billion-dollar industrial corporation. A devout Baptist, Rockefeller felt convinced
that "God gave me my money" and that the South Improvement Company was "right between
60   me and my God."
When the captains of industry retired or died off, many of the major corporations they had
formed remained in existence. These large corporate organizations were not dependent on a
single leader nor limited to the time span of one life. They took advantage of a simple fact: the
bigger the output, the cheaper the unit cost. By gaining nationwide and, when possible,
65   worldwide markets, they magnified profits. Even greater profits could be earned if competition
could be cut out. Sometimes competing companies agreed to limit production or to charge the
same prices. These agreements were not legally binding, and the "pools," as they were called,
broke down when one member pulled out.
A lawyer for Standard Oil invented a stronger device—the trust. Competing companies were
70   "invited" to have their securities administered by a common board of trustees while keeping the
profits for themselves. In this way they coordinated their operations instead of competing with
one another. Soon there were trusts controlling petroleum, cottonseed oil, whiskey, sugar,
lead, and other products. When the trusts were attacked by state and federal governments, they
reorganized into holding companies. A corporation was formed to hold a controlling interest in
75   a group of related companies. These arrangements were legal. The simple merger, where one
company bought out another, was yet another route. In the late 1890s a wave of mergers hit
the manufacturing and mining industries.
So strong was the trend toward concentration that in a number of industries it looked as if
one company would completely dominate the field by the end of the century. In 1870 there
80   were nineteen locomotive makers; thirty years later there were only two. Standard Oil of Ohio
refined 80 to 90 percent of the oil in 1879. At first bigness resulted in lower prices for the
consumer. But when a producer established a monopoly, consumers had to pay any price the
company set.
Say what one will of the "robber barons"—that they were crude and ruthless and exploited
85   their workers mercilessly—it is also true that they contributed in a revolutionary way to the
creation of new material wealth. They did so by bringing together labor power, resources, and
intelligence at a particular moment in time when they could make a lasting mark on American
history.   /1308

• *Skill Development*

Answer the following with *T* (true), *F* (false), or *CT* (can't tell).

_____ 1. The author's intent in this selection is to show the positive force of big
business on America's industrial development.

_____ 2. The author includes Vanderbilt's quotation, "The public be damned!" to
illustrate the public's indifference to big business.

_____ 3. The author mentions that Rockefeller was a devout Baptist and quotes him
in order to dramatize the irony between his philosophy and his practices.

_____ 4. The author implies that the railroads engaged in corruption to obtain land
from the government.

Which of the following word(s), as used in this selection, is the least emotional?

_____   5. a. *ruthless power*
                b. *empire builders*
                c. *self-made men*
                d. *robber barons*
_____   6. a. *graft*
                b. *management*
                c. *rebates*
                d. *cutthroat competition*
_____   7. a. *worldwide market*
                b. *goons*
                c. *lobbying*
                d. *exploited their workers*

For each of the following sentences, indicate *a* for fact and *b* for opinion.

_____   8. "The railroads were the first of the giant corporations that were to assume such a commanding place in American life."
_____   9. "While the new tycoons were thought of as self-made men, it is misleading to ignore the help they got from Uncle Sam and from state governments."
_____ 10. "Standard Oil of Ohio refined 80 to 90 percent of the oil in 1879."

• Comprehension Questions

After reading the selection, answer the following questions with *a, b, c,* or *d.*

_____   1. The best statement of the main idea of this selection is
                a. big business corrupted the nation and exploited the workers and the land
                b. though corrupt in many ways, big business was a force that helped make America the leading industrial nation
                c. the railroad was the unifying factor that allowed the rise of the robber barons
                d. big business stole from federal and state governments to create jobs for the laboring masses
_____   2. According to the author the railroad spurred a cause-and-effect relationship with all of the following except
                a. lending institutions
                b. labor unions
                c. government regulatory agencies
                d. natural resources
_____   3. By organizing subsidiaries to store grain, drill oil, etc., the railroad's main purpose was to
                a. contribute to America's growth
                b. get the maximum profit from its land holdings
                c. create additional jobs for its labor force
                d. force the government to give it more land

_____ 4. According to the author the railroads acquired government land by
   a. trading oil, timber, and iron ore
   b. paying the market price
   c. organizing subsidiaries
   d. illegally influencing political figures

_____ 5. The author primarily includes the quoted paragraph beginning with "Two pounds of . . . ." to illustrate
   a. Pittsburgh's function as an industrial center
   b. Carnegie's control of the resources
   c. the cheap price paid by the consumer for steel
   d. the diversity of ingredients used in steel manufacturing

_____ 6. The author implies that Rockefeller made his fortune through all of the following except
   a. bribery   c. espionage
   b. coercion   d. religion

_____ 7. The major purpose of establishing a trust is to
   a. eliminate competition, control price, and increase profits
   b. shift to central management for policy decisions
   c. stimulate competition among businesses of common interest
   d. secure control in order to lower consumer prices

_____ 8. Trusts were primarily attacked by the federal government because they
   a. bribed politicians   c. offered rebates
   b. established monopolies   d. earned profits

_____ 9. The primary rationale for trusts and holding companies was the desire of a large company to
   a. control the marketplace
   b. open worldwide markets
   c. avoid government regulations
   d. shelter tax benefits

_____ 10. The reduction in the number of locomotive makers from nineteen to two in a thirty-year period is an example of
   a. the inefficiency of small companies
   b. the need for industrial centralization
   c. the control of big business
   d. the restrictions of regulatory agencies

Answer the following with *T* (true), *F* (false), or *CT* (can't tell).

_____ 11. The east and west railroad lines were joined together at Promontory Point, Utah.

_____ 12. The author implies that most of the leading business tycoons rose to success from very meager beginnings.

_____ 13. Without the need for railroad tracks, Andrew Carnegie would not have become a tycoon.

_____ 14. The general public was not aware that Standard Oil illegally paid salaries to six U.S. Senators.

_____ 15. Major corporations formed by the robber barons continued the same ruthless practices of their predecessors.

• *Vocabulary*

According to the way the boldface word was used in the selection, indicate *a, b, c,* or *d* for the word or phrase that gives the best definition.

_____ 1. "the first **transcontinental** line"
a. oceanic
b. international
c. worldwide
d. across the continent

_____ 2. "**vision** spanned the continent"
a. eyeballs
b. influence
c. foresight
d. commands

_____ 3. "their own **subsidiaries**"
a. warehouses
b. labor leaders
c. freight cars
d. auxiliary companies

_____ 4. "The **era** gave rise to"
a. period of time
b. year
c. timetable
d. trend

_____ 5. "their **ruthless** competition"
a. keen
b. efficient
c. pitiless
d. magnanimous

_____ 6. "rugged **individualists**"
a. Westerners
b. believers in self-expression
c. slaves to industry
d. freedom fighters

_____ 7. "the new **tycoons**"
a. wealthy financiers
b. pioneers
c. sophisticates
d. workers

_____ 8. "secret **rebate** payments"
a. sale-priced
b. retroactive
c. kickback
d. reusable

_____ 9. "a wave of **mergers**"
a. antitrusts
b. bankruptcies
c. syndications
d. combination of companies

_____ 10. "**exploited** their workers"
a. took unethical advantage
b. mistrusted
c. physically abused
d. criminally attacked

• *Possible Essay Exam Question*

Illustrate how the ruthless power of big business was a vital factor in increasing America's wealth. (Hint: Select and discuss specific businesses and business-men and their contribution to the growth of America's wealth.)

• *Word Parts*

Study the meaning of the word parts and supply an additional example from your own vocabulary. In the second set of items, use the corresponding part to write the word that best fits the definition.

Word Parts	Meaning	Example	Your Example
1. dem, demo	people	demagogue	_____
2. post	after	posthumous	_____
3. idea, ideo	idea	ideology	_____
4. liber	free	liberal	_____

5. cura, cur	care, to take care of	curator	_____
6. pan	all	Pan-American	_____
7. dec, deca	ten	decimate	_____
8. ard, art	person who	drunkard	_____
9. cracy	rule	theocracy	_____
10. gon	angle	polygon	_____

1. government by the people _____
2. to delay or set back _____
3. visionary or dreamer _____
4. to set free from bondage _____
5. safe; free from care _____
6. relating to all the Greeks _____
7. athletic contest of ten events _____
8. one who boasts excessively _____
9. absolute rule by a single person _____
10. five-sided figure _____

Selection 3: Political Science

Charles P. Sohner, from *American Government and Politics Today*

The Nature of Politics:*
What's It All About?

Aristotle, often called the father of political science, wrote that man is a political animal. One can argue about whether this was a compliment or an insult. As the United States (a political creation) approaches its two-hundredth birthday, most Americans seem to believe that politicians are a pretty bad lot. According to a 1973 Harris survey, 60 percent feel that "most elective officials are in politics for all they personally can get out of it for themselves." Fifty-five percent believe that our leaders really don't care what happens to the average person. In addition, 74 percent think that "special interests get more from the government than the people

*LEARNING STRATEGY: Be able to explain why people feel a sense of alienation toward government and how this affects our social system.

do.''[1] Given these attitudes, it is not surprising that nearly two-thirds of the people, the highest percentage in 20 years, would not like to see their children go into politics.[2] If the survival of a free nation depends on faith and confidence, as Walter Lippmann said in the quotation on page 1, then America is in trouble. Only about a third of the people put much faith in those running the national government or sitting on the Supreme Court.[3]

Yet Americans have contradictory feelings about their political leaders. They reserve their greatest respect for Washington, Lincoln, and other famous presidents. Even among the living, a 1974 Gallup poll showed that eight out of the ten most admired men were politicians. A ninth, Secretary of State Henry Kissinger, was appointed by a politician.[4]

What is the truth of the matter? Is politics a ''dirty game'' or a ''noble calling''? Probably the best answer is that it is neither. Like a stick of dynamite, politics can be used for good purposes or bad ones, to build tunnels or to kill people. Such an answer is not a cop-out. It recognizes that an accurate picture of politics is painted with few blacks and whites but with many shades of gray. It is a portrait full of shadows. To understand it one must develop what social scientists call a ''tolerance of ambiguity,'' in other words, a willingness to live with complexity and contradictions. To accept these may be the mark of an educated human being.

With such acceptance, one can ask an even more important question: Can politics be made better? Can it be used more frequently for noble purposes? This book is written with the conviction that it can. Whether it will depends on all of us.

Corruption and Alienation

> The death of democracy is not likely to be an assassination from ambush. It will be a slow extinction from apathy, indifference, and undernourishment.
>
> Robert M. Hutchins

The sentiments expressed in the polls cited on page 2 indicate that while most people may still have a strong loyalty to the nation and its form of government, they distrust its political leaders. They feel cut off from the process of government, sensing that their faith in the system has somehow been betrayed. They believe they are powerless to control the institutions that affect their lives. This is the essence of what is often called *alienation*.

The Politician as Crook

Corruption is one of the major causes of alienation, recently dramatized by a single word: Watergate. Scarcely a week went by in 1973 and 1974 when television channels and newspapers did not sicken the American public with reports of new scandals, accusations of official misconduct, and charges of criminal deceit. The president to whom we gave more votes than anyone else in the nation's history resigned in disgrace. It was disclosed that two of the government's most secret bodies, the Federal Bureau of Investigation (F. B. I.) and the Central Intelligence Agency (C.I.A.), used their vast powers not only to fight domestic crime and foreign threats, but also to harass and discredit the political opponents of those in office.

Corruption in government is not limited to Watergate crimes. It seems like a spreading cancer, creeping into every branch and level of the political system. In 1974, two New York congressmen were found guilty of accepting money in return for political influence.[5] The same year, ten former or current state legislators in Illinois were indicted for similar offenses.[6] Other instances of misconduct are discussed in the following chapter and elsewhere in this book.

[1] *Confidence and Concern: Citizens View American Government* (Cleveland: Regal Books/King's Court Communications, 1974), pp. 6–7. This pamphlet is a summary of a poll by Lou Harris and Associates.
[2] Gallup Poll, *Los Angeles Times,* Oct. 14, 1973, Part IX, p. 4, and Feb. 3, 1974, p. 3
[3] *Confidence and Concern,* p. 8.
[4] *Los Angeles Times,* Dec. 29, 1974, p. 4. The only one not connected with the government was the Reverend Billy Graham, a friend of both President Johnson and President Nixon.
[5] *Los Angeles Times,* Jan. 2, 1974, p. 9 and July 20, 1974, p. 2. They were Representatives Bertram L. Podell and Frank J. Brasco, both Democrats.
[6] Ibid., Dec. 5, 1974, p. 18. They included six Republicans and four Democrats.

*Whatever the nature of politics in
the United States, the political
convention is here to stay.*

The Roots of Alienation

Corruption, of course, is not the only cause of alienation. Another contributing factor has been
the "credibility gap" of the late 1960s—a belief that officials were not telling the truth,
especially about the Vietnam war. In the mid 1970s, the situation has been worsened by the
apparent inability of the government to cope with such basic problems as unemployment,
prices, and crime rates which were too high and energy supplies which were too low.

Also contributing to the growing alienation of people is the "future shock" of change, the
dizzying speed with which old and familiar attitudes have had to be readjusted or replaced. In
little more than a generation, abortion was legalized, pot became popular, and Germany and
Japan rose from destitute and defeated enemies to prosperous and peaceful allies. Television
entered the living room, computers entered the office, blacks entered all-white schools, topless
dancers entered bars, men entered outer space, and Richard Nixon, staunch foe of communists
in America, entered Peking as a guest of the Communists in China. Within just four months,
President Ford recommended a tax increase to fight inflation and then a tax cut to fight
recession. Worst of all, perhaps, an economy of abundance suddenly became one of scarcity,
and a politics of speech-making and baby-kissing became one of spying and burglary. Many
people looked to their leaders to provide at least some cushion against these startling changes.
But they often looked in vain, while the trauma of change joined with corruption, loss of
credibility, and unsolved economic problems in further alienating people from their government.
A big segment of the population had the feeling that somehow public officials were too
powerful to control yet too weak or indifferent to solve the country's problems.

The Effects of Alienation

We have just attempted to explain some of the causes of alienation. Equally important are its effects. What happens when people lose faith in their government? Three things, all of them bad. First, this reduces participation in politics. Voter turnout at the 1972 and 1974 elections,
70   which will be discussed further in Chapter 9, dropped to its lowest levels since the 1940s. A 1974 poll of college freshmen disclosed that only 36.6 percent, the lowest in 9 years, think it important to keep informed about political events. Only 12.5 percent want to try to influence political affairs themselves.[7] Since 61 percent of the total population seem to believe that what they think doesn't count much any more,[8] it is not surprising that many college students also
75   "don't want to get involved." Many, no doubt, would follow the recommendation of Gordon Strachan, a former aide in the Nixon White House. He advised young people to "stay away" from government service. They don't have the necessary experience, he later explained, "to deal with such a crummy business." If this advice is heeded, however, the nation will surely lose the services of some of its most able and honorable citizens.[9]

80   Such a loss would lead to worse government, a second result of alienation. If good people are not involved in politics, corruption is likely to increase,[10] and even more problems are likely to go unsolved. It was the involvement of Rachel Carson, Ralph Nader, and Martin Luther King, Jr., along with thousands of others, that led to regulations on dangerous pesticides,[11] bans on automobile safety hazards, and new civil rights legislation. T. V. Smith, a philosopher
85   and congressman, said it well: "Democracy is government by politicians for citizens who too often reward them with disdain. This disdain of politicians is a dangerous disease. . . . Politicians, of course, are not perfect—not yet. They may be improved and should be improved . . . .Disdain, however, is a poor improver. Understanding is much better. . . . From it will flow replacement of the weak and corrupt. From it will flow larger participation in
90   politics by the strong and the good.[12]

The third effect of alienation is a decrease in the authority of government. If people disdain their political system, they will be less likely to obey even ordinary laws regulating things like fire hazards and traffic safety. This weakens the whole principle of rule of law which is so important in limiting excessive use of power in a democracy. It could also undermine
95   government efforts in an emergency such as a flood or enemy attack, when respect for government authority might be the key to survival itself.   /1419

• *Skill Development*

Answer the following with *T* (true), *F* (false), or *CT* (can't tell).

_____   1. The author believes that politics can be used more frequently for noble purposes.

_____   2. The author implies that government officials did not tell the truth about the Vietnam War.

_____   3. The author feels that the FBI and the CIA should be abolished.

_____   4. The author is probably an American citizen.

[7]Ibid., Jan. 12, 1975, p. 12. The poll was conducted by the American Council on Education.
[8]*Confidence and Concern*, p. 6.
[9]*Los Angeles Times,* March 11, 1975, p. 7.
[10]See Chapter 2, pp. 43–44 of this book.
[11]Rachel Carson, *Silent Spring* (Greenwich, Conn.: Fawcett Publications, 1962).

Which of the following word(s), as used in this selection, is the least emotional?

_____ 5. a. *political animal*
　　　　　 b. *national government*
　　　　　 c. *trauma of change*
　　　　　 d. *disdain of politicians*
_____ 6. a. *Watergate*
　　　　　 b. *Communists in China*
　　　　　 c. *Aristotle*
　　　　　 d. *the Nixon White House*
_____ 7. a. *dangerous disease*
　　　　　 b. *criminal deceit*
　　　　　 c. *in return for political influence*
　　　　　 d. *respect for government authority*

For each of the following sentences, indicate *a* for fact and *b* for opinion.

_____ 8. "According to a 1973 Harris survey, 60 percent feel that 'most elective officials are in politics for all they personally can get out of it for themselves.' "
_____ 9. "Like a stick of dynamite, politics can be used for good purposes or bad ones, to build tunnels or to kill people."
_____ 10. "In 1974, two New York congressmen were found guilty of accepting money in return for political influence."

• *Comprehension Questions*

After reading the selection, answer the following questions with *a, b, c,* or *d.*

_____ 1. The best statement of the main idea of this selection is
　　　　　 a. democratic government breeds corruption and fosters alienation
　　　　　 b. politics is both good and bad and the swing of the pendulum depends on the involvement of the people
　　　　　 c. more laws are needed to control corruption and prevent alienation
　　　　　 d. popular opinion polls indicate that people are losing interest in their government
_____ 2. The author's opinion about the future of politics in America might best be described as
　　　　　 a. optimistic　　　　　 c. fatalistic
　　　　　 b. pessimistic　　　　　 d. antagonistic
_____ 3. According to the author, America is in the biggest trouble politically if
　　　　　 a. corruption in the government continues
　　　　　 b. citizens cannot tolerate ambiguity
　　　　　 c. politics does not become a more noble calling
　　　　　 d. the American people lack confidence in the government

———————— 4. The author points out that the 1973 Harris survey and the 1974 Gallup polls are contradictory because
   a. the data were collected in two different years
   b. one professes disdain and the other admiration for the same group of people
   c. different questions were asked in the two different studies
   d. the Presidents who were most admired are now dead

———————— 5. The candidate who received the highest number of votes in a presidential election in American history is
   a. Washington
   b. Lincoln
   c. Nixon
   d. Ford

———————— 6. According to the author, the "credibility gap" causes alienation because
   a. people do not want to fight an unpopular war
   b. citizens no longer believe what the government says
   c. unemployment exists on a national level
   d. the cities suffer from crime

———————— 7. According to the author "future shock" breeds political alienation because people feel
   a. topless dancers should not enter bars
   b. past enemies cannot become political friends
   c. our country is a land of abundance
   d. politicians do not provide adequate leadership in the face of change

———————— 8. The author feels that the reason fewer college students expressed an active interest in politics in the 1974 polls is because
   a. they comprise a small percent of the total population
   b. they had lost faith in their ability to influence government
   c. Gordon Strachan advised against involvement
   d. politics in general is a "crummy business"

———————— 9. The author uses Rachel Carson as an example of
   a. involvement that decreases corruption
   b. political disdain
   c. supporters of civil rights litigation
   d. alienation of philosophers

———————— 10. The author sees running a red light as a possible chain reaction effect of
   a. alienation
   b. power
   c. democracy
   d. rule by law

Answer the following with *T* (true), *F* (false), or *CT* (can't tell).

———————— 11. The author believes that corruption in the country began with Watergate.

———————— 12. The author implies that the FBI and CIA were used as political pawns.

———————— 13. Two New York congressmen were indicted in 1974 for accepting bribes from a major oil company.

———————— 14. The author feels that Nixon should not have gone to China.

———————— 15. T. V. Smith believes politicians need more understanding from the public.

- ## *Vocabulary*

According to the way the boldface word was used in the selection, indicate *a, b, c,* or *d* for the word or phrase that gives the best definition.

_____ 1. "tolerance of **ambiguity**"
a. confidence
b. more than one meaning
c. mismanagement
d. the unexpected

_____ 2. "This is the **essence**"
a. name
b. formula
c. choice
d. fundamental nature

_____ 3. "charges of criminal **deceit**"
a. lying
b. suicide
c. negligence
d. murder

_____ 4. "**credibility** gap"
a. responsibility
b. believability
c. reliability
d. indoctrination

_____ 5. "to **cope** with"
a. agree
b. solve
c. argue
d. contend

_____ 6. "growing **alienation** of people"
a. anger
b. involvement
c. selfishness
d. estrangement

_____ 7. "**prosperous** and peaceful allies"
a. thriving
b. helpful
c. ambitious
d. likeable

_____ 8. "the **trauma** of change"
a. moment
b. noise
c. shock
d. assault

_____ 9. "dangerous **pesticides**"
a. bug killers
b. politicians
c. animals
d. infections

_____ 10. "automobile safety **hazards**"
a. risks
b. headaches
c. controls
d. requirements

- ## *Possible Essay Exam Question*

Explain why the author feels that America is in trouble if people lose faith in the government. (Hint: Discuss the specific causes and effects of alienation.)

- ## *Word Parts*

Study the meaning of the word parts and supply an additional example from your own vocabulary. In the second set of items, use the corresponding part to write the word that best fits the definition.

Word Part	Meaning	Example	Your Example
1. popul, public (pop)	people	populace	_____
2. nil, nul	nothing	nullify	_____

3. later	side	equilateral	_____
4. quir	question	inquisition	_____
5. judic	judge, lawyer	judiciary	_____
6. ultra	over, above	ultraconservative	_____
7. semi, hemi, demi	half	semicircle	_____
8. calc	lime or stone	calcify	_____
9. en	make, made of	wooden	_____
10. eer	one who	electioneer	_____

1. quality of being liked by many people _____

2. to invalidate a marriage _____

3. action that is one-sided _____

4. investigation _____

5. discrimination _____

6. beyond the violent end of visible light _____

7. every six months _____

8. machine for mathematical operations _____

9. made of fine fabric produced by worms _____

10. one who directs bidding at a sale _____

Chapter Ten

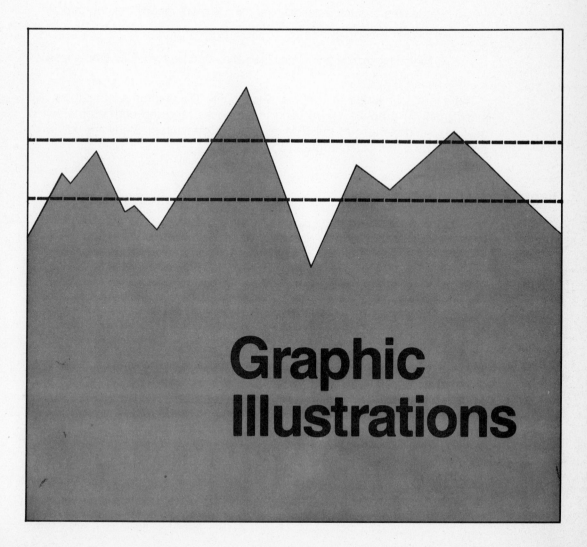

Graphic
Illustrations

If a picture is worth a thousand words, a graphic illustration is worth at least several pages of facts and figures. Graphics express complex interrelationships in simplified form. Instead of plodding through repetitious data, you can glance at a chart, a map, or a graph and immediately see how everything fits together as well as how one part compares with another. Instead of reading several lengthy paragraphs and trying to visualize comparisons, you can study an organized design. For understanding many small bits of information, the graphic illustration is a logically constructed aid.

Graphic illustrations are generally used for the following reasons:

1. To condense
   Pages of repetitious, detailed information can be organized into one explanatory design.
2. To clarify
   Processes and interrelationships can be more clearly defined through visual representations.
3. To convince
   Developing trends and gross inequities can be forcefully dramatized.

There are four kinds of graphic illustrations: (1) diagrams, (2) tables, (3) maps, and (4) graphs. All are used in textbooks, and the choice of which is best to use depends on the type of material presented. Study the following explanations of the different graphic forms.

Diagrams

A diagram is an outlined drawing or picture of an object or a process. It shows the labeled parts of a complicated form such as the muscles of the human body, the organizational make-up of a company's management and production teams, or the directional flow of a natural ecological system. (See Exercise 1)

Tables

A table is a listing of facts and figures in columns for quick and easy reference. Small bits of information such as the nutritional content of meats and vegetables can be simplified in an ordered pattern. (See Exercise 2)

Maps

A map is a geographic designation or distribution. It shows differences in physical terrain, direction, or variations indicative of specified areas. The legend of a map explains the symbols, distance scales, and shading. (See Exercise 3)

Graphs

There are five different types of graphs: (1) pie, (2) bar, (3) column, (4) line, and (5) surface.

(1) A **pie graph** is a circle that is divided into wedge-shaped slices. The complete pie or circle represents a total of 100 percent. Each slice is a percent or fraction of that whole. Budgets, such as the annual expenditure of the federal or state governments, are frequently in pie graphs. (See Exercise 4)

(2) A **bar graph** is a series of horizontal bars in which the length of each bar symbolizes a particular amount of what is being discussed. A series of different items can be quickly compared by noting the different bar lengths. These graphs only measure horizontally and might be used as an example of the total production of different crops for a particular year. (See Exercise 5)

(3) A **column graph** is like a bar graph that is standing upright and measures not only horizontally, but vertically. Thus, the column graph gives two kinds of information. It can compare an item at different time intervals or at different stages of development. For example, this graph could show the growth of total crop production over the last hundred years. (See Exercise 6)

(4) A **line graph** is a continuous curve or frequency distribution. The horizontal scale measures time and the vertical scale measures amount. As the data fluctuate, the line will change direction and with extreme differences become very jagged. This graph could be used to show the monthly rise and fall in steel production. (See Exercise 7)

(5) A **surface graph** is a line graph with a shaded area and might represent the supply of an item such as water over a period of time, and a line superimposed over it might represent the demand for the product; thus the differences between varying amounts can be dramatized on this graph. (See Exercise 8)

How to Read Graphic Material

1. Read the title and get an overview. What is it about?
2. Look for footnotes and read italicized introductory material.
   Identify the who, where, and how.
   How and when were the data collected?
   Who collected the data?
   How many persons were included on the survey?
   Do the researchers seem to have been objective or biased?
   Considering the above information, does the study seem valid?

3. Read the labels.
   What do the vertical columns and the horizontal rows represent?
   Are the numbers in thousands or millions?
   What does the legend represent?
4. Notice the trends and find the extremes.
   What are the highest and lowest rates?
   What is the average rate?
   How do the extremes compare with the total?
   What is the percentage of increase or decrease?
5. Draw conclusions and formulate future questions.
   What does it mean?   What wasn't included?
   What needs to be done?   Where do we go from here?

Each of the described graphic illustrations is represented in the following exercises. Study the illustrations and then respond to the statements as instructed.

● **Exercise 1: Diagram**

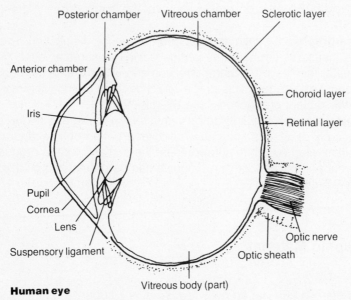

Human eye

Willis H. Johnson et al., *Essentials of Biology*

Answer the following with *T* (true), *F* (false), or *CT* (can't tell).

_____ 1. The cornea covers the front of the eye.
_____ 2. The retinal layer is directly touching the sclerotic layer.
_____ 3. The vitreous chamber or the vitreous body are one and the same as
             indicated by the diagram.

_____ 4. The iris of the eye regulates the size of the pupil.
_____ 5. The front of the lens is called the pupil.
_____ 6. The anterior chamber and the vitreous chamber are filled with the same
type of jelly-like material.
_____ 7. An optic sheath surrounds the optic nerve.
_____ 8. The lens is supported by suspensory ligaments.
_____ 9. The cornea encircles the vitreous chamber.
_____ 10. The image is reflected on the retina.

• *Exercise 2: Table*

Occupational Backgrounds of the Members of the House and Senate, 1973

	House			Senate		
Occupation	D	R	Total	D	R	Total
Agriculture	14	24	38	4	7	11
Business or banking	72	83	155	12	10	22
Education	41	18	59	7	3	10
Engineering	1	1	2	2	0	2
Journalism	16	7	23	4	1	5
Labor leader	3	0	3	0	0	0
Law	137	84	221	42	26	68
Law enforcement	1	1	2	0	0	0
Medicine	3	2	5	1	0	1
Public service/politics	201	152	353	55	42	97
Minister	2	2	4	0	0	0
Scientist	2	0	2	0	0	0
Veteran	175	142	317	42	31	73

*Senate total = 100 House total = 435, Data from *Congressional Quarterly Weekly Report,* January 6, 1973, p. 3.
Theodore J. Lowi, *American Government: Incomplete Conquest*

Answer the following with *T* (true), *F* (false), or *CT* (can't tell).

_____ 1. In 1973 more congressmen had backgrounds in law than any other
occupational area.
_____ 2. The majority of the members of the 1973 Senate at some time served in
the U.S. military.
_____ 3. Congressmen were allowed to list more than one occupational background
for this study.
_____ 4. In 1973 only three Republican congressmen had occupational
backgrounds as labor leaders.

_____ 5. Because of the occupational background of its members, the House has passed more bills than the Senate that are favorable to business and banking interests.

_____ 6. According to this data a minister would seem to be less likely than a journalist to be elected to the House.

_____ 7. In the 1973 Congress more Democrats than Republicans were lawyers.

_____ 8. Most of the senators who listed public "service/politics" as a previous occupation also listed at least two other occupational areas.

_____ 9. In 1973, two hundred eighty-nine of the Democratic congressmen had occupational backgrounds in law.

_____ 10. In this study about fifty percent of the House members listed occupational backgrounds in education.

• *Exercise 3: Map*

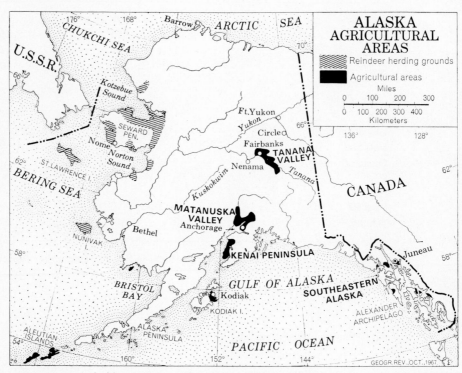

FIG. 1—Agricultural areas. *Sources:* Alaska Crop and Livestock Reporting Service and the Bureau of Indian Affairs, Juneau.

Geographical Review

Answer the following with *T* (true), *F* (false), or *CT* (can't tell).

_____ 1. The major concentration of reindeer-herding grounds in Alaska is on Seward Pennisula.

_____ 2. There are no major highways in Alaska north of Anchorage.
_____ 3. Bethel is the largest city in Alaska.
_____ 4. Anchorage is less than 300 miles from Juneau.
_____ 5. The Matanuska Valley and the Tanana Valley are two of the major agricultural areas in Alaska.
_____ 6. The Yukon River extends into Canada.
_____ 7. Eskimos live in the areas around Nome and Barrow.
_____ 8. Reindeer herding is more prevalent than agriculture on the islands in the Bering Sea.
_____ 9. Because of the cold, no farming exists in Southeastern Alaska.
_____ 10. The northernmost city in the United States is Fort Yukon.

• *Exercise 4: Pie Graph*

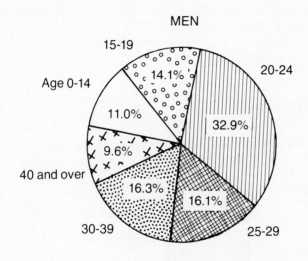

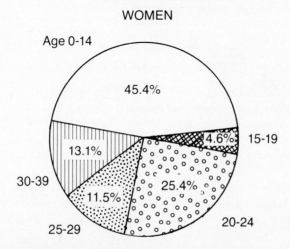

Virginia in 1625: an age profile

Keith Ian Polakoff et al., *Generations of Americans, Part 1*

Answer the following with *T* (true), *F* (false), or *CT* (can't tell).

_____ 1. The majority of the children in the Virginia colony were females.
_____ 2. There were more men than women in Virginia in 1625.
_____ 3. Only approximately one quarter of the men in Virginia in 1625 were thirty years or more of age.
_____ 4. The population of Virginia in 1625 was thirty percent younger than Virginia's population today.
_____ 5. Almost half the women in Virginia in 1625 were under eighteen years of age.
_____ 6. A greater number of women than men in Virginia in 1625 were 20–24 years of age.
_____ 7. According to the graph there were no women in Virginia in 1625 over 40 years of age.
_____ 8. More women than men left the Virginia colony.
_____ 9. There was a greater number of men than women between the ages of 30–39 in Virginia in 1625.
_____ 10. Because of the availability of females, men married women much younger than themselves in the Virginia colony.

• *Exercise 5: Bar Graph*

Projected Percentage Increase in Occupations: 1970-1980

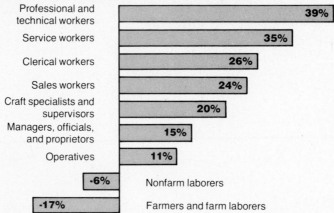

Louis E. Boone and David L. Kurtz, *Contemporary Business*

Answer the following with *T* (true), *F* (false) , or *CT* (can't tell).

_____ 1. The decrease in farmers and farm laborers will be greater than the increase in managers, officials, and proprietors.
_____ 2. The greatest projected increase will be in professional and technical workers.

_____ 3. The greatest projected increase will be in nonfarm laborers.

_____ 4. A greater number of people will be working in the towns and cities than on the farms.

_____ 5. Farmers will be moving to the cities and becoming managers.

_____ 6. The projected increase in operative positions is approximately one third the increase in service worker positions.

_____ 7. In 1980, twenty-six percent of all workers will be clerical workers.

_____ 8. This graph was published to help people find jobs.

_____ 9. There will be a greater demand for service workers than for sales workers in 1980 because more things will need to be fixed.

_____ 10. The combined projected increase in sales and clerical workers will be greater than the projected increase in professional and technical workers.

• *Exercise 6: Column Graph*

Mean income of men by level of education and age, 1972

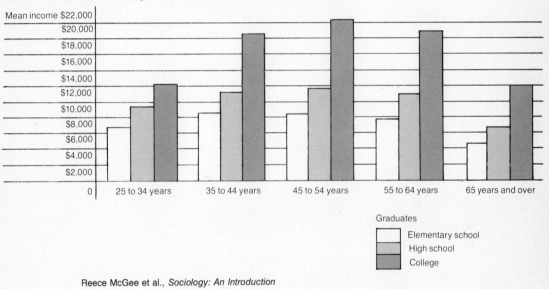

Reece McGee et al., *Sociology: An Introduction*

Answer the following with *T* (true), *F* (false), or *CT* (can't tell).

_____ 1. Only a person between 45 and 54 years of age with a college education made over $20,000 in 1972.

_____ 2. For all ages over twenty-five in 1972, the average income of college graduates was higher than the average income of noncollege graduates.

_____ 3. The greatest difference in the average income of college graduates and noncollege graduates is in the 35 to 44 age group.

_____ 4. In 1972 the average 25-to-34-year-old college graduate made about $2500 more than the average high-school graduate of the same age.

_____ 5. According to this information a college education on the average means more financially at 50 than it does at 30.

_____ 6. In 1972 the average high-school graduate reached his peak earning potential at 54 years.

_____ 7. The 1972 figures show that, on the average, more education means more money.

_____ 8. In 1972 the average college graduate made about the same at age 65 as a college graduate would make at age 30.

_____ 9. In the 1972 figures an average elementary-school graduate never made as much as an average college graduate.

_____ 10. College graduates work harder than noncollege graduates and thus have higher incomes.

• **Exercise 7: Line Graph**

U.S. population by place of residence, 1910-1970

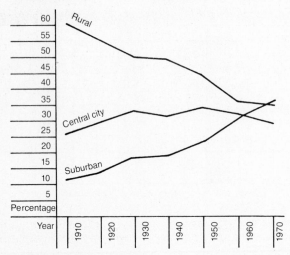

The percentage of the population living in rural areas declined drastically during the period shown. The percentage in central cities rose steadily until 1950, except for a slight decline during the Depression of the 1930s. The percentage in suburban areas grew throughout this period, and particularly so after 1940. Since 1940, suburban living has gained so steadily at the expense of both central city and rural living that by 1970 there were more suburbanites than either of the other two groups.

Reece McGee et al., *Sociology: An Introduction*

Answer the following with *T* (true), *F* (false), or *CT* (can't tell).

_____ 1. In 1910 about six times more people lived in rural areas than lived in suburban areas.

_____ 2. The greatest growth in population since 1918 has been in suburban areas.

_____ 3. The percentage of the population living in the central city in 1910 and in 1970 is exactly the same.

_____ 4. Since 1910, the periods of the least decline in rural population were in the 1930's and 1960's.

_____ 5. The graph shows the number of people leaving the farms to become factory workers.

_____ 6. In 1920 about half of the U.S. population lived in rural areas.

_____ 7. In 1970 more people work in suburban areas than in the central city.

_____ 8. The increase in suburban population was greater in the 1930's than in the 1950's.

_____ 9. The suburban population approximately tripled between 1910 and 1960.

_____ 10. More of the people who left the rural areas between 1910 and 1970 went to surburban areas than central city areas.

• ## Exercise 8: Surface Graph

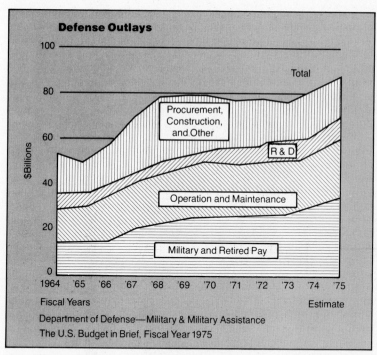

Burns, Peltason and Cronin, *Government by the People*

Answer the following with _T_ (true), _F_ (false,) or _CT_ (can't tell).

_____ 1. The amount of money spent on defense outlays has doubled from 1964 to 1975.

_____ 2. Military and retired pay accounted for less than one fourth of the total defense budget for 1975.

_____   3. From 1964 to 1965 there was a slight drop in the total military expenditure.

_____   4. In 1967 approximately 40 billion dollars was spent in "military and retired pay" and "operation and maintenance."

_____   5. This graph was prepared in 1972.

_____   6. In 1969 approximately 88 billion dollars was spent in "procurement, construction, and other."

_____   7. In the late 1960's more money was spent on military construction than on procurement.

_____   8. By 1977 the total defense outlay is expected to reach one hundred billion.

_____   9. The amount of money spent on "procurement, construction, and other" has decreased since the late 1960's.

_____   10. The area marked "R & D" denotes the expenditure for the military railroad system.

Selection 1: Psychology

Jerome Kagan and Ernest Havemann, from *Psychology: An Introduction*

Overlearning*

Adults are often surprised by how well they remember something they learned as children but have never practiced in the meantime. A man who has not had a chance to go swimming for years can still swim as well as ever when he gets back in the water. He can get on a bicycle

*LEARNING STRATEGY: Be able to define the terms and to use research findings to support the opinions expressed.

after several decades and still ride away. He can play catch and swing a baseball bat as well as his son. A mother who has not thought about the words for years can teach her daughter the poem that begins "Twinkle, twinkle, little star" or recite the story of Cinderella or Goldilocks and the three bears.

One explanation is the *law of overlearning,* which can be stated as follows: Once we have learned something, additional learning trials increase the length of time we will remember it. A laboratory demonstration of this law is shown in Figure 4-14.

In childhood we usually continue to practice such skills as swimming, bicycle riding, and playing baseball long after we have learned them. We continue to listen to and remind ourselves of jingles such as "Twinkle, twinkle, little star" and childhood tales such as Cinderella and Goldilocks. We not only learn but overlearn.

Earlier in the chapter, it was mentioned that the multiplication tables are an exception to the general rule that we tend to forget rather quickly the things that we learn in school by rote. An explanation was promised later—and now, of course, you have it, for the multiplication tables are another of the things we overlearn in childhood.

The law of overlearning explains why cramming for an examination, though it may result in a passing grade, is not a satisfactory way to learn a college course. By cramming, a student may learn the subject well enough to get by on the examination, but he is likely soon to forget almost everything he learned. A little overlearning, on the other hand, is usually a good investment toward the future.

Distribution of Practice

Another argument against cramming is that it represents an attempt to learn through what is called *massed practice*—that is, a single long learning session. Studies of a wide range of situations involving both human and animal learning have indicated that massed practice is generally less efficient than *distributed practice*—that is, a series of shorter learning periods. As Figure 4–15 shows, the same total amount of time spent in learning is often strikingly more efficient when invested in short, separated periods than all at once.

Three possible explanations have been suggested for the superiority of distributed practice:

1. Distributed practice reduces the fatigue that often accompanies massed practice in motor learning and the boredom that often occurs in massed practice in verbal learning.

4–14 How Overlearning Aids Remembering

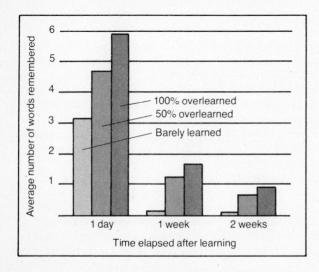

These are the results of an experiment in which subjects learned a list of twelve single-syllable nouns. Sometimes they stopped studying the list as soon as they were able to recall it without error—in the words used in the chart, as soon as they had "barely learned" the words. At other times they were asked to continue studying the list for half again as many trials as bare learning required (50 percent overlearned) or to continue studying for the same number of extra trials as the original learning had required (100 percent overlearned). Whether measured after a day or at later intervals, the subjects who had overlearned by 50 percent remembered considerably more than those who had barely learned, and the subjects who had overlearned by 100 percent remembered most of all. (20)

4–15 Massed Versus Distributed Practice

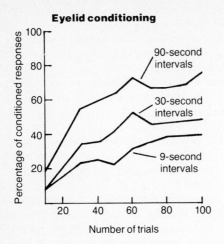

Eyelid conditioning

90-second intervals

30-second intervals

9-second intervals

Percentage of conditioned responses

Number of trials

This graph shows the results of an experiment in which the eyelid-blinking reflex, produced by a puff of air directed at the eye, was conditioned to a light. More conditioned responses were obtained when there were 90-second intervals between trials than when the intervals were shorter—that is, when the practice was more massed. (21)

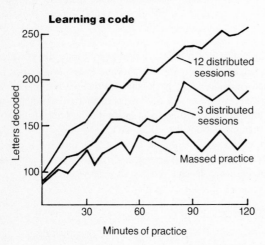

Learning a code

12 distributed sessions

3 distributed sessions

Massed practice

Letters decoded

Minutes of practice

This graph shows the results of an experiment in which the subjects learned to substitute numbers for letters. Progress was slowest in a single massed session of 120 minutes of practice, higher when the subjects worked in three 40-minute sessions spread over six days, and highest of all when twelve 10-minute sessions were spread over six days. (22)

2. In the intervals between distributed practice sessions the learner may continue to mull over the material he has learned, even without knowing that he is doing so. This process is called *covert rehearsal* and results in what is called *consolidation* of what has been learned.

3. In many kinds of learning it seems likely that we learn not only what we want to learn but a number of useless and irrelevant habits that may actually interfere. A student learning to type, for example, might at the same time learn to grit his teeth, squint, and blink his eyes— habits that do not help his skill but hurt it. During the intervals between distributed practice sessions these extraneous habits may be forgotten more quickly than the basic subject matter of the learning. The process is called *differential forgetting*.

It must be added, however, that distributed practice does not always give such spectacular results as those shown in Figure 4–15. It seems less helpful in learning by logical rule than in learning by rote, possibly because rule learning involves less boredom. In learning situations that require a lot of "cranking up" time—getting out several books and notebooks, finding some reference works on the library shelves, and finding a comfortable and well-lighted place to work—short practice periods may be less efficient than long ones. Moreover, distributed

practice does not appear to have much effect if any on how well the learning is remembered; even when it results in substantial savings of the time required for learning, it does not seem to
50 improve retention. But the general idea of distributed practice is a useful tool in the management of learning. Probably all learning tasks can be best accomplished through some pattern of distributed practice—in some cases many short periods separated by long intervals, in some cases fewer and longer periods separated by shorter intervals, and in some cases perhaps a combination. The trick is to find the pattern that best suits the particular situation.

Recitation

55 We come now to the last of the questions posed at the beginning of the chapter: Is it better just to keep reading when you study or to read a while and then attempt to recite? . . .

Experimenters have found that it makes no difference whether the subjects are children or adults or whether the material being learned is nonsense syllables, spelling, mathematics, or a foreign vocabulary. In every case it is more efficient to read and recite than to read alone.

60 Let us say that you have eight hours to devote to learning this chapter and that reading through the chapter takes you two hours. The least efficient way to spend your study time would be to read through the chapter four times. You would do much better to spend more time in trying to recite what you have learned than in reading—for, . . . devoting as much as 80 percent of study time to recitation may be more efficient by far than mere reading.

65 Recitation seems to assist learning in a number of ways. It certainly helps make the stimulus more distinctive; it casts a telling searchlight on what you have grasped quickly and what you have not, on what you understand and what you still find obscure. It provides a form of feedback that sharpens your attention. It helps you find meaningfulness and logical principles in the material. Of all study techniques, recitation is the one of most clearly proved value.

70 Recitation is the heart of a widely recommended study method called the SQ3R system (24), which holds that the most efficient way to study a chapter is to approach it through five steps:

1 *Survey*. That is, study the outline at the beginning of the chapter (if there is one, as in this book) and then glance through the chapter to get a general idea of how much attention is devoted to each point in the outline and to the subheadings.

75 2. *Question*. Look through the chapter again in a more inquisitive fashion, asking yourself questions that the headings and subheadings suggest; let the topics you find there whet your curiosity.

3. *Reading*. Now read the chapter straight through, without taking notes.

4. *Recitation*. You have made a survey of the chapter, asked some questions about it, and
80 read it. Now see how much of the chapter you can recite, either silently to yourself or out loud to a cooperative friend.

5. *Reviewing*. Go through the chapter again, making another survey of its topics and noting how much of it you were able to recite and what points you left out. The reviewing process will show you where you must devote further study. /1328

• *Skill Development*

Study the indicated graphs and then respond to the following statements with *T* (true), *F* (false), or *CT* (can't tell).

Figure 4–14

_____ 1. After a time lapse of one day the 100 percent overlearned group could recall almost twice as many words as the barely learned group.

_____ 2. Each of the three groups, barely learned, 50 percent overlearned, and 100 percent overlearned have the same number of subjects.

_____ 3. Two weeks after the initial learning, the barely learned group remembered almost no words.

_____ 4. The 50 percent overlearned group did not forget as much as the 100 percent overlearned group after a week.

_____ 5. According to the results of the study, 50 percent overlearning is better than 100 percent overlearning because it takes less time in proportion to words later remembered.

Figure 4–15

_____ 6. Letters decoded in twelve 10-minute sessions as opposed to one massed learning session of an equal amount of time resulted in twice as much learning.

_____ 7. Boredom accounts for the fluctuation in the number of letters decoded in the massed practice group.

_____ 8. By a close approximation, the 12 distributed sessions group knew as much about decoding after 45 minutes of practice as the 3 distributed sessions knew after 85 minutes of practice.

_____ 9. After 60 trials the difference between the percentage of conditioned responses for the 90- and 30-second intervals was twice the difference between the 30- and 9-second intervals.

_____ 10. In the eyelid conditioning experiment the hundred trials at 90-second intervals required less than twice the amount of time to complete the experiment as the hundred trials at 9-second intervals.

- **Comprehension Questions**

   After reading the selection, answer the following questions with *a, b, c,* or *d.*

_____ 1. The best statement of the main idea of this selection is
   a. recitation explains why cramming for an exam is an ineffectual method of study
   b. overlearning, distributed practice, and recitation improve the efficiency of the learning process
   c. effective learning means remembering the material at least two weeks later
   d. forgetting is caused by a failure to apply the principles of learning in an efficient manner

_____ 2. The author uses all of the following as examples of the success of overlearning except
   a. bicycling
   b. nursery jingles
   c. multiplication tables
   d. examination cramming

_____ 3. The difference between distributed practice and mass practice is
   a. the number of hours spent studying
   b. the complexity of the material studied
   c. the time intervals between study periods
   d. the recitation after study units

_____ 4. The process of covert rehearsal between distributed practice sessions is
   a. a conscious recitation
   b. an unconscious review
   c. an organized consolidation
   d. a selective forgetting

_____ 5. The author implies that the differential forgetting process that occurs between distributed practice sessions would probably be the most important in
   a. learning to play tennis
   b. memorizing a poem
   c. studying for a history examination
   d. learning multiplication tables

_____ 6. Distributed practice sessions have been shown to do all of the following except
   a. cut down on fatigue
   b. improve retention
   c. save time
   d. relieve boredom

_____ 7. The author feels that the most effective method of spending four hours studying a chapter for an exam would be to
   a. read it once and then recite
   b. read it once, recite, and then read it again
   c. read it twice and then recite
   d. read it three times and recite after each reading

_____ 8. The author feels that the key success factor in the SQ3R study method is
   a. recitation
   b. a combination of distributed practice and recitation
   c. the final review that follows the recitation
   d. looking over the material and asking questions before beginning the reading

_____ 9. The author feels that the most valuable practice for a college student to use in remembering material is
   a. overlearning
   b. distribution of practice
   c. covert rehearsal
   d. recitation

_____ 10. The author would consider an adult's forgetting how to tie a shoe an example of a failure in
   a. overlearning
   b. distribution of practice
   c. recitation
   d. SQ3R

Answer the following with *T* (true), *F* (false), or *CT* (can't tell).

_____ 11. The author implies that short distributed practice periods would be the most efficient method for writing a research paper.

_____ 12. The author suggests that recitation is similar to a self-imposed examination.

_____ 13. Remembering the words to a popular hit song usually would combine the laws of overlearning, distributed practice, and recitation.

_____ 14. Recitation lessens fatigue and boredom.

_____ 15. The author considers the initial reading to be the most important key to learning.

• *Vocabulary*

According to the way the boldface word was used in the selection, indicate *a*, *b*, *c*, or *d* for the word or phrase that gives the best definition.

____1. "learn in school by **rote**"
a. rules
b. short time sessions
c. logic
d. repetition without meaning

____2. "to **mull** over"
a. ponder
b. work
c. progress
d. refine

____3. "**covert** rehearsal"
a. planned
b. hidden
c. required
d. repetitious

____4. "**consolidation** of what has been learned"
a. unification
b. reorganization
c. magnification
d. repetition

____5. "**irrelevant** habits"
a. annoying
b. conditioned
c. detrimental
d. unrelated

____6. "these **extraneous** habits"
a. extraordinary
b. nonessential
c. dangerous
d. disliked

____7. "still find **obscure**"
a. unnecessary
b. ridiculous
c. vague
d. uninteresting

____8. "a form of **feedback**"
a. rekindling
b. reminding review
c. instructions
d. demonstrating

____9. "a more **inquisitive** fashion"
a. vindictive
b. intellectual
c. curious
d. studious

____10. "**whet** your curiosity"
a. kill
b. fancy
c. find
d. excite

● *Possible Essay Exam Question*

Explain why a series of study periods is better than cramming when studying for an exam. (Hint: Define both methods, point out the advantages of short, separate periods, and use the research findings to corroborate your statements.)

● *Word Parts*

Study the meaning of the word parts and supply an additional example from your own vocabulary. In the second set of items, use the corresponding part to write the word that best fits the definition.

Word Part	Meaning	Example	Your Example
1. pute	think	dispute	_____
2. jac, jec, ject	throw, lie	objection	_____
3. end, endo	within	endogeny	_____
4. dorm	sleep	dormant	_____
5. sat, satis	enough	insatiability	_____
6. gest	carry, bear	digestion	_____
7. mega	large	megalomania	_____
8. migra	wander	migratory	_____
9. monstr	show	remonstrate	_____
10. sphere	ball, sphere	atmosphere	_____

1. to calculate _____

2. refused, denied _____

3. internal secretion, especially relating to a gland _____

4. a residence hall _____

5. thoroughly soak _____

6. clogged and overcrowded _____

7. device for amplifying sound _____

8. to come into a country _____

9. to present or display _____

10. half the earth _____

Selection 2: Political Science

James M. Burns, J. W. Peltason and Thomas E. Cronin, from *Government by the People*

Millions of Nonvoters*

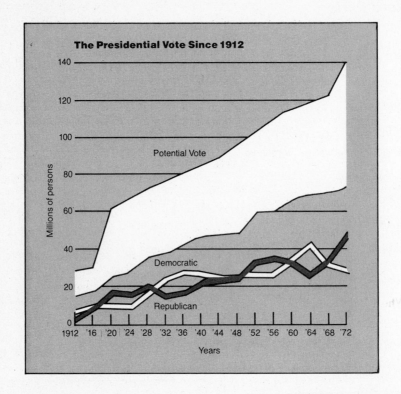

On the average, the proportion of Americans who vote is smaller than that of the British, French, Italians, West Germans, Scandinavians, or Canadians. Talk as we will about democratic suffrage, the fact remains that millions of Americans do not choose to vote or somehow fail to get to the polls on election day. Our record has not always been so poor. Voting was generally high (among those legally *able* to vote) during the latter nineteenth century; in 1876, 86 percent of the adult enfranchised males voted. In this century our voting ratio has been erratic. Turnout dropped between the early 1900s and the mid-twenties, rose in the late 1920s and 1930s, declined in the mid- and late 1940s, climbed in 1952 and 1956, and has decreased in the last three presidential elections—three elections, incidentally, that were thought to be unusually significant and compelling.

Americans have an absolute right *not* to vote. But in a democracy where voting is considered a civic virtue and a prudent means of self-defense, the extent of nonvoting is startling. In the last two presidential elections about 40 percent of the eligible voters did not go to the polls.

*LEARNING STRATEGY: Be able to describe who the nonvoters are and why they are not going to the polls.

15 *Over 60 percent* of them stayed home in the congressional elections of 1974. Participation in
state and local elections is usually even *lower*.

Why do people fail to vote? Aside from outright denials of the right to vote—happily no
longer a significant factor—important reasons are registration requirements and being absent
from the voting district on election day. As we noted in Part Three, registering to vote (not
required in many other democracies) is bothersome and time-consuming and often compels a
20 potential voter to initiate action long before he or she faces election issues.[1] Although the
Supreme Court has ruled that states may not impose residency requirements of longer than fifty
days, almost a third of the potential voters are not even registered to vote. Disturbed by the
low turn-out, Congress in 1970 established for *presidential elections* a uniform thirty-day
residency requirement and set simpler procedures for absentee voting.

25 The *prime* reasons for not voting, however, are not institutional. They are *personal*.
Millions of Americans are just not interested enough to go to the polls to vote for president,
and even fewer vote for state and local candidates. They feel—if they think about the matter at
all—that politics is not important, or that there is no real choice between candidates, or that
they do not know enough to vote, or that they are "disgusted with politics." Some fear losing
30 business or wages if they go to the polls. Much nonvoting probably results from a combination
of low interest and inconvenience: An elderly person might vote if the polls were around the
corner—but actually they are two miles away and he or she lacks transportation. Of course,
sometimes the inconvenience is simply a rationalization for basic lack of interest.

Should such apathy surprise us? When students mobilized for action after President Nixon's
35 Cambodia "incursion" of 1970, it was estimated that half a million of them would take part in
the ensuing national elections. In fact only a tiny minority was active. That minority was
effective in a number of congressional elections, but the vast majority of interested students did
more talking than electioneering. Some were alienated from the whole election process; most
were simply not interested in the issues of the day.[2] Indeed, of all major categories of voters,
40 the lowest percentage of voter turnout in the 1964 and 1968 presidential elections was among
the eighteen to twenty-year-olds in the states that permitted them to vote.

Who Fails to Vote?

The extent of voting varies among different types of persons, areas, and elections. Voting
studies generally agree on the following patterns, which are listed here roughly in order of
declining importance:

45 **1.** People with high incomes are more likely to vote than people with low ones. Why do low-
income people vote in fewer numbers than the wealthy? They have less economic security; they
feel less of a sense of control over their political environment; they feel at a disadvantage in
social contacts; and their social norms tend to deemphasize politics. Their nonvoting thus is part
of a larger political and psychological environment that discourages political activity, including
50 voting.[3]

2. The college-educated are more likely to vote than the noncollege-educated. High school
alumni are more likely to vote than those with only a grade school education. "Practically
speaking," writes Warren Miller, "almost everybody who has been to college votes."[4] Even
college-educated persons who profess little interest in or knowledge about political issues turn
55 out to vote. People with college backgrounds exist in a climate of opinion in which voting is
considered a civic duty; they tend to be more exposed to ideas, active people, newspapers,

[1]See Stanley Kelley, Jr., Richard E. Ayres, and William G. Bowen, "Registration and Voting: Putting First
Things First," *American Political Science Review* (June 1967), pp. 359–77.
[2]Walter T. Murphy, Jr., "Student Power in the 1970 Elections: A Preliminary Assessment," *Political Science*
(Winter 1971), pp. 27–32. See also Sidney Hyman, *Youth in Politics* (Basic Books, 1972).
[3]See Angus Campbell, Philip E. Converse, Warren E. Miller, and Donald E. Stokes, *The American Voter*
(John Wiley, 1960).
[4]Warren Miller, "The Political Behavior of the Electorate," *American Government Annual, 1960–1961* (Holt,
Rinehart & Winston, 1960), p. 50.

political leaders. The college education itself may have an independent effect in exposing the graduates to political ideas and personalities.

60 **3.** Middle-aged people are more likely to vote than the younger and older. Many young people are busy getting established, moving about, having babies, raising young children. The new husband is occupied with getting ahead; the young wife is immersed in home affairs, or has a job of her own. They find little time for politics. The more established, between thirty-five and fifty-five, are more active; then voting falls off sharply in the sixties and seventies, owing partly to the infirmities of old age.

65 **4.** Men are more likely to vote than women. This variation—not very great in most elections—exists in many foreign countries as well. In recent presidential elections about 61 in every 100 women have voted, about 75 in every 100 men. Women feel less social pressure to vote than men. Morality issues such as birth control, however, generally bring out a high women's vote, and college-educated women tend to be more active in political party work than 70 college-educated men. There are indications that the traditional difference in the rate of voting between men and women is decreasing.

5. Partisans are more likely to vote than independents. ''By far the most important psychological factor affecting an individual's decision to vote is his identification with a political party.''[5] When the election outcome is doubtful, strong partisanship is even more 75 likely to induce a person to vote. A partisan is likely to have a personal interest and to be concerned about the outcome. If partisanship has this influence, however, the recent decline in party feeling and loyalty could bring a decline in voting turnout.

6. Persons who are active in organized groups are more likely to vote. This is especially true when the organized groups are themselves involved in community activity.[6] People in groups 80 are more likely to be exposed to stimuli that engage them with civic and political problems.

[5]*Report of the President's Commission on Registration and Voting Participation* (U.S. Government Printing Office, 1963), pp. 9–10.
[6]Sidney Verba and Norman H. Nie, *Participation in America* (Harper & Row, 1972), pp. 197–200.

Summing up, if you are a young woman with a low income and little sense of partisanship, the chances that you will turn out even for an exciting presidential election are far less than if you are a wealthy man in your fifties, a strong partisan, and a member of a civic group. Thus nonvoting influences are cumulative. But there also appear to be psychological or attitudinal differences between nonvoters and voters. Even when sex, age, education, and income are controlled, the chronic nonvoter, more characteristically than the voter, is a person with a sense of inadequacy, more inclined to accept authority, more concerned with personal and short-range issues, less sympathetic toward democratic norms, and less tolerant of those who differ from himself.

85

/1164

• *Skill Development*

Study the graph and then respond to the following statements with *T* (true), *F* (false), or *CT* (can't tell).

_____ 1. In 1956 almost half of the potential voters actually voted in the presidential election.
_____ 2. In 1920 a greater percentage of the nonvoters were registered Republicans than registered Democrats.
_____ 3. The approximately equal turnout of Republican and Democratic voters for the 1948 presidential election accounts for a leveling off in the total vote from the previous election year.
_____ 4. More votes were cast for the Republican candidate in 1952 than for the Democratic one.
_____ 5. Approximately 60 million people voted in the presidential election of 1952.
_____ 6. In the presidential election of 1972 there were more total voters as well as more total nonvoters than in any other presidential election since 1912.
_____ 7. Between 1916 and 1920 the number of potential American voters doubled.
_____ 8. In the 1924 presidential election more of the nonvoters were registered Democrats than registered Republicans.
_____ 9. In the presidential election of 1940 there were approximately 80 million nonvoters.
_____ 10. Republicans have enjoyed a steady, uninterrupted increase in presidential votes since 1912.

• *Comprehension Questions*

After reading the selection, answer the following questions with *a, b, c,* or *d.*

_____ 1. The best statement of the main idea of this selection is
   a. all Americans must vote regardless of age, sex, or wealth to maintain our democratic system
   b. millions of Americans are failing to vote and studies show that this voting behavior varies according to the type of person, the area, and the election

    c. even though all Americans are allowed to vote, wealthy, middle-aged men are still the dominant political force because of their voting patterns

    d. the percentage of voting Americans is lower than any other major democratic world power

_____ 2. In the following, the only definitely true statement about the American voter is

    a. more people voted in 1876 than in any of the last three presidential elections

    b. voter turnout has been on a continual decline since the early 1900's

    c. in 1974, voter turnout was lower for state and local elections than for congressional elections

    d. about the same number of people voted in the late 1920's as voted in 1952

_____ 3. The author feels that the major cause for the high number of nonvoting Americans is

    a. registration requirements   c. failure to register

    b. absenteeism   d. apathy

_____ 4. The effect at the polls of President Nixon's Cambodia "incursion" of 1970 was

    a. equal to the amount of student protest

    b. less than anticipated

    c. an example of the powerful influence of a discontented voter group in a presidential election

    d. a strong danger to Nixon when he ran for reelection

_____ 5. According to the author, wealthy people are more likely to vote than people with low incomes because of all of the following except

    a. a greater feeling of control over their political environment

    b. less trouble in getting time off from work

    c. a stronger emphasis on voting in their social group

    d. greater financial security

_____ 6. Voting studies show that generally the most important of the following comparative factors in describing voters and nonvoters is

    a. education   c. political party affiliation

    b. income   d. sex

_____ 7. According to the selection, all of the following are true of the college educated except

    a. they are more likely to vote than those who have not been to college

    b. the men are less likely to be involved in political party work than the non-college-educated men

    c. they seem to vote even if they are not interested in the political issues

    d. they are more likely to have high incomes

_____ 8. The author feels that women are less likely to vote than men because of

    a. education   c. raising young children

    b. less social pressure   d. morality issues

_____ 9. The author believes that the most important characteristic distinguishing the voter from the nonvoter is

    a. education   b. sex   c. attitude   d. income

_____ 10. Of the following, the author would probably feel that Americans
   a. should all fulfill a civic duty and go to the polls and vote
   b. should vote only if they feel that their actual vote can make a difference
   c. should penalize the citizens who fail to vote
   d. should launch a massive campaign in the six listed areas to insure greater voter turnout

Answer the following with _T_ (true), _F_ (false), or _CT_ (can't tell).

_____ 11. All democracies require voters to be registered before the actual day of voting in the election.

_____ 12. Fewer eighteen- to twenty-year-olds voted in the 1972 presidential election than in the presidential election of 1968.

_____ 13. Members of civic organizations are more likely to vote than sixty- or seventy-year-olds.

_____ 14. The author implies that there has been a recent feeling toward voter independence as opposed to political-party membership.

_____ 15. The author believes that most nonvoters use inconveniences as an excuse.

• _Vocabulary_

According to the way the boldface word was used in the selection, indicate _a, b, c,_ or _d_ for the word or phrase that gives the best definition.

_____ 1. "adult **enfranchised** males"
   a. educated
   b. enlisted in the military
   c. endowed with a vote
   d. certified

_____ 2. "has been **erratic**"
   a. enormous
   b. unsteady
   c. regular
   d. erroneous

_____ 3. "a **prudent** means of self-defense"
   a. wise
   b. satisfactory
   c. encouraged
   d. continuing

_____ 4. "to **initiate** action"
   a. complete
   b. begin
   c. regulate
   d. terminate

_____ 5. "students **mobilized** for action"
   a. assembled
   b. got into automobiles
   c. rioted
   d. shouted

_____ 6. "Cambodia **incursion**"
   a. mistake
   b. concession
   c. invasion
   d. adventure

_____ 7. "**ensuing** national elections"
   a. previous
   b. illegal
   c. contested
   d. following

_____ 8. "High school **alumni**"
   a. graduates
   b. seniors
   c. teachers
   d. students

_____ 9. "strong **partisanship**"
   a. friendship
   b. adherence to a political party
   c. civic involvement
   d. business affiliations

_____ 10. "influences are **cumulative**"
   a. important
   b. added one to another
   c. predictable
   d. relevant

- ## *Possible Essay Exam Question*

  Explain why millions of Americans fail to vote. (Hint: Discuss general reasons and then mention specific examples of types of persons, areas, and elections.)

- ## *Word Parts*

  Study the meaning of the word parts and supply an additional example from your own vocabulary. In the second set of items, use the corresponding part to write the word that best fits the definition.

Word Part	Meaning	Example	Your Example
1. mis	ill, wrong	misjudge	_____
2. civi	citizen	uncivil	_____
3. leg	law	legal	_____
4. claim, clam	declare, cry	acclaim	_____
5. mem	remember	commemorate	_____
6. clud, clus	shut	exclusive	_____
7. cause, cus	cause, motive	accuser	_____
8. ade	action	blockade	_____
9. lic, licit	permit	license	_____
10. test	to bear witness	testimony	_____

1. hater of mankind _____
2. man's cultural development _____
3. a law-making assembly _____
4. a sudden outcry _____
5. inter-office reminder; a note _____
6. to finish _____
7. reason for not acting _____
8. act of decaying _____
9. illegal _____
10. to demonstrate against _____

Selection 3: Geography

Jesse H. Wheeler, Jr., J. Trenton Kostbade and Richard S. Thoman, from *Regional Geography of the World*

The British Isles*

The two main islands and the major political divisions of the British Isles.

The British Isles lie off the northwest coast of Europe. There are approximately 5500 islands in the group, but most of them are small, and only two islands, Great Britain and Ireland, are of major consequence. The largest island, Great Britain, lies only 21 miles across the Strait of Dover from France, and the whole island group is generally considered part of Europe.

5   Two countries occupy the islands: the Republic of Ireland, with its capital at Dublin, and the United Kingdom of Great Britain and Northern Ireland, with its capital at London. The latter country is usually referred to by shorter names such as "United Kingdom," "UK," "Britain," or "Great Britain." It incorporates the island of Great Britain, plus the northeastern corner of Ireland and most of the smaller islands, including the Isle of Wight, Isle of Man, Hebrides,

10   Orkneys, Shetlands, and Channel Islands. Altogether the United Kingdom comprises about four-fifths of the area and has about 95 percent of the population of the British Isles (Table 3).

Political Subdivisions of the United Kingdom

The United Kingdom is sometimes incorrectly referred to as "England." However, England is merely the largest of four main subdivisons of the country, the others being Scotland, Wales, and Northern Ireland (map). These were originally independent territories. Wales was

*LEARNING STRATEGY: Be able to define, locate, and describe the unique characteristics of the British Isles.

Table 3 British Isles: Area and Population Data

Political Unit	Area (Thousand Square Miles)	Population (Millions: 1973 Estimates)	Density (Per Square Mile: to Nearest Multiple of 5)
United Kingdom	94.5	56.8	600
England	50.3	46.9	930
Wales	8.0	2.8	345
Scotland	30.4	5.3	175
Northern Ireland	5.5	1.6	280
Isle of Man[a]	0.225	0.05	220
Channel Islands[a]	0.075	0.13	1735
Republic of Ireland	27.1	3.0	110
British Isles	121.7	59.8	490

[a]In a strict sense the Isle of Man and Channel Islands are not included in the United Kingdom, both being dependencies of the British Crown. But in practical effect they are part of the United Kingdom and are so regarded in this chapter.

15   conquered by England in the Middle Ages, but preserves some cultural distinctiveness associated with the Welsh language, still spoken by about a quarter of its population. Northern Ireland, together with the rest of Ireland, was twice conquered by England. The earlier conquest in the Middle Ages was followed by a lapse of English control during the Wars of the Roses in the second half of the fifteenth century. A second conquest was completed in

20   the 17th century. One of its outcomes was the settlement of Scottish and English Protestants in the North, where they became numerically and politically dominant. In 1921, when the Irish Free State (later the Republic of Ireland) was established in the Catholic part of the island, the predominantly Protestant North, for economic as well as religious reasons, elected to remain with the United Kingdom. Today Northern Ireland retains a certain amount of political

25   autonomy within the United Kingdom. For example, it has its own parliament, which meets at Belfast and legislates in matters of local concern. This parliament was restructured in 1973, in an attempt to end several years of grim guerrilla civil war between the region's contending religious factions by giving proportional representation to the Catholic minority. Northern Ireland, like the other subdivisions of the United Kingdom, sends representatives to the

30   Parliament at London. Scotland was first joined to England when a Scottish king inherited the English throne in 1603, and the two became one country under the Act of Union passed in 1707. Scotland has no separate parliament, but it does have special administrative agencies in Edinburgh which deal with Scottish affairs. It also has its own system of courts and law.

Food and Agriculture in Britain

     One of the major characteristics of the United Kingdom is its dependence on imported food. It

35   is estimated that Britain now produces about half of its total food requirements or two-thirds of all that can be grown in temperate climates. Importation of the remainder makes the United Kingdom the greatest net importer of food in the world. It is the leading importer of meat, dairy products (except fluid milk), and tea; is generally second only to Japan as an importer of grains; and is the world's third largest import market for sugar. These and many other food

40   imports make it the single most important market for many food-exporting countries.

Norwich, England, open-air market.

In most of the country, crop production is unrewarding or impossible. Poor soils, steep slopes, cool summers, and excessive cloudiness and moisture are the principal handicaps. Highland Britain suffers the most on all these counts, but various parts of Lowland Britain are also affected. Comparatively slight rises in elevation bring sharp decreases in temperature and
45 increases in precipitation. In Highland Britain the warmest month generally averages below 60°F, and precipitation is nearly always over 40 inches and in many places over 60 inches a year. Moorland, often waterlogged and boggy, is estimated to cover 25,000 of the 88,000 square miles of land in the island of Great Britain. In terms of economic use, such land is mainly unimproved natural pasture ("rough grazing"), generally with a low density of both
50 animals and men.

Land and climate are more favorable to agriculture in Lowland Britain, and especially in the drier and warmer east. Even in Lowland Britain, however, much of the land is in pastures and meadows, though these are usually sown and tended and have a high carrying capacity. About one-third of the land in the United Kingdom is regularly plowed and planted in tilled crops.
55 Eastern England is the largest section in which such arable land is predominant over grass. This dependence on imported food is not due to lack of efficiency in British agriculture, but to the high density of population and the relatively high plane of living. Crop yields and the output of animal products per unit of land are among the highest in the world, being exceeded only by a few extremely productive countries in western continental Europe. Output per man is probably
60 the highest in Europe, as farms are larger on the average in Britain than in the rest of Europe, and mechanization has now reached a point that is matched by very few countries anywhere. Total food production has more than doubled in the last thirty years, mainly an outcome of various government policies aimed at reducing imports. Results have been achieved principally by inducing farmers to more than double the acreage in feed crops, mainly barley, at
65 the expense of grassland, since a given acreage of such crops can generally feed more animals than the same acreage of grass—though the feed crops may well be more expensive to produce. Production of wheat has also been sharply increased. These expansions have required various subsidies to farmers and have been expensive. However, despite the high cost in

70 subsidies and food prices, Britain's entry into the Common Market in 1973 probably means a
continuation of the tendency to expand British agricultural production. Up to now, the
agricultural policy of the Common Market has emphasized subsidies to agriculture, including
high import tariffs on agricultural products entering the Market from outside. Thus British
farmers will now receive further incentives in the form of high and protected prices, and the
British people, like the other peoples in the Common Market, will eat more expensive food,
75 produced to a greater degree within the home country. /1207

• *Skill Development*

Study the map and Table 3 and then respond to the following statements with
T (true), *F* (false), or *CT* (can't tell).

_____ 1. England is another name for the United Kingdom of Great Britain.
_____ 2. The Republic of Ireland and the United Kingdom are separate countries within the British Isles.
_____ 3. England makes up over half of the total area of the United Kingdom.
_____ 4. In 1973 more people lived in Wales and Northern Ireland than lived in Scotland.
_____ 5. Considering the amount of land, there are more people per square mile living on the Isle of Man than living in Scotland.
_____ 6. The largest city in the British Isles is London.
_____ 7. The Isle of Man and the Channel Islands combined had more than a quarter of a million people in 1973.
_____ 8. According to the data, more people live in less space in England than in Scotland.
_____ 9. The islands off the coast of northern Scotland are owned by Northern Ireland.
_____ 10. A river divides Scotland and England.

• *Comprehension Questions*

After reading the selection, answer the following questions with *a, b, c,* or *d.*

_____ 1. The best statement of the main idea of this selection is
a. the United Kingdom should grow more of its own food supplies because it is expensive to import agricultural products
b. because of unfavorable climate and unyielding land, the United Kingdom, composed of several subdivisions and islands, is forced to import a large amount of its food and agricultural products
c. political disputes have divided the British Isles into two countries, the United Kingdom and the Republic of Ireland.
d. the failure of British agriculture is due to the land and climate, and not to the people

_____ 2. The United Kingdom of Great Britain and Northern Ireland can also be correctly referred to as
    a. The Republic of Ireland
    b. England
    c. UK
    d. Wales

_____ 3. The part of the United Kingdom which is called Wales is
    a. an independent territory
    b. made up mostly of Welsh-speaking people
    c. the smallest British subdivision
    d. a subdivision that was conquered by England

_____ 4. According to the selection, the island of Ireland is presently divided into two countries because
    a. the Catholics did not want Protestants to be included in the Irish Free State
    b. the Protestants did not choose, for political and economic reasons, to become a part of the new country
    c. the Wars of the Roses ended British control
    d. the two religious groups were unable to choose a prime minister

_____ 5. Being a major importer of food, the United Kingdom, according to the article,
    a. outranks Japan as a net importer
    b. imports more sugar than tea
    c. produces enough fluid milk to engage in minor exporting
    d. imports meat before sugar

_____ 6. Highland Britain might be correctly described as all of the following except
    a. cool in the summer
    b. cloudy
    c. weak in agricultural productivity
    d. cultivated in rich pastureland

_____ 7. In the United Kingdom, crops are planted on approximately
    a. 25,000 square miles
    b. two thirds of the temperate climate area
    c. one third of the land
    d. one third of Lowland Britain

_____ 8. The author attributes Britain's high food importation primarily to
    a. agricultural inefficiencies
    b. high national demand
    c. farm subsidy programs
    d. a shortage of farmers

_____ 9. The author feels that the policies of the Common Market discourage
    a. importation of agricultural products
    b. increased food prices
    c. subsidies to farmers
    d. increased national food production within Britain

_____ 10. The author feels that in general the British farmer
      a. is inadequate   c. is inefficient
      b. is uneducated   d. lacks modernization

Answer the following with *T* (true), *F* (false), or *CT* (can't tell).

_____ 11. The United States exceeds Britain in the output of animal products per unit of land.

_____ 12. The author feels that Britain's entry into the Common Market was a mistake.

_____ 13. Britain is twenty-one miles from continental Europe.

_____ 14. The Republic of Ireland was conquered twice by Britain.

_____ 15. The United Kingdom produces more food per unit of land than Ireland.

• *Vocabulary*

According to the way the boldface word was used in the selection, indicate *a*, *b*, *c*, or *d* for the word or phrase that gives the best definition.

_____ 1. "of major **consequence**"
a. trouble
b. importance
c. territory
d. result

_____ 2. "the **Strait** of Dover"
a. sea
b. river
c. bay
d. narrow waterway

_____ 3. "**incorporates** the island"
a. includes
b. largely composes
c. reduces
d. features

_____ 4. "a **lapse** of English control"
a. slip
b. renewal
c. abdication
d. withdrawal

_____ 5. "**numerically** and politically dominant"
a. newly
b. nervously
c. religiously
d. with respect to numbers

_____ 6. "Amount of political **autonomy**"
a. alliance
b. dictatorship
c. self-rule
d. dignity

_____ 7. "greatest **net** importer"
a. natural
b. resulting after allowances have been made
c. gross
d. pertaining to ocean fishing

_____ 8. "waterlogged and **boggy**"
a. marshy
b. cloudy
c. rainy
d. cold

_____ 9. "**Output** per man"
a. salaries
b. union labor
c. production
d. expenses

_____ 10. "**subsidies** to farmers"
a. learning programs
b. grants of money
c. legislation
d. taxes

• *Possible Essay Exam Question*

Define the United Kingdom and explain its dependence on imported food. (Hint: Locate the United Kingdom geographically and give specific reasons for its import needs in food.)

• *Word Parts*

Study the meaning of the word parts and supply an additional example from your own vocabulary. In the second set of items, use the corresponding part to write the word that best fits the definition.

Word Parts	Meaning	Example	Your Example
1. pon, pos	place, set	composition	_____
2. counter	against	countervailing	_____
3. iso	equal	isomagnetic	_____
4. mer, mar, mari	sea	mermaid	_____
5. hydra	water	hydroplane	_____
6. pict, picto	paint	pictograph	_____
7. prim, prime	first	primeval	_____
8. ian	native of	Italian	_____
9. wise	way, position	clockwise	_____
10. volcan, vulcan	fire	vulcanize	_____

1. to assume a position; pose   _____
2. illegally made money   _____
3. equal measure of pressure   _____
4. underwater ship   _____
5. motorboat that lifts on air   _____
6. to portray or describe   _____
7. crude; basic; self-taught   _____
8. a native of Australia   _____
9. against the direction of the clock _____
10. erupting mountain   _____

Acknowledgments

Chapter One

9–11 From UNDERSTANDING HUMAN BEHAVIOR by James V. McConnell. Copyright © 1974 by Holt, Rinehart and Winston, Inc. Reprinted by permission of Holt, Rinehart and Winston.

16–18 "The American Man" from SOCIOLOGY, by Donald Light, Jr. and Suzanne Keller. Copyright © 1975 by Alfred A. Knopf. Reprinted by permission of Alfred A. Knopf, Inc.

22–4 From HUMAN ANATOMY AND PHYSIOLOGY: PRINCIPLES AND APPLICATIONS by Roy Hartenstein. Copyright © 1976 by Litton Educational Publishing, Inc. Reprinted by permission of D. Van Nostrand Company.

Chapter Two

28 Willis H. Johnson et al., *Essentials of Biology* (New York: Holt, Rinehart and Winston, Inc., 1972), p. 143.

29 Theodore J. Lowi, *American Government: Incomplete Conquest* (Hinsdale, Ill.: The Dryden Press, 1976), p. 248.

29 From Introductory Psychology: The Modern View by Douglas Matheson, p. 175. Copyright © 1975 by The Dryden Press. Reprinted by permission of the author.

31 From A HISTORY OF THE WESTERN WORLD by Shepard B. Clough et al. Copyright © 1969 by Raytheon Education Company. Reprinted by permission of the author.

31 *ibid.,* p. 442.

31 Reece McGee et al., *Sociology: An Introduction* (Hinsdale, Ill.: The Dryden Press, 1977), p. 263.

31 *ibid.,* p. 188.

31 *ibid.,* p. 112.

31 Theodore J. Lowi, *American Government: Incomplete Conquest* (Hinsdale, Ill.: The Dryden Press, 1976), p. 116.

31 Willis H. Johnson et al., *Essentials of Biology* (Holt, Rinehart and Winston, Inc., 1972), p. 327.

31 *ibid.*

31 *ibid.,* p. 321.

31 Jesse H. Wheeler, Jr., J. Trenton Kostbade and Richard S. Thoman, *Regional Geography of the World* (Holt, Rinehart and Winston, 1975), p. 159.

31 *ibid.,* p. 371.

32 *ibid.,* p. 435.

32 Gardner Lindzey, Calvin Hall and Richard F. Thompson, *Psychology* (New York: Worth Publishers, Inc., 1975), p. 140.

32 *ibid.*

32 David J. Rachman and Michael Mescon, *Business Today* (New York: Random House, Inc., 1976), p. 115.

32 *ibid.,* p. 49.

32 From PHYSICAL GEOLOGY, 2nd edition, by Robert Foster. Copyright © 1971, 1975 by Bell & Howell Company. Reprinted by permission of Charles E. Merrill Publishing Company.

32–3 From the book, HOW TO BUILD A BETTER VOCABULARY by Nurnberg and Rosenblum. © 1961 by Maxwell Nurnberg and Morris Rosenblum. Published by Prentice-Hall, Inc., Englewood Cliffs, New Jersey 07632.

37–8 From INTRODUCTORY PSYCHOLOGY: THE MODERN VIEW by Douglas Matheson. Copyright © 1975 by The Dryden Press, a division of Holt, Rinehart and Winston. Reprinted by permission of Holt, Rinehart and Winston.

38–9 From ESSENTIALS OF BIOLOGY, Second Edition, by Willis H. Johnson, Louis E. DeLanney, Thomas A. Cole, and Austin E. Brooks. Copyright © 1969 and 1974 by Holt, Rinehart and Winston, Inc. Reprinted by permission of Holt, Rinehart and Winston.

Chapter Three

43 From HOW TO STUDY IN COLLEGE, 2nd edition, by Walter Pauk. Copyright © 1974 by Houghton Mifflin Company. Reprinted by permission of the publisher.

45 John H. Gagnon and Cathy S. Greenblat. LIFE DESIGNS. Copyright © 1978, Scott, Foresman and Company.

46–8 Peter C. Kratcoski and Donald B. Walker. CRIMINAL JUSTICE IN AMERICA. Copyright © 1978, Scott, Foresman and Company.

51–2 David Dempsey and Philip Zimbardo. PSYCHOLOGY AND YOU. Copyright © 1978, Scott, Foresman and Company.

52   Carl N. Degler et al., THE DEMOCRATIC EXPERIENCE, 4th edition. Copyright © 1977, Scott, Foresman and Company.

52–3   Willis H. Johnson et al., *Essentials of Biology,* p. 173.

54–6   From CONTEMPORARY BUSINESS by Louis E. Boone and David L. Kurtz. Copyright © 1976 by The Dryden Press, a Division of Holt, Rinehart and Winston. Reprinted by permission of Holt, Rinehart and Winston.

60–2   Selection is reprinted from BIOLOGICAL SCIENCE, 2nd edition, by William T. Keeton, by permission of W. W. Norton & Company, Inc. Copyright © 1972, 1967 by W. W. Norton & Company, Inc.

67–70   "Unity in Diversity" from SOCIOLOGY, by Donald Light, Jr. and Suzanne Keller. Copyright © 1975 by Alfred A. Knopf. Reprinted by permission of Alfred A. Knopf, Inc.

Chapter Four

75, 76, 77   From A CONCISE HISTORY OF THE AMERICAN REPUBLIC: AN ABBREVIATED AND NEWLY REVISED EDITION OF THE GROWTH OF THE AMERICAN REPUBLIC by Samuel Eliot Morison, Henry Steele Commager and William E. Leuchtenburg. Copyright © 1977 by Oxford University Press, Inc. Reprinted by permission.

76   Willis H. Johnson et al., *Essentials of Biology,* p. 315.

77   From A HISTORY OF THE WESTERN WORLD by Shepard B. Clough et al. Copyright © 1969 by Raytheon Education Company. Reprinted by permission of the author.

77   Multiple Contributing Consultants, eds., *Society Today* (Del Mar, Calif.: Communications Research Machines, Inc., 1973), p. 91.

78   W. H. Auden, *The Dyer's Hand* (New York: Random House, 1968).

78   From PHYSICAL GEOLOGY, 2nd edition, by Robert Foster. Copyright © 1971, 1975 by Bell & Howell Company. Reprinted by permission of Charles E. Merrill Publishing Company.

78   William Faulkner, "The Bear" (Curtis Publishing Company, 1942).

79   From PHYSICAL GEOLOGY, 2nd edition, by Robert Foster. Copyright © 1971, 1975 by Bell & Howell Company. Reprinted by permission of Charles E. Merrill Publishing Company.

79   John Raynor, *Anatomy and Physiology* (New York: Harper and Row, 1977), p. 29.

79   Stephen Crane, "The Open Boat."

80   Wheeler, Kostbade and Thoman, *Regional Geography of the World,* p. 16.

80   "The Snake" from COLLECTED POEMS by D. H. Lawrence, Copyright 1929 by Jonathan Cape and Harrison Smith, Inc. and renewed © 1957 by Freida Lawrence Ravagli. Used by permission of Viking Penguin Inc.

80   Morison, Commager, and Leuchtenburg, *A Concise History of the American Republic,* p. 131.

81   Henry F. Bedford and Trevor Calbourn. THE AMERICANS. New York: Harcourt Brace Jovanovich, Inc., 1976.

81   From A HISTORY OF THE WESTERN WORLD by Shepard B. Clough et al. Copyright © 1969 by Raytheon Education Company. Reprinted by permission of the author.

82   George Meredith, "Love in the Valley."

82   Lloyd C. Gardner and William L. O'Neill, *Looking Backward* (New York: McGraw-Hill Book Co., 1974), p. 38.

82   From A CONCISE HISTORY OF THE AMERICAN REPUBLIC: AN ABBREVIATED AND NEWLY REVISED EDITION OF THE GROWTH OF THE AMERICAN REPUBLIC by Samuel Eliot Morison, Henry Steele Commager and William E. Leuchtenburg. Copyright © 1977 by Oxford University Press, Inc. Reprinted by permission.

83   *ibid.*

83   E. B. White, "Once More on the Lake" in *One Man's Meat* (New York: Harper and Row, 1938).

84–6   From A HISTORY OF THE WESTERN WORLD by Shepard B. Clough et al. Copyright © 1969 by Raytheon Education Company. Reprinted by permission of the author.

91–3   William Wordsworth. "Lucy Gray", 1800.

99–100   From PHYSICAL GEOLOGY, 2nd edition, by Robert Foster. Copyright © 1971, 1975 by Bell & Howell Company. Reprinted by permission of Charles E. Merrill Publishing Company.

Chapter Five

109–11   From INTRODUCTORY PSYCHOLOGY: THE MODERN VIEW by Douglas Matheson, pp. 3, 38–39, 42, 79, 103, 135. Copyright © 1975 by The Dryden Press, a division of Holt, Rinehart and Winston. Reprinted by permission of the author.

111   Wheeler, Kostbade and Thoman, *Regional Geography of the World,* p. 290.

111   Roy Hartenstein, *Human Anatomy and Physiology* (New York: D. Van Nostrand Co., 1976), p. 250.

112   Gardner and O'Neill, *Looking Backward,* p. 210.

112   *ibid.,* p. 27.

112   McGee et al., *Sociology: An Introduction,* p. 271.

112   Henry F. Bedford and Trevor Calbourn. THE AMERICANS. New York: Harcourt Brace Jovanovich, Inc., 1976.

112   Leonard Pitt. WE AMERICANS. Copyright © 1976, Scott, Foresman and Company.

112   John Raynor, *Anatomy and Physiology* (New York, Harper and Row, 1977), p. 26.

112   Gerard J. Tottora and Nicholas P. Anagnostakos, *Principles of Anatomy and Physiology* (San Francisco: Canfield Press, 1975), p. 274.

112   Louis E. Boone and David Kurtz, *Contemporary Business* (Hinsdale, Ill.: The Dryden Press, 1976), p. 453.

112   From SOCIOLOGY, by Donald Light, Jr. and Suzanne Keller. Copyright © 1975 by Alfred A. Knopf. Reprinted by permission of Alfred A. Knopf, Inc.

113   *ibid.,* p. 298.

113   McConnell, *Understanding Human Behavior,* p. 428.

113   Carl N. Degler et al., *The Democratic Experience* (Glenview, Ill.: Scott, Foresman and Co., 1977), p. 133.

113   Victor A. Gruelach and Vincent J. Chiapetta. BIOLOGY: THE SCIENCE OF LIFE. Copyright © 1977, Silver Burdett Company.

114   David Dempsey and Philip Zimbardo, *Psychology and You* (Glenview, Ill.: Scott, Foresman and Co., 1978), p. 291.

114   Charles P. Sohner. AMERICAN GOVERNMENT AND POLITICS TODAY, 2nd edition. Copyright © 1976, Scott, Foresman and Company.

115–7   Marilu Hurt McCarty. DOLLARS AND SENSE, 2nd edition. Copyright © 1979, 1976, Scott, Foresman and Company.

120–4   From UNDERSTANDING HUMAN BEHAVIOR by James V. McConnell. Copyright © 1974 by Holt, Rinehart and Winston, Inc. Reprinted by permission of Holt, Rinehart and Winston.

127–8   A. Lee McAlester, THE EARTH, © 1973, pp. 140–142. Reprinted by permission of Prentice-Hall, Inc., Englewood Cliffs, New Jersey.

Chapter Six

133   Mark Twain, *Life on the Mississippi.*

135   Edward J. Fox and Edward W. Wheatley. MODERN MARKETING. Copyright © 1978, Scott, Foresman and Company.

135   David Dempsey and Philip Zimbardo. PSYCHOLOGY AND YOU. Copyright © 1978, Scott, Foresman and Company.

136   Marilu Hurt McCarty. DOLLARS AND SENSE, 2nd edition. Copyright © 1979, 1976, Scott, Foresman and Company.

136   Frederick Douglass. "Narrative of an American Slave," from NARRATIVE OF THE LIFE OF FREDERICK DOUGLASS, AN AMERICAN SLAVE, 1845.

137   Carl N. Degler et al., THE DEMOCRATIC EXPERIENCE, 4th edition. Copyright © 1977, Scott, Foresman and Company.

140   Burton Wright II, John Weiss and Charles M. Unkovic. PERSPECTIVE: AN INTRODUCTION TO SOCIOLOGY. New York: The Dryden Press, 1975, p. 145.

140   Shelby D. Gerking. BIOLOGICAL SYSTEMS 2nd. ed. Philadelphia: W. B. Saunders Company, 1974, p. 286.

141   From INTRODUCTION TO GEOGRAPHY, Fifth Edition by Henry M. Kendall et al., © 1976 by Harcourt Brace Jovanovich, Inc. Reprinted by permission of the publisher.

141   Ambrose Bierce, *The Boarded Window,* 1899.

142   From HUMAN ANATOMY AND PHYSIOLOGY: PRINCIPLES AND APPLICATIONS by Roy Hartenstein. Copyright © 1976 by Litton Educational Publishing, Inc. Reprinted by permission of D. Van Nostrand Company.

143–5   "The Eskimos" from ANTHROPOLOGY: THE EXPLORATION OF HUMAN DIVERSITY, by Conrad Phillip Kottak. Copyright © 1974 by Random House, Inc. Reprinted by permission of Random House, Inc.

149–50   From "Mountain Climbing and Scuba Diving" from BIOLOGICAL SYSTEMS by Shelby D. Gerking. Copyright © 1974 by W. B. Saunders Company. Reprinted by permission of the publisher.

155–7   Leonard Pitt. WE AMERICANS. Copyright © 1976, Scott, Foresman and Company.

Chapter Seven

164–5   Victor A. Greulach and Vincent J. Chiapetta. BIOLOGY: THE SCIENCE OF LIFE. Copyright ©

1977, Silver Burdett Company.

165–6 David Dempsey and Philip Zimbardo. PSYCHOLOGY AND YOU. Copyright © 1978, Scott, Foresman and Company.

166–7 Edward J. Fox and Edward W. Wheatley. MODERN MARKETING. Copyright © 1978, Scott, Foresman and Company.

167–8 Charles P. Sohner. AMERICAN GOVERNMENT AND POLITICS TODAY, 2nd edition. Copyright © 1976, Scott, Foresman and Company.

168 Lawrence J. Gitman. PERSONAL FINANCE. Hinsdale: The Dryden Press, 1978, pp. 395–396.

169–70 David Dempsey and Philip Zimbardo. PSYCHOLOGY AND YOU. Copyright © 1978, Scott, Foresman and Company.

170–1 Leonard Pitt. WE AMERICANS. Copyright © 1976, Scott, Foresman and Company.

172–5 Karen Carlson and Alan Meyers. SPEAKING WITH CONFIDENCE. Copyright © 1977, Scott, Foresman and Company.

179–81 Edward J. Fox and Edward W. Wheatley. MODERN MARKETING. Copyright © 1978, Scott, Foresman and Company.

185–8 From Lindzey, Hall, Thompson, PSYCHOLOGY, Worth Publishers, New York, 1975, pp. 291–295.

Chapter Eight

195 Leonard Pitt. WE AMERICANS. Copyright © 1976, Scott, Foresman and Company.

196 Stephen Crane, "The Open Boat."

197 Alfred Lord Tennyson, "The Eagle."

198 Mary Wilkins Freeman, *A Village Singer.*

198–9 Wheeler, Kostbade and Thoman, *Regional Geography of the World,* p. 204.

199–204 "The Death of the Hired Man," by Robert Frost from THE POETRY OF ROBERT FROST edited by Edward Connery Lathem. Copyright 1930, 1939 © 1969 by Holt, Rinehart and Winston. Copyright © 1958 by Robert Frost. Copyright © 1967 by Lesley Frost Ballantine. Reprinted by permission of Holt, Rinehart and Winston Publishers.

209–10 Samuel Clemens. THE ADVENTURES OF HUCKLEBERRY FINN, 1844.

214–6 From A HISTORY OF THE WESTERN WORLD by Shepard B. Clough et al. Copyright © 1969 by Raytheon Education Company. Reprinted by permission of the author.

Chapter Nine

223 Reece McGee et al., *Sociology: An Introduction* (Hinsdale, Ill.: The Dryden Press, 1977), p. 384.

223 Wheeler, Kostbade and Thoman, *Regional Geography of the World,* p. 291.

223 Louis Boone and David Kurtz, *Contemporary Business* (Hinsdale, Ill.: The Dryden Press, 1976), p. 244.

224 James McConnell, *Understanding Human Behavior* (New York: Holt, Rinehart and Winston, 1974), p. 321.

224 James M. Burns, J. W. Peltason and Thomas E. Cronin, *Government by the People* (New York: Prentice-Hall, 1975), p. 333.

224 Kenneth Prewitt and Sidney Verba, *An Introduction to American Government* (New York: Harper and Row, 1977), p. 114.

224 From PHYSICAL GEOLOGY, 2nd edition, by Robert Foster. Copyright © 1971, 1975 by Bell & Howell Company. Reprinted by permission of Charles E. Merrill Publishing Company.

224 From SOCIOLOGY, by Donald Light, Jr. and Suzanne Keller. Copyright © 1975 by Alfred A. Knopf. Reprinted by permission of Alfred A. Knopf, Inc.

224 From A HISTORY OF THE WESTERN WORLD by Shepard B. Clough et al. Copyright © 1969 by Raytheon Education Company. Reprinted by permission of the author.

224 Edward M. Burns, *Western Civilizations,* 8th ed. (New York: W. W. Norton and Co., 1973), p. 463.

224 Burns, Peltason, Cronin, GOVERNMENT BY THE PEOPLE, 9th Ed. Basic Ed., © 1975, p. 267. Reprinted by permission of Prentice-Hall, Inc., Englewood Cliffs, New Jersey.

225 William Lee Stokes. ESSENTIALS OF EARTH HISTORY. Englewood Cliffs: Prentice-Hall, Inc., 1973, pp. 504–505.

226 Reece McGee and Others. SOCIOLOGY: AN INTRODUCTION. Hinsdale: The Dryden Press, 1977, pp. 426–427.

227 Ambrose Bierce. THE DEVIL'S DICTIONARY, 1911.

228 From A CONCISE HISTORY OF THE AMERICAN REPUBLIC: AN ABBREVIATED AND NEWLY REVISED EDITION OF THE GROWTH OF THE AMERICAN REPUBLIC by Samuel Eliot Morison, Henry Steele Commager, and William E. Leuchtenburg. Copyright © 1977 by Oxford University Press, Inc. Reprinted by permission.

229–32 Jonathan Swift. "A Modest Proposal", 1728.

237–9   Leonard Pitt. WE AMERICANS. Copyright © 1976, Scott, Foresman and Company.
243–6   Charles P. Sohner. AMERICAN GOVERNMENT AND POLITICS TODAY, 2nd edition. Copyright © 1976, 1973, Scott, Foresman and Company.

Chapter Ten

262–5   From PSYCHOLOGY: AN INTRODUCTION, Second Edition by Jerome Kagan and Ernest Havemann, © 1972 by Harcourt Brace Jovanovich, Inc. Reprinted by permission of the publisher.
270–3   Burns, Peltason, Cronin, GOVERNMENT BY THE PEOPLE, 9th ed., © 1975, pp. 280–284. Reprinted by permission of Prentice-Hall, Inc., Englewood Cliffs, New Jersey.
277–80 From REGIONAL GEOGRAPHY OF THE WORLD, Updated Third Edition, by Jesse H. Wheeler, Jr., J. Trenton Kostbade, and Richard S. Thoman. Copyright © 1975, 1969, 1961, 1955 by Holt, Rinehart and Winston. Reprinted by permission of Holt, Rinehart and Winston.

Picture Credits

Chapter One

9   Thomas McAvoy, Life Magazine, © 1955, Time, Inc.
16 Wide World Photos
22 Riboud/MAGNUM

Chapter Three

54   Courtesy of The Great Atlantic & Pacific Tea Co.
67b Inell Jones

Chapter Four

85 Francis Tyrwhitt-Drake
93 Ron Martig
99 U.S. Dept. of the Interior Geological Survey

Chapter Five

115 Courtesy of The Chicago Tribune
121 U. of Wisconsin Primate Lab
128 U.S. Coast Guard

Chapter Six

143 Tom Stack & Associates
151 U.S. Naval Photographic Center
156 The Sophia Smith Collection, Women's History Archive, Smith College

Chapter Seven

172 Mary Elyse Ebright
179 c. 1980 by Sidney Harris.
186 U.S. Dept. of Interior, National Parks Service, Edison National Historic Site

Chapter Eight

201 Tom Stack & Associates
208 Wisconsin Center for Film & Theater Research
215 Scottish National Portrait Gallery

Chapter Nine

230 Metropolitan Museum of Art, Harris Brisbane Dick Fund, 1932
237 Culver Pictures
245 Bill Stanton/MAGNUM

Chapter Ten

254 From ESSENTIALS OF BIOLOGY, Second Edition, by Willis H. Johnson, Louis E. DeLanney, Thomas A. Cole, and Austin E. Brooks. Copyright © 1969 and 1974 by Holt, Rinehart and Winston, Inc. Reprinted by permission of Holt, Rinehart and Winston.
255 From AMERICAN GOVERNMENT: INCOMPLETE CONQUEST by Theodore J. Lowi. Copyright © 1976 by The Dryden Press, a Division of Holt, Rinehart and Winston. Reprinted by permission of Holt, Rinehart and Winston.
256 Reprinted from the Geographical Review, Vol. 57, 1967, with the permission of the American Geographical Society.
257 From Keith Ian Polakoff et al., GENERATIONS OF AMERICANS, PART 1, p. 25. Copyright 1976, St. Martin's Press, Inc.

258 From CONTEMPORARY BUSINESS by Louis E. Boone and David L. Kurtz. Copyright © 1976 by The Dryden Press, a Division of Holt, Rinehart and Winston. Reprinted by permission of Holt, Rinehart and Winston.

259 From SOCIOLOGY: AN INTRODUCTION by Reece McGee and Others. Copyright © 1977 by The Dryden Press, a Division of Holt, Rinehart and Winston. Reprinted by permission of Holt, Rinehart and Winston.

260 From SOCIOLOGY: AN INTRODUCTION by Reece McGee and Others. Copyright © 1977 by The Dryden Press, a Division of Holt, Rinehart and Winston. Reprinted by permission of Holt, Rinehart and Winston.

261 Burns/Peltason/Cronin, GOVERNMENT BY THE PEOPLE, National, State and Local Edition, 9th Edition, © 1975, pp. 281, 581. Reprinted by permission of Prentice-Hall, Inc. Englewood Cliffs, New Jersey.

262 Jean-Claude Lejeune

263–4 From Jerome Kagan and Ernest Havemann, PSYCHOLOGY: AN INTRODUCTION, 2nd edition, pp. 139 & 140. Copyright © 1968, 1972 by Harcourt Brace Jovanovich, Inc.

270 Burns/Peltason/Cronin, GOVERNMENT BY THE PEOPLE, National, State and Local Edition, 9th Edition, © 1975, pp. 281, 581. Reprinted by permission of Prentice-Hall, Inc. Englewood Cliffs, New Jersey.

272 P. Karas/FPG

277–8 From REGIONAL GEOGRAPHY OF THE WORLD, Updated Third Edition, by Jesse H. Wheeler, Jr., J. Trenton Kostbade, and Richard S. Thoman. Copyright © 1975, 1969, 1961, 1955 by Holt, Rinehart and Winston. Reprinted by permission of Holt, Rinehart and Winston.

279 Michael D. Sullivan

To the Student

You, the student, are the final test of the success of our textbooks. We need your reactions and ideas if we are to serve you better. On the following page is a simple questionnaire which, if you would take a few moments to fill it out, will greatly help us to publish more informative and interesting books for you and your instructor.

When completed, simply tear out the page, fold and staple it with the post-paid label showing, and drop it in the mail.

Thank you.

Bridging the Gap: College Reading

Your Name (If you wish): _____ Date: _____

School: _____ Your Major: _____

Size of Class: _____

1) What did you like best about this book?

fold here

2) What did you like least about this book?

3) Which chapters were easiest for you?   Why?

4) Which chapters were most difficult for you?   Why?

5) In general, how might the book be improved?

May we quote you in our advertising efforts? Yes_____   No_____

Thank you,
Scott, Foresman, College Division

fold here

NO POSTAGE
NECESSARY
IF MAILED
IN THE
UNITED STATES

‖‖‖

BUSINESS REPLY MAIL
FIRST CLASS   PERMIT NO. 282   GLENVIEW, IL.

POSTAGE WILL BE PAID BY ADDRESSEE

Scott, Foresman, College Division
1900 East Lake Avenue
Glenview, Illinois   60025